COMPUTER-BASED INSTRUCTION
A State-of-the-Art Assessment

Edited by

HAROLD F. O'NEIL, JR.

*Army Research Institute for
the Behavioral and Social Sciences
Alexandria, Virginia*

ACADEMIC PRESS   1981

A Subsidiary of Harcourt Brace Jovanovich, Publishers

New York   London   Toronto   Sydney   San Francisco

To the memory of
JOSEPH W. RIGNEY
our esteemed colleague

COPYRIGHT © 1981, BY ACADEMIC PRESS, INC.
ALL RIGHTS RESERVED.
NO PART OF THIS PUBLICATION MAY BE REPRODUCED OR
TRANSMITTED IN ANY FORM OR BY ANY MEANS, ELECTRONIC
OR MECHANICAL, INCLUDING PHOTOCOPY, RECORDING, OR ANY
INFORMATION STORAGE AND RETRIEVAL SYSTEM, WITHOUT
PERMISSION IN WRITING FROM THE PUBLISHER.

ACADEMIC PRESS, INC.
111 Fifth Avenue, New York, New York 10003

United Kingdom Edition published by
ACADEMIC PRESS, INC. (LONDON) LTD.
24/28 Oval Road, London NW1 7DX

Library of Congress Cataloging in Publication Data
Main entry under title:

Computer-based instruction.

(Educational technology series)
Includes bibliographies and index.
1. Computer-managed instruction--Addresses, essays, lectures. I. O'Neil, Harold F., Jr. Date. II. Series.
LB1028.46.C66   371.3'9445   81-1308
ISBN 0-12-526760-6   AACR2

PRINTED IN THE UNITED STATES OF AMERICA

81 82 83 84   9 8 7 6 5 4 3 2 1

COMPUTER-BASED INSTRUCTION
A State-of-the-Art Assessment

THE EDUCATIONAL TECHNOLOGY SERIES

Edited by

Harold F. O'Neil, Jr.

U.S. Army Research Institute for
the Behavioral and Social Sciences
Alexandria, Virginia

Harold F. O'Neil, Jr. (Ed.) Learning Strategies

Harold F. O'Neil, Jr. (Ed.) Issues in Instructional Systems Development

Harold F. O'Neil, Jr. (Ed.) Procedures for Instructional Systems Development

Harold F. O'Neil, Jr. and Charles D. Spielberger (Eds.) Cognitive and Affective Learning Strategies

Jane Close Conoley (Ed.) Consultation in Schools: Theory, Research, Procedures

Harold F. O'Neil, Jr. (Ed.) Computer-Based Instruction: A State-of-the-Art Assessment

In preparation

Gary D. Borich and Ron P. Jemelka. Programs and Systems: An Evaluation Perspective

Contents

List of Contributors   ix
Preface   xi

1

Introduction and Overview of Computer-Based Instruction   1

HAROLD F. O'NEIL, JR. and JUDITH PARIS

Introduction   1
Overview of the Remaining Chapters   4
References   20

2

Computer-Managed Instruction: A Context for Computer-Based Instruction   23

FRANK BAKER

Introduction   23
System Overview   27
Functions Performed by the CMI System   32
CMI Software System Concept   38
CMI Hardware System   55
Instructional Management under the CMI Concept   58
Evaluation Capabilities   61
References   64

3

Hardware–Software 65

CRAIG FIELDS and JUDITH PARIS

Introduction 65
Knowledge, Data, and Information in CBI Systems 67
Hardware and Software Technologies 69
Man–Machine Relations 87
Recommendations for Research 89
References 90

4

Courseware 91

C. VICTOR BUNDERSON

Courseware: Conceptions and Definitions 91
The Importance of Courseware in a Total Delivery System 94
Where Are We Now? 99
Prospects through the Early 1980s 116
Prospects for the Late 1980s and Beyond 120
References 122

Learning Strategies 127

J. W. RIGNEY and ALLEN MUNRO

What Are Learning Strategies? 127
Why Do Research on Learning Strategies? 129
Where Are We Now? 133
Prospects for the Immediate Future 149
Prospects for the Late 1980s 153
Summary and Conclusions 154
References 155

6

Evaluation 161

GARY D. BORICH and RON P. JEMELKA

Overview of Evaluation 161
Where We Are Now: History and Current Status of Evaluation 163
Prospects for the Immediate Future: Emerging Trends in Educational Evalution 180

Contents

Prospects for the 1980s and 1990s: Implications of the Emerging Trends   197
References   206

7

Management   211

ROBERT J. SEIDEL and HAROLD WAGNER

Introduction   211
Organizational Structures for Project Management   212
Management Issues   214
Lessons Learned and Recommendations   225
References   229

8

Computer-Based Instruction in Europe and Japan   231

KARL L. ZINN

Introduction   231
Hardware and Software   232
Courseware   235
Learning Strategies   237
Evaluation   239
Management   241
Needed Developments   243
References   246
Supplementary Reading   248

List of Contributors

Numbers in parentheses indicate the pages on which the authors' contributions begin.

FRANK BAKER (23), Department of Educational Psychology, University of Wisconsin—Madison, Madison, Wisconsin 53706

GARY D. BORICH (161), Instructional Systems Laboratory, College of Education, The University of Texas at Austin, Austin, Texas 78712

C. VICTOR BUNDERSON (91), WICAT, Inc., University Plaza, Orem, Utah 84057

CRAIG FIELDS (65), Cybernetics Sciences Division, Defense Advanced Research Projects Agency, Arlington, Virginia 22209

RON P. JEMELKA (161), Instructional Systems Laboratory, College of Education, University of Texas at Austin, Austin, Texas 78712

ALLEN MUNRO (127), Behavioral Technology Laboratories, University of Southern California, Redondo Beach, California 90277

HAROLD F. O'NEIL, JR. (1), Army Research Institute for the Behavioral and Social Sciences, Alexandria, Virginia 22333

JUDITH PARIS (1, 65), Advanced Information Management Technology, Inc., McLean, Virginia 22101

J. W. RIGNEY* (127), Behavioral Technology Laboratories, University of Southern California, Redondo Beach, California 90277

ROBERT J. SEIDEL (211), Educational and Training Systems Division, Human Resources Research Organization, Alexandria, Virginia 22314

HAROLD WAGNER (211), Educational and Training Systems Division, Human Resources Research Organization, Alexandria, Virginia 22314

KARL L. ZINN (231), Center for Research on Learning and Teaching, University of Michigan, Ann Arbor, Michigan 48104

*Deceased.

Preface[1]

In recent years individualized instruction and the use of computer technology to facilitate learning at all levels of education and training has received increased emphasis. Computer-based instruction (CBI) is the discipline that supports this activity. The term *computer-based instruction* is used because *computer-based* is sufficiently broad to cover a multitude of computer uses and *instruction* can refer to either education or training.

Civilian education and training systems tend to be highly decentralized, relatively inflexible, and dependent upon increasingly costly instructional procedures. For post-secondary education and training, the problem for the future is the decreasing quantity and quality of available human resources. For example, it is expected that because of decreased fertility rates the quantity of available labor will be 25–30% smaller in 1995 than it was in 1979. The product of the public educational systems, as gauged by the intellectual skills of high school graduates, appears to be lower than it was in the past (decreasing quality). These problems are compounded by consistent political pressure to reduce education and training budgets. In addition, the increasing technological sophistication of our society will require that people learn more complicated subject material and skills and perform these skills at higher standards of performance.

It is evident that these trends will continue and the need will grow to develop instructional systems that lead to more proficient performance at a reduced cost. Costs can be reduced to the extent that reductions in instructional time can be

---

[1]The views and conclusions that are expressed in this preface and the rest of the volume are those of the respective authors and should not be interpreted as necessarily representing the official policies, either expressed or implied, of the U.S. Army Research Institute for the Behavioral and Social Sciences, or the U.S. government.

achieved. A major advantage of CBI systems is that they can reduce instructional time while maintaining equivalent performance when compared with the traditional type of lecture–discussion techniques. Thus, the application of CBI techniques can lead to increased cost-effectiveness of education and training systems; CBI also provides an ideal research environment because we can study learning with almost as much rigor as carefully controlled laboratory conditions.

The intent of this book is to provide an intellectual framework for recent and future CBI research. To this end, state-of-the-art assessments were commissioned. These assessments, all by experts in the field, comprise the chapters in this volume. The chapters reflect current knowledge and future trends, but the treatment offered here is not exhaustive.

Chapter 1 is a general introduction to CBI and provides an overview of the rest of the book. An idealized computer-managed instructional system described in Chapter 2, provides a conceptual framework for the field of CBI. CBI hardware and software are summarized in Chapter 3; courseware developments are the focus of Chapter 4. In Chapters 5 and 6, learning strategies and evaluation are reviewed. Chapter 7 focuses on the management aspects of CBI projects. The final chapter is a discussion of CBI in Europe and Japan.

This book summarizes our knowledge and information to date in these fields and presents our collective wisdom concerning the state of the art in computer-based instruction. One of this book's uses is to plan future computer-based instructional systems for the public sector. We feel that our intellectual community consists of advanced students and researchers in the fields represented by the chapters.

In completing this book, I am indebted to a number of people for their support, help, and encouragement. In particular, I would like to acknowledge the invaluable support of Dr. Joseph Zeidner, Mr. James Baker, and Dr. Leon Nawrocki of the U.S. Army Research Institute for the Behavioral and Social Sciences who afforded me the technical and administrative opportunity to complete this volume. I also wish to note the excellent administrative support of Eileen Balasko. Finally, I acknowledge my appreciation for the help and moral support I have received from the staff of Academic Press.

1

Introduction and Overview of Computer-Based Instruction[1]

HAROLD F. O'NEIL, JR.
JUDITH PARIS

INTRODUCTION

In recent years there has been increased emphasis on individualized instruction and computer technology to facilitate learning at all levels of education and training. The discipline that supports this activity is computer-based instruction (CBI). We prefer the term *computer-based instruction* to others because "computer-based" is sufficiently broad to cover a multiple of uses [e.g., computer-managed instruction (CMI) or computer-assisted instruction (CAI)] and "instruction" can refer to either education or training. The terminology of our co-authors is consistent with our usage of CBI.

This book focuses both on the "lessons learned" in this area as well as future endeavors. The chapters are meant to be reflective, not all-encompassing, of the available literature. One of our uses for this information is to plan future CBI systems for the public sector. The purpose of this chapter is to provide a focus and overview for the remaining chapters.

The Problem

The civilian education and training systems tend to be highly decentralized, relatively inflexible, and dependent on increasingly costly instructional proce-

[1] The work reported in this chapter was supported in part by the Army Research Institute for the Behavioral and Social Sciences, contract number MDA 903-79-C-0558. Views and conclusions contained in this document are those of the authors and should not be interpreted as necessarily representing the official policies, either expressed or implied, of the Army Research Institute for the Behavioral and Social Sciences, or the United States Government.

COMPUTER-BASED INSTRUCTION
A State-of-the-Art Assessment

Copyright © 1981 by Academic Press, Inc.
All rights of reproduction in any form reserved.
ISBN 0-12-526760-6

dures. For postsecondary education and training the most obvious problem for the future is the decreasing quantity and quality of available human resources. For example, it is expected because of decreased fertility rates that the available labor pool (i.e., quantity) will be 25-30% smaller in 1995 than in 1979 (National Center for Educational Statistics, DHEW). The product of the civilian educational systems, that is, the intellectual skills of high school graduates, is assumed to be lower than in the past ("decreasing quality"). Compounding these problems is consistent political pressure to reduce education and training budgets.

In addition, the increasing technological sophistication of our society will require people to master an increased variety of complicated subject material, to master an increased set of sophisticated skills, and to perform these skills at higher standards of performance. We expect that these trends will continue, and that there will be an increased need to develop instructional systems that lead to more proficient performance at a reduced cost.

Most of the direct costs in education and training are associated with instructor and administrator salaries and benefits. In training environments such as industry and the military, students are also paid. For these reasons, in training environments the relationship between time and costs is a direct one—costs can be reduced to the extent that reductions in instructional time can be achieved. A major advantage of CBI systems is that they can reduce instruction time while maintaining equivalent levels of performance when compared to the traditional type of lecture-discussion techniques.

Computer-Based Instruction as a Solution

The application of CBI techniques is one way of increasing the cost effectiveness of education and training systems. Instruction of uniformly high quality is possible with computers (i.e., by eliminating variability caused by differences between instructors). With this technology, a long-term goal of educators and trainers can be realized by distributing instruction to students rather than by distributing students to instruction. With capabilities of centrally updating instructional materials, many logistical problems can be avoided. Furthermore, technological advances indicate that electronic transfer of information is expected to be cheaper in the 1980s than paper transmission of information. In addition, in the computer hardware arena we are entering into an area of computational plenty fostered by the explosion of silicon-integrated circuit technology. The commercial world is already exploiting this revolution (e.g., videogames, digital watches, and pocket calculators). All of these factors provide a "technological push" to the field of CBI.

In the past, one of the major drawbacks in the institutionalization of CBI has been the fragmented nature of the education and training market. Industry has not been able to bring to bear its strengths, that is, its financial, personnel, marketing, and dissemination expertise. However, the home entertainment market is likely to provide a firm base on which CBI can rest. The home entertainment market, which includes products such as videogames with their embedded microprocessors, and videodisks can provide this kind of mechanism.

Finally, in training environments where time saved is potentially money saved, there is compelling evidence that training time is reduced up to 30% with equivalent mastery with CBI (Orlansky & String, 1978). The advantages of CBI in a training–education environment are summarized in Table 1.1. The advantages are viewed in terms of cost reduction and improvement of effectiveness. Although other media share some of these advantages, we believe the entire set is unique to CBI.

Much of what we have discussed focuses on CBI applications in education and training. However, CBI also provides an ideal environment for research because we can study learning with almost as much rigor as carefully controlled laboratory conditions, coupled with the meaningfulness and realism of actual school or on-the-job learning.

State-of-the-Art Assessments

To provide an intellectual context for research in CBI, several activities broadly defined as assessments were commissioned. These assessments focus on documenting the state-of-the-art by experts in the area of CBI. The subsequent chapters are the results of these assessments.

The state-of-the-art assessments are an idealized computer-managed instructional system; hardware–software; courseware; learning strategies; evaluation; management; and overseas research and development (R&D). In each of these areas, the particular topics were chosen because we saw them as most relevant to the field of CBI. An expert in each area was asked to produce a chapter addressing "what we know now," "what we can reasonably expect to know 3 years from now," and some projections of 10 years from now. An example in the hard-

TABLE 1.1
Advantages of Computer-Based Instruction

Predominantly reducing cost	Predominantly increasing effectiveness
1. Reduce training time	1. Provide consistent high-quality instruction available on large scale
2. Reduce reliance on trained instructors	
3. Reduce need for using expensive or possibly dangerous operational equipment	2. Provide high-quality training at remote sites
	3. Provide hands-on, performance-oriented instruction
4. Provide rapid update of instructional material	4. Permit individualization of instruction

ware area would be that microprocessors are here now, videodisks are expected to be available widely 3 years from now, and handheld PDP-10s will be available 10 years from now. The state-of-the-art of CBI in the Soviet Union (or Eastern Europe) was not assessed because of the difficulties of a closed society and security reasons.

OVERVIEW OF THE REMAINING CHAPTERS

Computer-Managed Instruction

In Chapter 2, Baker provides the background of idealized CBI systems. A system is documented in the form of a systems concept document. The document serves several goals: It provides a conceptual framework for a computer-managed instructional (CMI) system, serves as the guide for the design and implementation of the CMI system(s), and acts as a baseline document for evaluation purposes. To provide a concrete example, Baker has chosen the world of training rather than education. The intent of Chapter 2 is to supply a conceptual framework for the field of CMI. The Training School setting, as envisioned by Baker, provides an excellent opportunity for the use of individualization based on progress rates because of the school's student diversity; the linkage between jobs, skills, and advancement within a field; and the continuous asynchronous flow of students.

Chapter 2 includes a description of the elements of the Training School environment and the role of CMI within that context. Briefly, Baker describes the six major elements of the Training School that function singularly and interactively: the marketplace, the personnel system, the school administration, the CMI system to support the instruction process, the instructional delivery and curriculum development systems, and the logistics support.

The functions performed by the CMI system and implemented via the CMI are divided into two classes: instructional management and support-type functions. These functions support four basic groups of users: students, instructors, administrators, and curriculum developers–evaluators. The major instructional management-related functions are diagnosis and prescription, performance monitoring, resource allocation, scheduling, and reporting. Representative definitions of each of these five functions can be found in Table 1.2.

The diagnosis function exists at the module level as well as at the course and program level, whereas the prescription function is both forward and remedial. Continuous and effective performance monitoring of students, curriculum, and instructors is ongoing. Both instructional and administrative scheduling, and resource allocation interact with performance monitoring through the curriculum. A key component of the CMI design—the reporting function—provides the administration, instructor, and student with a diverse range of reports.

1. Introduction and Overview of Computer-Based Instruction

TABLE 1.2
Instructional Management Functions

Diagnosis—Process of testing in some form for a student's instructional strengths and weaknesses.

Prescription—Process by which a range of instructional alternatives are suggested based on diagnosis to either the student or teacher. A subfunction is guidance-counseling, a process of helping individuals achieve adjustments such as conveying of information and skills necessary for effective functioning in a learning environment.

Performance monitoring—The process by which an individual's and group's rate of progress is watched and supervised closely. Both student and instructor performance is monitored. This function supports evaluation and planning.

Resource allocation/scheduling—The process of allocating instructional resources specified by the prescriptive process within a particular time frame to make the most effective use of the available resources.

Reporting—The process by which one retrieves and updates information based on characteristics of the information via a data management system and by which information is tabulated and formatted in a form interpretable by a human.

Baker's CMI system is an on-line management information system resting on a powerful and flexible data-base management system that interacts with a well-designed, man-machine interface function to provide the design philosophy foundation underlying the CMI software concept. Both hardware and software to support his idealized systems are described. However, the major focus in this book for hardware and software can be found in Chapter 3 by Fields and Paris.

Hardware-Software

In Chapter 3, Fields and Paris summarize and forecast the status of hardware and software technology for CBI. In one sense their predictions are the ones most grounded in reality: If a capability will exist in the industrial market 10 years from now, it exists *now* in an R&D laboratory. Ten years is the average length of time it takes to move an innovation from the laboratory to the marketplace. Fields and Paris conclude that the trend will be toward the development of smaller standalone CBI systems used, or possibly owned, by individuals. Their conviction, which we share, is based on the economics of mass production, unregulated computer costs and consumer preference for systems that are ownable, personal, and physically available. Chapter 3 focuses on four major areas: (*a*) the kinds of knowledge stored in CBI systems; (*b*) summaries and forecasts of hardware and software technologies; (*c*) man-machine relations; and (*d*) potential R&D projects that could influence significantly the development of CBI systems.

In CBI systems, knowledge representation can vary from English text to an animated cartoon. For example, similar information (e.g., rain) could be represented as either a written text, a cartoon, or a spoken word. Fields and Paris assert that although there is no theory that can assist the system designer in choosing among appropriate knowledge representations, there are cost considerations that can and should serve as guidelines. Speech and cartoons, for example, have proven to be bargains among competing knowledge representations. This process is being facilitated by the marketing of videodisks, which provide the capability to store a variety of different knowledge representations at very low cost.

The authors also forecast that the main implication of large-scale integration (LSI) will be inexpensive speech compression and techniques for low-cost computing based on multiprocessor microprocessors. They forecast that the trend will be away from many-user, remote time-sharing systems and will be toward single-user, standalone systems. Moreover, speech and English comprehension systems will become available to the CBI designer. It is possible that by 1985 both English and speech understanding will be practicable in CBI systems.

In the section on hardware, Fields and Paris describe in detail devices used to support such functions as optical character recognition; drawing, sketching, and pointing; image and text inputting; printing on paper and electronic displays; and speech input–output. In the area of input and output technology, they forecast that speech output will shortly be common in CBI systems. Moreover, in the 1980s very low-cost printers, large, flat television displays, and limited-quality speech input will become part of CBI systems.

In the area of communications, Fields and Paris discuss credible communications technologies by dividing their comments into two parts: short distance, low and high bandwidth; and long distance, low and high bandwidth. As is shown in Table 1.3, examples of short distance, low bandwidth are power lines within buildings used for home intercom systems or electronic devices for on–off appliances. Short distance, high bandwidth communication is provided at present

TABLE 1.3
Communications Technologies

Type	Example
Short distance	
Low bandwidth	Home intercom system
	Power lines within buildings
High bandwidth	Cable television
	Optical cable television
Long distance	
Low bandwidth	Packet switching (e.g., ARPANET)
	Packet radio
	Dial-up telephones
High bandwidth	Broadband satellite channels
	Television broadcast equipment

1. Introduction and Overview of Computer-Based Instruction

by cable television and, in the future, will be provided by optical cable technology. The most common long distance, low bandwidth technology is the telephone; whereas long distance, high bandwidth communication technology is provided by broadband satellite channels and television broadcast equipment.

In the area of electronic storage technology in CBI systems, Fields and Paris highlight four major categories: (*a*) semiconductor and core memories; (*b*) charge-coupled devices (CCD), bubble memories, and floppy disks; (*c*) large magnetic disks and tapes; and (*d*) mass memories. In their comments on hardware-software forecasts, Fields and Paris conclude that the advantages and benefits of the digital optical videodisk over the analog videodisk for picture storage and economical high-capacity storage are important issues to the future design of CBI systems.

The success of a CBI system resides in the fact that the system must also be accepted and used by its user community. Fields and Paris list more than 30 major design variables that typically are neglected by the CBI system designer. This list includes such characteristics as appearance, simplicity, prestige, and portability. In response to some of these issues, they suggest to CBI system designers that computers, to the extent that they look expensive, may be valued. The authors conclude Chapter 3 with six major recommendations for research, for example, development of laboratory experiments that can test and validate-invalidate credible man-machine relations hypotheses.

Courseware

The term *courseware* originally distinguished computer code for instructional application (i.e., courseware) from computer code for general computer applications (i.e., software). In Chapter 4, Bunderson's definition of courseware emphasizes three major new concepts: educational work, delivery system, and economical replication. In Table 1.4, representative definitions of his key concepts are provided.

TABLE 1.4
Key Concepts in Courseware Definition

Delivery system—consists of physical objects and structures designed to perform or facilitate the work necessary to achieve education and training, and incorporates a human culture.

Educational work—consists a wide array of categories in which tasks are conducted on an individual basis: coaching and counseling in the use of the delivery system, learning motivation, diagnosis and prescription, modeling of process, presenting accurate information, and management of administrative information.

Economical replication—refers to the potential for educational work to be duplicated and disseminated rapidly and inexpensively and to reproduce the replicated product reliably. Examples include the book and the videodisk.

Because of the enormous cost and amount of work required to provide individualization, courseware seems to be the key way to perform the major portions of this work. Bunderson likens the current courseware revolution to the invention of the book. The book provided the ability to replicate information at low cost. With courseware, it is now possible to replicate interactions as well as information at low cost.

In his discussion of current product and process aspects of courseware, Bunderson considers product forms that have continued to exist. By "product form" he means conventional presentational packages (e.g., printed media), packages that replicate interactions (e.g., CAI), packaged performance aids (Statistical Packages for Social Sciences), and testing systems (e.g., CMI systems).

In his discussion of the current state in courseware *process,* the major thrust of his comments concern instructional systems development (ISD) models. In particular, Bunderson points to the interservice procedures ISD model (IPISD), which is rapidly becoming a standard for communication in the military and civilian training environment (O'Neil, 1979). However, there are several major areas in which ISD models need to be improved, such as explanations on "how to" in addition to "what to." We share his belief that interactive computer programs offer the greatest technological aids in the further development of the ISD model.

Bunderson also recommends that artistic, analytical, and empirical traditions be wed with intelligent use of technological tools to develop ISD models. Table 1.5 presents representative definitions of each of these traditions.

To discuss lessons learned about the ISD process for computer courseware, Bunderson uses two well-known major systems built within the last 20 years—TICCIT (Time-Shared Interactive Computer-Controlled Information Television) and Control Data PLATO (Program Logic for Automatic Teaching Operations)—that reflect two different authoring approaches. The former reflects an attempt to merge analytical, empirical, and artistic traditions, whereas the latter is a blending of the artistic and empirical traditions only.

TABLE 1.5
Artistic, Analytical, and Empirical Traditions

Artistic approach—is practiced by media developers (i.e., film and television), and emphasizes action and movement, dramatic content, and other visual artistic aspects of a presentation.

Analytical approach—concerns the application of instructional theorems that have been validated to the production of courseware components. These theorems have been validated on cognitive and psychomotor objectives.

Empirical approach—validates the claim that courseware produced by either the artistic or analytical approach does achieve its desired outcomes. The affective outcomes of the artistic approach and the instructional theorems of the analytical approach are validated by empirical testing to discover bugs.

1. Introduction and Overview of Computer-Based Instruction

In the near future, Bunderson foresees the ability of personal computers to administer more complex courseware product forms as well as the proliferation of new kinds of distributed systems through the availability of intelligent terminals. Games and personal programming will increase in the commercial sector, whereas job aids and testing systems will dominate the military and industrial sectors. These events will open the door to further courseware distribution in offices and homes. His vision of the future is consistent with Fields's and Paris's regarding hardware and software.

Learning Strategies

In Chapter 5, Rigney and Munro define learning strategies as those "human information-processing activities that facilitate acquisition, retention, and retrieval of representational and procedural knowledge in long-term memory [p. 128]." New emphasis is being placed on the development of various techniques and strategies to help the student create and use efficient and effective learning strategies (O'Neil, 1978; O'Neil & Spielberger, 1979). Prototype learning strategies are being developed to assist students to modify or replace the learning strategies they have created spontaneously and relied on. Dansereau (1978) has classified learning strategies as either primary strategies or support strategies. Primary strategies are concerned with the comprehension–retention, retrieval, and use of information. Support strategies focus on: (*a*) cultivation of a positive learning attitude; (*b*) coping with internal and external distractions; and (*c*) monitoring or meta comprehension.

The Rigney and Munro chapter reviews the contributions of cognitive science and educational psychology to the field of learning strategies. The area of cognitive science has fostered the creation of a variety of interdisciplinary tools and concepts with which researchers are forging ahead in the investigation of the cognitive processes and the design of effective and successful learning strategies.

The authors describe the cross-disciplinary parentage of cognitive science and cite the diverse lines of research, such as the processes of basic skills and sentence comprehension; and the nature of mental imagery and the different processes that support acquisition, retention, and remembering. They especially note that the theory of strategy transformations may provide the key assistance in the design of easily learned novice strategies that could be transformed into expert strategies.

Rigney and Munro also cite various studies involving the modeling of cognitive processes: (*a*) semantic memory models and production systems; (*b*) information processing models of mental abilities; (*c*) ad hoc computer simulation models; and (*d*) conscious and unconscious processing. They suggest that these four types of models provide the vehicles with which researchers can describe how certain kinds of learning strategies operate. For example, they state that conscious and unconscious processing reflects a duality in the human information-processing system architecture with which the other process models have not yet come to terms. One example of this duality is the issue of test anxiety, which is considered by some researchers to be a product of unconscious automatic processes aroused by conscious, unhealthy, self-evaluation.

The field of educational psychology has contributed to the study of learning strategies by the creation of learning-to-learn or studying-skills centers in universities. The primary significance of these centers is their function as the principal vehicle for bringing students into contact with learning strategies. The authors recommend that these centers be aligned with ongoing research, and thus provide a laboratory setting for research into learning strategies.

In their discussion of the prospects for the immediate future, Rigney and Munro comment on four major areas: cognitive process analyses, processing resources, individual differences, and trainability of basic skills. In the area of cognitive process analysis, the authors project that processes involved in the acquisition and retrieval of information can be described and taught as learning strategies.

Among the prospects for learning strategies in the late 1980s is an electronics industry that will continue to revolutionize computer technology with changes that will help to create automatic portable tutors and more efficient, less costly

TABLE 1.6
Contrasts between Research and Evaluation[a]

Research	Evaluation
1. Problem selection and definition are the responsibility of the individual doing the study.	Many people may be involved in the definition of the problem, and because of its complexity, it is difficult to define.
2. Given the statement of the problem and the hypothesis, the study can be replicated.	The study is unique to a situation and seldom can be replicated, even approximately.
3. The data to be collected are determined largely by the problem and hypothesis.	The data to be collected are influenced heavily if not determined by feasibility.
4. Tentative answers may be derived by deduction from theories or by induction from an organized body of knowledge.	Precise hypotheses usually cannot be generated; rather the task becomes one of testing generalizations, some of which may be basically contradictory.
5. Value judgments are limited to those implicit in the selection of the problem.	Value judgments are made explicit by the selection and definition of the problem as well as by the development and implementation of the study.
6. Relevant variables can be manipulated or controlled by including them in the design.	Only superficial control of potentially confounding variables can be achieved.

[a] Adapted from Hemphill, 1969, pp. 190-191.

1. Introduction and Overview of Computer-Based Instruction

TABLE 1.7
Some Contributions Associated with Four Milestones in the Field of Evaluation

Milestones	Contributions
1. Operationalism	Defining constructs by the procedures used to measure them Use of behavioral objectives for program design and evaluation Programmed instruction Computer-assisted instruction
2. Curriculum reform	Increased federal expenditure in education New initiatives in instructional techniques and materials Cooperation of scientists and teachers on the design of curricula Integration of curriculum development and evaluation as a unitary process (formative evaluation) Doctoral training programs in evaluation
3. Elementary and Secondary Education Act of 1965	Federal commitment to evaluation Federally mandated and funded evaluations The principle of refunding contingent on evaluation results Project accountability at the local level
4. School accountability	Teacher and administrator accountability Pupil behavior as criterion of program (teacher) success State-mandated evaluations Process evaluation techniques and instruments Evaluation as feedback for professional development.

software programs to teach learning strategies. Rigney and Munro suggest that growth in learning strategy research will be slow, but robust.

Evaluation

In Chapter 6, Borich and Jemelka distinguish between research and evaluation (see Table 1.6, reproduced from Table 6.2, Chapter 6). The authors describe six distinct, existing contrasts between research and evaluation: problem selection and definition, problem and hypothesis statement, data collection, deductive reasoning, value judgments, and relevant variables. Their working definition of evaluation would include determining the worth or value of an activity.

They also provide a historical overview of developments in educational evaluation by outlining the four major movements of the past and their contributions to the field of evaluation: operationalism, curriculum reform, Elementary and Secondary Education Act of 1965 (ESEA), and school accountability. As seen in Table 1.7 (reproduced from Table 6.1, Chapter 6), operationalism defined constructs by the procedures used to measure them. Eventually, operationalism was incorporated into the behavioral sciences, providing evaluators behavioral objectives for program design and evaluation.

Curriculum reform provided the basis of formative evaluation as well as new initiatives in instructional techniques and materials. The infusion of federal monies in education by ESEA encouraged cooperation of scientists and teachers on curriculum design and the creation of new doctoral programs in evaluation. The fourth development, school accountability, was embraced by teachers, school administrators, and community members. As an outgrowth of ESEA, it mandated state evaluations and encouraged the use of pupil behavior for program criteria. The resultant evaluation served as feedback for teacher and school administration development.

The different conceptions of evaluation have resulted in a diverse group of implementation models for evaluation studies, which in turn represent different concepts of evaluation. Borich and Jemelka list three popular evaluation models, emphasizing their general nature: (a) the discrepancy evaluation model; (b) the Stake model; and (c) the Context Input Process Product (CIPP) evaluation model. Table 1.8 (reproduced from Table 6.4, Chapter 6) describes these models. Essentially, these models represent general aids or heuristics to the conceptualization of evaluation designs.

One of the problems in choosing an evaluation model is the desire to perceive it as a methodology that actually conducts the evaluation rather than as a conceptual framework that must be placed into more specific constructs and methods. Thus, a main thesis in Chapter 6 is that evaluation models provide pragmatic heuristics to assist in organizing how an evaluation should be approached. They suggest that evaluators borrow appropriate components from other models to ensure the best match of program purpose and context to an evaluation model.

In recent years, there has been recognition of the need for a stronger foundation for evaluation theory. Four trends of evaluation have emerged as new conceptualizations have been built upon old ones: (a) decision-oriented; (b) value-oriented; (c) naturalistic; and (d) systems-oriented.

The decision-oriented evaluation approach helps to provide the evaluator with the kinds of information wanted by decision makers. This style establishes prespecified criteria for judging a program's effectiveness and reflects the perception that evaluation is a shared function between decision maker and evaluator. In this approach, the evaluator is dependent on the decision maker. On the other hand, the value-oriented evaluation approach emphasizes value judgments and assigns the act of judgment to the evaluator. This approach calls for a goal-free evaluation because goals may inhibit the evaluator's ability to perceive program effects. Moreover, the social responsibility of the evaluator in terms of concern for the welfare of the consumer is another component of the evaluator's role. However, the decision-maker's efforts to maintain the status quo may result in the evaluator designing evaluations that only examine the efficacy of the decision maker.

Naturalistic evaluation is a process that relies on observation as a means to discovery and verification. Naturalistic evaluation does not necessarily require

1. Introduction and Overview of Computer-Based Instruction

TABLE 1.8
Characteristics of Three Evaluation Models

Characteristic	CIPP	Stake	Provus
1. Purpose of evaluation	To make better, more defensible decisions	To describe and judge the merit of a thing	To uncover discrepancies between standards and performance
2. Implied role of evaluator	Information provider serves the decision maker	Makes judgments about the effectiveness of a program from descriptions and standards	Compares standards with performance at various stages to revise or terminate program
3. Relationship to objectives	High	High, "intents" are objectives	High, "standards" are objectives
4. Types of evaluation activities proposed	Context, input process, product	Description, judgment, logical and empirical contingency, congruency	Program definition, installation, process, product, cost-benefit
5. Unique constructs	Context	Logical contingency	Discrepancy
6. Relationship to decision maker	Integral	Unclear	High
7. Some criteria for judging evaluations	Did the evaluator collect context input, process, and product data?	Did the evaluator look for logical contingencies and collect judgment data?	Did the evaluator collect data and check for discrepancies within each stage?
8. Implications for evaluation designs	Mostly qualitative decisions except for product evaluation, where a control group is applicable	Deals mostly with descriptions and judgments. Control group helpful but not necessary, judgments can be absolute	Comparisons between standards and performance at each stage are essential. Control group is needed for cost-benefit stage

the subject's cooperation nor the subject's awareness. Moreover, this approach requires that the phenomena in question not be changed by being measured. Thus, it breaks ties with traditional forms of measurement and data analysis and represents a movement away from such formal definitions of evaluation.

The fourth, and last, evaluation model Borich and Jemelka describe is the systems-oriented evaluation, which includes the evaluator in the predevelopment and planning stages for instructional development projects. Specifically, this approach unifies and integrates the planning, development, and evaluation processes. Borich and Jemelka discuss the system approach using the interservice procedures for instructional systems development (IPISD) as a prime example.

The IPISD is composed of five basic sequential phases to analyze, design, develop, implement, and maintain instructional quality control (i.e., evaluation). Through the use of needs assessment and systematic program evaluation, the systems approach blends humanistic and behavioral psychological principles by deriving tools from fields including engineering, computer science, management science, and economics.

Borich and Jemelka divide their discussion of the implications for the emerging trends in the 1980s into the following categories: system approaches, naturalistic observation, needs assessment, policy assessment, and the role of the evaluator.

A major implication for the future is the early conduct of policy assessment in the planning process. These policy assessments should be performed prior to the needs assessment because they help to decide the appropriate kind of needs assessment required. Borich and Jemelka describes four basic elements that should be included in a policy assessment: (a) clarification; (b) identification of underlying goal assumptions; (c) definition of goal consequences; and (d) portrayal of alternative strategies. Whereas needs assessments contain quantitative data, policy assessments often include a mix of quantitative and qualitative. Another key difference is the focus policy assessment places on goal legitimization. As a fast-growing methodology, policy assessment has a variety of democratically oriented techniques (e.g., risk–benefit and trends extrapolation), which emphasize the participation of both laypersons and experts in making policy judgments. Thus, Borich and Jemelka maintain, policy assessments will be a crucial means to bridge the gap between new technological advances and the effects of programs created by these advances.

We have found their conceptualization of the field of evaluation to be extremely useful in conceptualizing the evaluation of CBI (see Orlansky and String, 1978, for an analysis of CBI evaluation studies).

Evaluation of CBI

Using the concepts discussed in Chapter 6 as an organizational framework, in the following discussion we will articulate the evaluation issues, problems, and concerns raised by these studies. These ideas are intended as an argumentative "think piece" for discussing desired ways of evaluating CBI.

For the studies reviewed, the evaluation of CBI seemed to have followed many of the same trends that influenced the growth and development of the larger field of evaluation. Within this context the evaluation of CAI–CMI courseware development seemed influenced most by the principles of operationalism and behavioral objectives, influenced moderately by the ESEA Legislation of 1965, and influenced least by the school and teacher accountability movement. The use of models of courseware development stemming from the curriculum reform movement also could be noted, particularly the team authorship of instructional courseware and the formative evaluation and pilot testing of prototype materials.

The evaluations of CBI that we reviewed were generally indistinguishable from applied research. Although these investigations were often called evaluations, they were, in essence, applied research studies indistinguishable from textbook definitions of experimental and quasi-experimental research. The statistical control of potentially confounding (interactive) variables, the terminal availability of data, and the use of control groups and statistical decision rules (e.g., $p < .05$) were standard ingredients of these studies.

Most CBI evaluations we reviewed did not employ evaluation models. The applied research nature of these studies made the use of evaluation models difficult because many fell outside the traditional definition of applied research. Given the applied research nature of these studies, the matching of any particular evaluation model to a particular CBI context was not possible. For example, only Provus's "cost-benefit" stage and Stufflebeam's "product" stage clearly matched the stated purposes of CBI evaluations, whereas such concepts as Stake's "logical contingency," Stufflebeam's "context evaluation," and Provus's "program definition" seemed too far removed from the conclusion-oriented and hypothesis-testing intent of these evaluations to be of use. An exception to these comments is a planned evaluation of an Army computer-managed instructional (CMI) system (Berkowitz, Wagner, & O'Neil, 1979).

Most studies reviewed seemed to fit the Phi Delta Kappa (PDK) National Study Committee's definition of educational evaluation stated as "the process of delineating, obtaining, and providing useful information for judging decision alternatives (Stufflebeam *et al.*, 1971, p. 4). The purpose of many of these studies was to provide decision makers with information as to whether or not previously articulated program goals and objectives were being met. This purpose seemed to add a decidedly summative emphasis to many evaluations, resulting in considerably less emphasis on formative evaluation and program modification. Sometimes conclusions were used in an all-or-none manner: The program was either accepted or rejected, adopted or discontinued. But, at other times the data were too ambiguous to point to such all-exclusive alternatives, and, hence, were ignored in making recommendations for program improvements.

Naturalistic inquiry played little, if any, role in the CBI evaluations reviewed. If naturalistic inquiry is defined as "any form of research that aims at discovery and verification through observation... [Willems & Rauch, 1969, p. 81]" or "slice of life episodes documented through natural language... [Wolf & Tymitz, 1976-1977, p. 12]," then little in the manner in which these CBI evaluations were conducted would suggest such a theme. Thus, naturalistic inquiry as a series of observations that are directed alternately at "discovery and verification" generally did not characterize CBI studies. Also, evaluators seldom approached the data collection with a minimum of preconceived categories or notions of what would be seen, or as though the phenomena were being observed for the first time. Thus, data were tabulated and analyzed in traditional ways with traditional statistical techniques, allowing little to be discovered other than that which was expected at the onset of the study.

If the system approach is viewed as a coherent, integrated, approach to planning, development, and evaluation, then few CBI projects evidenced this concept. To the contrary, planning, development, and evaluation generally were compartmentalized with the evaluator arriving at the end of the development task to fill an applied research or summative role. Characteristics of the systems approach, such as its capacity to deal simultaneously with multiple dimensions of the instructional environment, its reliance on program modeling to describe this environment, and the conceptualization of parts within wholes (programs within larger programs), also were not in evidence. CBI evaluations seldom considered the effects of the system in which the program operated or traced program effects to other than the immediate stimuli under consideration. In summary, evaluations of CBI that we have reviewed reflect the state-of-the-art during the time period that they were conducted (1969-1979). Because all of the evaluations had an applied focus this is not surprising. However, we hope that subsequent evaluations reflect the ideas in the Borich and Jemelka chapter.

Management

In Chapter 7, Seidel and Wagner focus on the management aspects of computer-based instructional projects. They draw on their extensive and varied experience in their descriptions of management factors, which typically are overlooked. They select complex CBI projects and use these examples to illustrate how the purposes of CBI projects (which vary widely in complexity, adaptability, and comprehensiveness) dictate personnel requirements and resource allocations, types of management functions and activities, and appropriate evaluation (e.g., formative and summative) models.

The authors briefly describe the three basic organizational structures used in CBI project management: (*a*) functional (pyramidal); (*b*) project; and (*c*) matrix (a combination of functional and project). They suggest specific criteria, such as budget cycle and existing hardware and software, on which to base the choice of the management organizational structure. Their experience with these three types leads them to conclude that either matrix or project is the most appropriate management organizational structure for CBI projects.

However, regardless of the type of organizational structure chosen, there are several key issues that must be dealt with successfully, if the CBI project itself is to be successful. For successful project management, the hopes, goals, and expectations of the user, researcher, and sponsor must be communicated clearly

1. Introduction and Overview of Computer-Based Instruction

and shared mutually. To support this thesis the authors relate numerous implementation examples: the Computerized Training System at Fort Gordon, the PLATO Project at Chanute Air Force Base, the National Science Foundation (NSF) sponsored TICCIT implementation. They also cite their own research including Project IMPACT and the implementation of a prototype computer-based training system for the U.S. Postal Service. Their experience has led them to conclude that if *any* of the major participants fail to understand the nature of the project and its products, serious problems will develop and the implementation of the CBI system will be, at best, only partially successful. The lack of agreement in the expectations of the project staff, the school administration, and the instructional staff adversely affected the implementation of all of the preceding systems.

Another major concern is in the area of evaluation. If the type of evaluation model used is inappropriate and inconsistent with the project then difficulties will ensue. Based on their extensive and diverse experiences the authors provide guidelines on the appropriateness of both formative (testing and improvement of a prototype system) and summative (comparison of alternative systems after debugging period) systems. Seidel and Wagner include implementations that were successful because the appropriate evaluation model was used, such as the IBM Field Engineering Division CMI implementation. They point to this case as an example of the importance of agreement when it occurs among the sponsor, user, and researcher within the same organization and its impact on successful implementation. The authors also describe cases of internal organizational agreement where ambiguities and difficulties have developed because of mismatched project purposes and evaluation models. The views expressed in Chapter 6 by Borich and Jemelka are consistent with those of Seidel and Wagner.

Another important issue the authors raise concerning internal project management is the need to create a balanced multidisciplined staff headed by a manager of competent interpersonal skills. Seidel and Wagner encourage the manager to recognize the importance of such issues as personnel turbulence and turnover, skill mixes, and continuing staff training and educational needs.

Based on their experiences, Seidel and Wagner state that CBI personnel need to understand the necessity to establish a stable hardware and software environment prior to the development of course materials on the system. In many cases the effect of parallel development of system components resulted in the instructors's lack of confidence in the reports generated by the system; consequently, the instructors depended on their own manual system.

In terms of the management of the technology transfer process, Seidel and Wagner conclude that a key factor contributing to the resistance to CBI implementation is a lack of understanding of CBI's advantages and limitations. Thus, it is essential that multilevel training programs include such topics as general awareness of computers, and build on multidisciplinary knowledge (e.g., evaluation versus courseware). To illustrate the need for and limitations of such a training program, the authors cite several examples in which the training program was affected adversely by a high degree of personnel turbulence at top management levels and the consequent need to provide additional training for new personnel. Because the new personnel did not perceive the project as their own, the training was not as effective as it was with the original personnel.

Based on these experiences the authors outline several conditions that must exist to assist in a successful technology transfer process: (a) a clear line of project control with a congruent allocation of authority and responsibility; (b) expectations and understandings monitored by frequent communications; and (c) the project manager mediating continuous communication.

In summary, Seidel and Wagner emphasize that the areas of control and communications over resources, project activities, and lines of communication are crucial to the successful implementation of a CBI system. Essentially, the lessons they have culled from their experiences include the need for (a) clear communication and shared understanding of the project's nature among all participants; (b) the use of appropriate evaluation models; and (c) proper and sufficient control over personnel and material resources as well as participant coordination. The authors suggest that it would be very useful to conduct a study that analyzes the major CBI systems according to purpose, including all management functions. They urge that the closure of the loop between research, development, and implementation be accomplished, in part by creating an instructional technology evaluation center. This center could control operational testing and the development of new technologies including in their design an experimental educational or training experience to provide feedback from the user to the researcher in a timely fashion.

CBI in Europe and Japan

In Chapter 8, Zinn focuses on CBI in Europe and Japan and contrasts developments, advances, and planning in the United States with current and projected activities in both Europe and Japan. His comments are based on the conviction that the monitoring and tracking of international CBI developments can assist in the planning of U.S. R&D programs. His chapter parallels the organization of the book and includes descriptions of activities in the areas of hardware, software, courseware, learning strategies, evaluation, and management.

In his discussion of hardware and software developments, Zinn notes that Fields and Paris's chapter on U.S. software and hardware technology developments can be generalized to the European and Japanese CBI experiences. In fact, other countries are increasing their reliance on small CBI systems more than is the United States because of low costs and higher reliability. Actions in the United Kingdom have provided direction, assessment, and information to potential buyers of these small, portable, and personal CBI systems.

1. Introduction and Overview of Computer-Based Instruction

In the area of hardware technology, Japan is concerned with the problems of character input and display because of difficulties germane to the Japanese language (i.e., a large character set). They have developed a technology that may be applicable to special character sets in English and to line drawings along with the display of complex graphics that follow sophisticated but well-established rules. West Germany and France have been pacing the advancement of the videodisk industry in Europe and their developments have been parallel to those in the United States.

Although the Unites States leads in software development, other nations such as France have concentrated on creating projects that foster local school acceptance of computers and programming. In France, teachers are given sabbaticals during which time they are expected to learn about computer programming and educational computer applications in their areas of expertise. Afterward, they are required to author computer-related units for use by teachers in the classroom using a new language created especially for them.

The products and procedures for developing courseware are not as impressive in Europe and Japan as they are in the United States. In Sweden, West Germany, and the United Kingdom, the emphasis is on content. In Japan, however, the emphasis is on language and how to build courseware that will help reduce the instructor's burden. The European courseware experience reflects small group and individual efforts that are more creative but less productive than are American projects. This is caused, in part, by the European tendency to integrate subject expertise and technical computing skills. An area of noteworthy importance in courseware is the development of intelligent computer-assisted instructional (ICAI) projects at Leeds and Edinburgh. These ICAI projects are capable of generating examples and matching them to a profile of the student's performance under a set of built-in decision rules.

Evaluation activities in Europe and Japan reflect a commonsense approach that, Zinn feels, is not taken usually by American educational researchers and psychologists. Typically, non-American CBI activities emphasize and encourage the transfer of CBI and other types of educational packages, sharing the costs for software development, purchase of communication equipment, and time-sharing systems. The field of evaluation per se, however, is not as advanced as it is in the United States.

Management activities in Europe and Japan have focused on four major areas: politics, technology, economics, and pedagogy. Because of limited CBI resources, the majority of these countries have pooled their available resources, emphasizing the development of standards for software and communications and the creation of a clearinghouse and other sources for technical information. The French experience reflects close cooperation and the mutual concerns of the computer educator, student, teacher, and potential government and industrial employers. Japan's computer industry is working together through a program of national economic and development cooperation to develop a new generation of computers and new markets for microelectronic products. Sweden's educational decision-making process is decentralized and thus encourages the active support and involvement of schools and the local community in managing the educational process.

Zinn's discussion of developments needed in the United States is based on his analysis of activities in Japan and Europe: (*a*) the involvement of CBI designers in the development and expansion of microelectronics technology; (*b*) appropriate application of this technology to such groups as the isolated, gifted, and disabled; and (*c*) design and implementation of national computer literacy programs.

He also stresses the need to foster national coordination of planning and funding for CBI programs designating centers as sites for CBI training, and research and development as they have been created in the United Kingdom. Seidel and Wagner echo this suggestion. These centers could assist in the development of additional courseware and its testing, which, Zinn believes, is in need of special attention. These centers could test alternative systems and approaches to CBI curriculum design. Zinn urges that the United States actively sponsor computing and information processing as part of the basic educational process to encourage national computer literacy.

His study of non-United States CBI experiences reveals the significant absence of U.S. national goals, priorities, and projects supported by federal funds. Zinn suggests that the United States should follow the example of the French and Japanese programs of government and industrial cooperation.

Postscript

In general, a major uncertainty regarding the state-of-the-art is *when* electronic transmission of information will be cheaper than paper. The uncertainty is based on policy decisions (communications are government-regulated) and market forces (extent and timing of videodisk and home computing market). If we hope to characterize the field in a sentence, we must say it has too few good ideas where we need them the most: measures of cost effectiveness in operational field environments, intelligent computer-assisted instruction systems, and media selection.

REFERENCES

Berkowitz, M., Wagner, H., & O'Neil, H. F., Jr. *A formative evaluation plan for the Automated Instructional Management System (AIMS)* (Tech. Rep.). Alexandria, Va.: Army Research Institute, June 1980.

Dansereau, D. The development of a learning strategy curriculum. In H. F. O'Neil, Jr. (Ed.), *Learning strategies.* New York: Academic Press, 1978.

O'Neil, H. F., Jr. (Ed.). *Learning strategies.* New York: Academic Press, 1978.
O'Neil, H. F., Jr. (Ed.). *Procedures for instructional systems development.* New York: Academic Press, 1979.
O'Neil, H. F., Jr., & Spielberger, C. (Eds.). *Cognitive and affective learning strategies.* New York: Academic Press, 1978.
Orlansky, J., & String, J. *Cost effectiveness of computer-based instruction in military training.* Arlington, Va.: Institute for Defense Analysis, 1978.
Stufflebeam, D. L., Foley, W. J., Gephart, W. J., Guba, E. G., Hammond, R. L., Merriman, H. D., & Provus, M. M. *Educational evaluation and decision making.* Itasca, Ill.: Peacock, 1971.
Willems, E. P., & Rauch, H. L. *Naturalistic viewpoints in psychological research.* New York: Holt, Rinehart & Winston, 1969.
Wolf, R. L., & Tymitz, B. Ethnography and reading: Matching inquiry mode to process. *Reading Research Quarterly,* 1976-1977, 12.

2

Computer-Managed Instruction: A Context for Computer-Based Instruction[1]

FRANK BAKER

INTRODUCTION

One of the persistent problems of computer-based instruction (CBI) is that of integrating it into the enduring fabric of the educational system. Far too many CBI systems have a short but often highly publicized life in the schools. Although the reasons for this are manifold and dealt with in other chapters, a significant factor is that they are often out of context. A CBI system that replaces part or all of a teachers instructional role will receive little if any long-term use. Sophisticated computer-based instructional systems that do not meet a perceived need also will not survive. Although such systems may be perfectly rational when considered in isolation, they do not fit within the framework of the existing instructional scheme of things. Thus, what is needed is a vehicle that in and of itself can be absorbed readily into the instructional milieu, yet provides the vehicle for a variety of other CBI systems to be incorporated at appropriate times. I believe that this vehicle is computer-managed instruction (CMI) because modern instructional strategies are becoming more complex and thus harder to manage from an instructional and administrative point of views. Individualized rate of progress schemes, in particular, pose severe management loads. Because of this, educators are turning to CMI as a means of bringing the power of digital computers to bear on the instructionally related management problems. Early

[1] The work reported in this chapter was supported in part by the Army Research Institute for the Behavioral and Social Sciences, contract number MDA 903-79-C-0558. Views and conclusions contained in this document are those of the author and should not be interpreted as necessarily representing the official policies, either expressed or implied, of the Army Research Institute for the Behavioral and Social Sciences, or the United States Government.

CMI systems were oriented heavily toward data processing and aimed at relieving teachers of burdensome clerical tasks (Baker, 1971). However, in my recent book (Baker, 1978) CMI was conceptualized as a six-part system consisting of the curriculum plan, the instructional model, diagnosis and prescription, reporting, management, and computing. Thus, the conceptualization of CMI was broadened and the emphasis changed from a computer orientation to an educational oreintation. Because my book provides an assessment of the state-of-the-art in CMI, this chapter provides an opportunity to broaden further the conceptualization of CMI with a view toward providing a context for other CBI systems. The vehicle chosen to do this is the highest level document in the software documentation chain: the system-concept document. In addition, the Training School was chosen as the target environment for the CMI system defined by this document. The systems concept document and the Training School were choosen on rather pragmatic grounds. First, because one of the most common failings of CBI systems is that they usually are underconceptualized and inappropriately documented. The system-concept document provides a high-level overview of a system in a form that is understood readily by all participants from the user to those funding the project. The existence of a first-rate system-concept document can do much to ameliorate the project management problems described by Seidel and Wagner in Chapter 7. Second, because I had indicated previously (Baker, 1978) that the short-term future of CMI lies with the training schools, especially military schools, rather than in elementary or secondary schools. Clearly, there is an excellent match between the state-of-the-art in CMI and the scientific management philosophy underlying rate-of-progress instructional schemes used in training schools. For these two reasons, the rest of this chapter is devoted to presenting a system-concept document for a state-of-the-art Training School CMI system.

The Training School Environment

The Training School constitutes a unique environment in which there is a premium on educational productivity by both the school and the student. The training programs are linked closely with particular jobs, skills, and advancement within a technical field. As a result, there is usually a well-defined body of knowledge and skills to be acquired by the student and the classic behavioral objectives–mastery learning paradigm is appropriate. Because of this and the diversity of the student's background, the Training School setting provides an ideal situation for the use of individualization based on rate-of-progress. Each student can proceed through a given program at a rate that is commensurate with past job experience, program-related background, and aptitudes. In addition, the program can be adapted to the individual student to maximize the rate-of-progress and the reaching of program goals. The total time it takes to train a given student is important because it is related to cost to the student and to the

2. Computer-Managed Instruction: A Context for CBI

school. Time to train also determines availability of the student and, in areas with rapidly changing personnel needs, availability is often an overriding consideration.

The individualization of instruction coupled with the curricular characteristics of most Training Schools results in a continuous, but asynchronous flow of students. Some students finish a program very quickly, others very slowly, and two students entering on the same day may finish days or weeks apart. The student flow, coupled with the number and variety of courses, leads to instructional management problems for both the school administration and the classroom instructor. It becomes very difficult simply to monitor the large numbers of students, let alone to optimize their learning experiences. Since its inception around 1966, CMI has evolved into an information system designed to facilitate the management of instruction and individualized instruction in particular. It provides the automated data collection, data processing, and reporting capability needed to cope with the managerial demands of individualized instruction. A CMI system frees the instructor and adminstrator from much of the low-level clerical work inherent in modern training curricula while providing the tools necessary to manage instruction. Experience has shown that it is not feasible economically to implement individualized instruction without supporting it with CMI. The enormous clerical and monitoring burden simply overwhelms existing instructional management paradigms when more than a handful of students are involved.

A CMI system benefits the student, the instructor, the school administration, and the eventual employer. The students are provided with continuous feedback and individualized assistance in their program. The instructor is freed of low-level clerical work, assisted in performing a managerial role, and provided additional time to work with students. The school administration is able to monitor student progress, optimally allocate resources, and manage a very dynamic educational environment. The eventual employer obtains students who are well trained, have known competencies, and are available on an individual basis rather than as groups such as a graduating class. Thus, it is clear that CMI will affect the role of everyone associated with a Training School. Most of the routine, time-consuming tasks will be automated, a wide range of information will be available for instructional and administrative decision making, and everyone will participate in the management of instruction. Finally, all this is accomplished at relatively modest operational costs.

Goals of the System-Concept Document

The system-concept document is the highest level document in a "top-down" documentation chain leading to the implementation of a CMI system. Its purpose in this chain is to present a high-level view of a state-of-the-art CMI system for the Training School setting. Within this context, the systems-concept document fulfills several goals that rarely are attended to in the usual documentation of computer-based systems. These goals are to:

1. Provide a conceptual framework for the CMI system. The system-concept document is intended to allow the reader to acquire an understanding of the philosophy of the CMI system. It shows the structure of the system, its interrelationships, and functional capabilities at a conceptual rather than an implementation level. Such a document enables the reader to develop a gestalt for the system. It is imperative that the system concept be understood fully by both those who develop CMI and those who actually will use it.

2. Serve as the guidance document for the design and implementation of the CMI system. The system-concept document serves as the touchstone of all subsequent efforts. It provides the system analyst, the curriculum specialist, and management with the conceptual framework within which the design trade-offs, the implementation choices, and the educational decisions are made. Thus, it provides a means for those responsible for the development of the CMI system to make enroute decisions within a conceptual framework rather than those made in a "fire-drill" mode or those deferred to the whim of the computer programmer. The end result is that at all stages of development the basic philosophy of the CMI system should be apparent to those involved.

3. Act as a baseline document for evaluation purposes. The document serves as the vehicle for the evaluation of the conceptual basis of the CMI system by those who will develop it and by those who will use the resultant system. The proper time to discover omissions, inconsistencies, or other difficulties is at the conceptual level before they become obscured by implementation and technical detail. It is much simpler and considerably less costly to iterate the conceptual-level document than the actual hardware–software implementation. In addition, the document can be used to evaluate whether or not subsequent levels of documentation are in accord with the system conceptualization.

4. Provide the basis for a "family" of systems implementation. The system concept can be used as the basis for the design of CMI systems implemented on microcomputers to supercomputers. In the latter case one could implement a full state-of-the-art system with hundreds of terminals supporting a school enrollment of many thousands. By eliminating functions, reducing certain capabilities, and limiting your ambitions, the CMI system could be implemented on a microcomputer. Such a microcomputer system could serve the students in a given program within a Training School (see McIsaac & Baker, 1978, for an example system). Attainment of these four goals will yield a systems-concept document that will be of significant value over the full life-cycle of the CMI system.

Underlying Assumptions

The system concept contained in the present chapter is based on the following assumptions:

2. Computer-Managed Instruction: A Context for CBI

1. The curriculum within each Training School program has been fractionated into segments. The lowest level of fractionalization is the behavioral objective. Within such a curriculum, extensive use is made of Criterion Referenced Tests and a mastery learning paradigm.
2. The major dimension of the individualization of instruction is rate-of-progress through the program.
3. The CMI system concept is independent of the instructional management philosophy of those who use the system.
4. The Training Schools using the system will vary considerably with respect to the number of programs, the duration of the programs, total student enrollment, and the flow of students through the programs.
5. The instructional delivery system is functionally independent of the curricular development and evaluation process. That is, a group of people distinct from the classroom instructors is responsible for the curriculum.
6. The CMI system is not targeted for implementation on a particular class of computers or manufacturer's line of products.
7. The computer hardware suite is dedicated to the CMI application.

SYSTEM OVERVIEW

In any educational system, the instructional process does not exist as an isolated entity. It is surrounded typically by a number of other activities whose roles are to provide the students, facilitate the instruction, handle the administrative aspects of a school, maintain the physical plant, deliver the needed logistic support, and provide the educational leadership. Because the basic role of CMI is to support the instructional process, it shares the latter's interfaces and interdependencies with the other aspects of the Training School. It also means that CMI can play a crucial role with respect to the overall functioning of the Training School. As a result, it is of fundamental importance that the CMI system be conceptualized as a component within the Training School. To do so, has important implications for the functions performed by the CMI system and hence for the design of the computer software. Consequently, this section attempts to define the Training School environment and the role of CMI within that context. This will be done in rather general terms because the intent is to identify those features that will have an impact upon the conceptualization of the CMI system.

Components of the Training School

Figure 2.1 presents a block diagram of a generalized view of a Training School. In this diagram there are six major components that perform particular roles and interact with each other. Each of these components are described briefly.

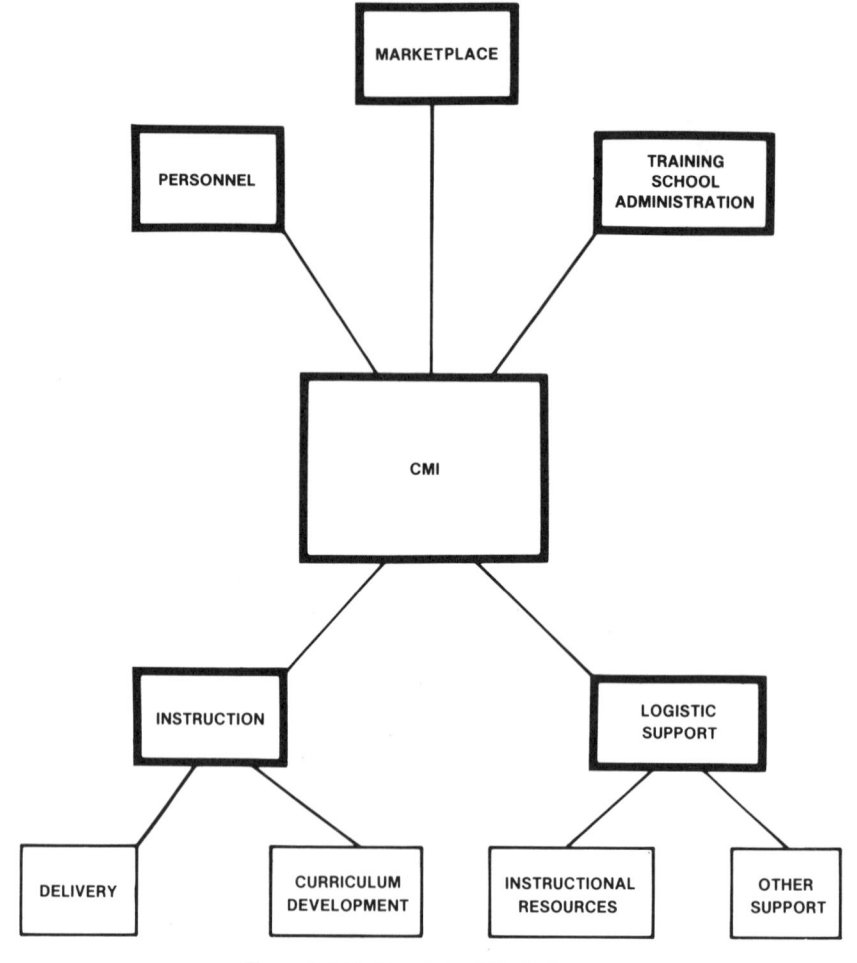

Figure 2.1 Training School block diagram.

The Marketplace

In the working world, needs arise for persons with particualr skills to perform certain functions. These needs can be caused by ordinary turnover of personnel, the introduction of new equipments, or the adoption of new technologies. As a result, there is a perceived need for a certain number of electronic technicians, diesel-truck mechanics, or carpenters. These needs are communicated to the Training School so that sufficient numbers of trained persons are available to meet the needs. The marketplace also evaluates the graduates of the Training School with respect to their on-the-job performance.

2. Computer-Managed Instruction: A Context for CBI

The Personnel Component

Whenever large numbers of students are involved in a training situation, it becomes necessary to implement a personnel system. Its role is to maintain records for each student that identify the student demographically, specify the student's program, record the courses completed, the levels of attainment or competencies, and subsequent on-the-job performance. The personnel component has interfaces with the marketplace, the school administration, and the CMI system. Because most student personnel systems are automated, the CMI interfaces will be computer-to-computer or via a computer compatible medium.

The Training School Administration

The administrative component is responsible for the overall functioning of the Training School. Its primary role is to see that the proper environment exists for the instructional process to be implemented. To fulfill this role, it must perform functions that range from providing educational leadership to ensuring that particular equipment will be available to certain students at a specified time. The actual structure of the administrative staff can vary; however, some form of hierarchical organization is usually found. In addition, the administrative lines of authority can extend into all of the other components.

The CMI System

CMI is a computer-based information system designed primarily to support the instructional process and secondarily the other components. The CMI system maintains an instructionally related data base that provides the classroom instructor with the information necessary to manage at the instructional unit, course, and program levels of management. Because of its close ties to the actual instructional process, the CMI system has interfaces with all of the other components, except the marketplace.

The Instructional Component

This component actually contains two subsets: The instructional delivery system (IDS) and the curriculum-development system. The instructional delivery system consists of the instructors and facilities used to train the students. The goal of the instructional delivery component is to train the students to their maximum potential within a minimal time frame and with the available resources. The curriculum-development staff designs the courses necessary to train a student to perform a particular job or role. It is responsible for creating the units of instruction, the assessment devices, the modes of presentation, as well as for the formative and summative evaluation of the resultant curriculum. In addition, it is often charged with the responsibility of teaching the instructors how to implement the particular course or program. For purposes of this chapter, it has been *assumed* that curriculum development and instructional delivery constitute separate aspects of the instructional component. This assumption was based on the knowledge that in industrial and military settings such a separation is the rule.

Logistic Support

The logistics component provides the expendable resources needed to operate a Training School. Two types of resources are involved: those directly expended during the course of instruction and those indirectly expended. The former would consist of test booklets, filmstrips, supplies, technical manuals, and so on. The latter would consist of those items needed to maintain the instructional facilities and environment. For example, the electronic components needed to maintain the computers in the CMI and computer-assisted instruction (CAI) systems, or parts needed to maintain noninstructional but school-related equipment or facilities. For present purposes, only the logistic support for the directly expended resources will be considered in the design of the CMI system.

Functional Flow

These five components can be placed in better relation to the CMI system through a short description of the functional flow. Let us assume that the marketplace generates a need for 720 technicians who are able to operate and maintain a new piece of electronic equipment, say, a radar set. This need will occur at the rate of 20 technicians per month over a 3-year period. This information is given to the school administration along with sufficient funds to both recruit the students and implement the necessary training program. The personnel system can be used to locate past and present students who have the prerequisite skills to be trained on the new equipment. This system can also be used to identify the students's previous training, which will provide a basis for the required training. The curriculum-development group then designs and develops the courses and trains the instructors. The logistic component is informed as to the logistic requirements unique to this new training program. The CMI system is prepared to accept instructionally related data from the program and the basic student data needed for instructional management.

Once all of this is in place the student flow begins. Students are registered, briefed, and provided with the appropriate instruction materials. Part of this initial procedure is to enter the students into the CMI system as individuals or members of instructional groups, and as members of administrative groups. Once instruction begins, the CMI system is used to collect data from the classroom. The students are provided continuous feedback as to their status in the program and their level of attainment: The program is individualized to the student. As instruction proceeds, the logistics support component is informed by the CMI system about the usage of expendables. When critical levels are reached the

2. Computer-Managed Instruction: A Context for CBI

resupply process is initiated. The CMI system also transmits summary-type data for each student to the personnel system as the various milestones are passed. The school administration can obtain summary reports of these data to determine student progress and predict course completions for a student or group of students. The data can also be used by the instructor to evaluate student performance. The detailed instructional-level data collected during the instructional process can be accessed by the curriculum developers for evaluation purposes. Initially this data can be used formatively. When students have completed the program and the marketplace provides on-the-job performance data, summative evaluation can be accomplished. The instructors stand at the core of this functional flow. They are in one-to-one contact with the students and are responsible for their performance. They use the CMI system to orchestrate both the day-to-day activities of the students as well as their progress through the curriculum. The various reports generated by the CMI system on either a scheduled or "on-demand" basis allow the instructor to examine the situation at many depths and implement actions necessary to achieve the instructional goals.

When the students complete the program, they will be trained properly to perform the job and the instructionally related data are transferred to archival storage. The personnel system retains the summary data and identifies the student as graduated. The administration informs the marketplace that the trained technicians are available, and the students move out to their new jobs.

Interface Considerations

The functional flow reveals a number of interfaces between the computer-managed instruction (CMI) system and other components that need to be clarified before a CMI system can be designed. The CMI-personnel interface is one that poses particular problems. To manage instruction, a certain amount of information is needed about student characteristics, their training program, and administrative grouping within the program. However, the usual student-records system maintains much of this same information. Thus, there is the choice of storing this information in only one system and accessing it when needed or duplicating basic data in both systems. In the present system it has been assumed that the basic demographic, academic, and administrative data of the student will originate in the personnel system, and a copy will be transferred to the CMI system when a student or group of students enter the school. The CMI system will transfer necessary instructionally related summary-data to the personnel system at appropriate times or milestones.

The interface between the CMI system and the instructional system is primarily via devices that are on-line to the computer including optical mark readers (OMR), keyboard terminals, and cathode ray tube (CRT) terminals as well as the usual computer peripherals. It is mandatory that the instructor have on-line access to the CMI component. These same terminals will provide the on-line feedback needed by the student to participate in the instructional management process. Because curriculum development is also a dynamic process, this subset of the instructional component also needs access to the data base maintained by the CMI system. Again, on-line terminals can be used for a certain level of access and reports produced via high-speed printers can provide the remaining access.

The interfaces between CMI and the logistic component involve information dealing with instructionally related expendables. Although this interface could be on a computer-to-computer basis, it is assumed in this chapter that the CMI system will generate the forms needed by the logistic component, and a bureaucratic interface is maintained.

The interface between the CMI and the school administration is similar to that with the instructional component. The basic difference is the level of detail of the reports and displays available to the administrators. Presumably, administrators would not need access to the fine-grain, instructionally related data used by the instructors. This interface also exposes a problem in the area of scheduling. Although scheduling of students and allocation of resources is an administrative function, under individualized instruction this process is linked very closely to ongoing instruction. As a result, the implementation of these functions will be accomplished via the CMI system.

FUNCTIONS PERFORMED BY THE CMI SYSTEM

The functions described in this section are those that will be implemented via the CMI software. They have been divided into two classes of functions: (*a*) those associated with instructional management; and (*b*) the support-type functions underlying the CMI software. Although these two classes interact extensively in the actual operation of the CMI system, this interaction will not be discussed in this chapter.

Instructionally Related Functions

Data Collection

To support the instructional management process, a wide variety of data must be collected by the CMI system. The data defining each student's instructional history are generated as the student passes through the curriculum. The results of pencil-and-paper tests used as pretests, curriculum-embedded tests, posttests for curricular units, and achievement tests encompassing larger curricular segments

2. Computer-Managed Instruction: A Context for CBI

are collected as they occur. In the Training School setting, extensive use can be made of other types of assessment procedures, such as: observational schedules completed by the instructors, checklists of tasks completed, and rating scales of level of performance in field exercises. All of these data must be collected in a form that can serve as computer input. In addition, considerable use is made of computer-based equipment during the training process, for example, simulators, laboratories, student carrells, and CAI. In each case, interfaces can be established and instructionally relevant data collected during the use of these equipments can be transmitted to the CMI computer. It is particularly important that any CAI that is employed be interfaced to the CMI system.

Administrative data also must be collected by the CMI system. Class attendance data can be obtained for each formally scheduled activity. The expenditures of instructional resources can be recorded either directly or indirectly. Finally, the time each student devotes to the various curricular entities or tasks can be recorded.

Although the CMI system directly collects only the data arising from the learning situation, considerable information that has many uses can be derived from these same data. Because of the dependence of the CMI system on the basic data it collects, the data elements to be collected must be chosen carefully, and their role in the creation of derived data fully explored. Data collection merely for the sake of collection cannot be tolerated because the overall storage requirements of a CMI system are very large even when only minimal data are collected at the instructional level.

Diagnosis and Prescription

From a student's point of view, diagnosis and prescription are the core of a CMI system. The diagnosis function is used to determine the basis of the students' observed performance. Unfortunately, the state-of-the-art in diagnosis is very rudimentary and descriptive at best. Nonetheless, a mechanism must be implemented in the CMI system to diagnose students' performance at the unit of instruction, course, and program levels. Unfortunately, most existing CMI systems only perform diagnosis at the unit of instruction level. In the Training School setting it is very important also to perform diagnosis at the course and program level. Failure to do so, will negate many of the advantages of the individualization based on rate-of-progress that is so necessary in a Training School. No two training programs will have the same diagnostic sequences or variables, yet they should share a common generalized diagnostic capability. Thus, considerable care must be exercised when designing the diagnostic function to provide the scope and flexibility needed to meet a variety of needs.

The prescription function implements two types of prescriptions: forward and remedial. The forward prescription is made when a student successfully completes a curricular segment and proceeds to the next segment. The forward prescription must take into account the intersection of the student's instruction history and the curricular requirements of the assignable segments. The remedial prescription is aimed at assisting the student in eliminating a performance deficiency. The prescription function should assign the student an optimum set of activities to eliminate the deficiency. Again, the state-of-the-art in prescription is very rudimentary and largely heuristic. Therefore, the prescriptive function of the CMI software should implement a generalized mechanism rather than actual prescriptions.

It should be noted that the specific diagnostic procedures and prescriptions associated with a given curricular segment or activity are created during the curriculum-development process. The CMI system provides the generalized capabilities needed to put diagnosis and prescription in operation for a given student.

Performance Monitoring

Several characteristics of the Training School environment result in the need for a performance-monitoring capability. Typically, a large number of courses are offered and they are of various lengths. In addition, large numbers of students are involved, often in several courses within a given program. When an individualized rate-of-progress scheme is superimposed upon this setting, performance monitoring becomes crucial to both instructional management and school administration. At the unit of instruction level it is necessary to monitor the progress of each student through the unit. This can be linked closely to the entry of assessment data into the CMI system and largely can be automated. Students and groups of students must be monitored relative to their progress through specific courses as well as the sequence of courses and activities that constitute their training syllabus. The key to performance monitoring of students is the use of a program of studies (POS). The POS is a list of all the training activities that a student must complete to graduate. It contains a specification of these activities at the unit of instruction, course, and program levels. The POS is generated by the CMI system when the student enters the school; it takes into account the student's abilities, past training, and current training requirements. As the student proceeds through the program of studies, data (such as units completed) are compared to the POS to provide the necessary performance monitoring. In many cases it will be necessary to alter dynamically the POS when it becomes apparent that the current one is not appropriate for a given student or group of students. It should be clear that the POS plays a crucial role in monitoring performance, and all of the other CMI functions depend on it to various degrees.

In the Training School environment, instructors often are obtained from the pool of persons experienced in various trades or technologies. These persons may lack extensive backgrounds in teaching and often serve as instructors for limited terms. As a result, performance monitoring of instructors also should be sup-

2. Computer-Managed Instruction: A Context for CBI

ported by the CMI system. Such monitoring should take into account the characteristics of the student body as well as that of the specific courses taught by the instructor. Performance monitoring of instructors long has been a difficult problem from a theoretical point of view, and a messy one from an administrative point of view. However, the CMI system should be designed to provide accurate and timely data to be used in this process.

Because of the rapidly changing technologies involved in the courses offered by a Training School, the curriculum is very dynamic. Often each new piece of equipment to be used in the field requires specialized courses to train the operators and maintenance technicians. The net result is a requirement for performance monitoring of the curriculum itself. The CMI system collects considerable data, such as, test scores, time-to-complete, number-of-attempts, student flow, and so on, that are useful in monitoring a curriculum. Such monitoring should be continuous and be available to the curriculum developers so that they function within a closed-loop rather than an open-loop system.

Performance monitoring of students, instructors, and the curriculum should be done within three time frames: past, present, and future. Monitoring of past performance is essential to evaluating the different facets of the Training School from an instructional as well as an administrative point of view. Monitoring of present performance underlies the management of the instructional process as well as of the Training School itself. One of the major functions of classical management theory is planning; hence monitoring of future performance must also be performed. Present and past performance can be used in conjunction with the students' POS to predict many future situations, for example, when students will complete a course or program. Achievement trends can be used to identify a curriculum that will become dysfunctional in the future. Usage rates of expendable instructional materials have implications for the future ability of the school to support certain instructional activities. In all these cases early awareness allows the students, instructors, and the administrators to plan future courses of action to meet the challenges.

Performance monitoring is dependent totally on the data collection function of the CMI system; thus, the design of the data collection function of CMI must take performance monitoring into account. Proper kinds of data must be collected; they should be collected at the proper points in time; and they also should be complete and accurate. In addition, the CMI system should incorporate quality control procedures to ensure the integrity of the data for performance monitoring as well as other management purposes.

Scheduling

Two types of scheduling are important in the Training School: instructional and administrative. Instructional scheduling is based on a student's POS. It specifies what the student should be doing relative to the curriculum. Schedules exist for the student at the unit of instruction level indicating the activities the student should be engaged in, the assessment instruments that will be used, and the timing of these events. At the course and program level, the POS is used to schedule the student through a curricular path that may or may not be unique to a given student. Although the POS is also used in performance monitoring the emphasis there is upon how well the student is achieving. In scheduling, the POS is used to indicate what activities students should be engaged in at any given point in time.

Administrative scheduling is a result of the composite of the POS of all the students in the Training School. Smooth functioning of the school requires that students have class schedules, that activities involving numbers of students be planned in advance, and that students and instructors be aware of the activities. Administrative scheduling is particularly important in Training Schools employing individualization of instruction because the asynchronous nature of the student flow in a Training School makes scheduling difficult. As a result, the instructionally related data, student status relative to the POS, and other data collected by the CMI system are the key to effective instructional and administrative scheduling. For this reason the scheduling function properly is considered an integral part of the CMI system.

Resource Allocation

Whereas scheduling is getting the right students to the correct places, resource allocation is positioning the proper materials, facilities, and staff to meet the student schedules. Because the allocation of these resources is tied directly to the instructional process, the CMI system should have the responsibility for implementing the resource allocation function. It has the proper data base to relate student schedules to resources and to determine both present and future allocations. Implicit in this function is the need to maintain an accurate inventory of the several classes of resources. Expended resources should be monitored so that future needs can be anticipated and the logistic component should be notified so that proper inventory levels are maintained. A well-designed resource-allocation function is necessary to support both the instructional process and the management of the Training School.

Reporting

Because CMI is basically a management information system, reporting is a crucial aspect of the system. Persons ranging from students to the head of the school rely on the reporting function. Each of these persons, from his or her own point of view, is interested in the instructional and other data stored by the CMI system. As a result, a variety of reports, defined in the next section, are needed. There is a temptation to provide a general computer-based query capability. However, experience has shown that such a facility is not viable in the CMI con-

2. Computer-Managed Instruction: A Context for CBI

text. Standard reports produced on a scheduled or demand basis have proven to be the best approach. Yet, there is a need for flexibility in the contents and formats of reports over a period of time. To meet this requirement, the reporting function should be based on a generalized report-generation function. Such a capability should allow the modification of existing reports or the creation of new reports with minimum impact on the total CMI system.

Computer-Related Functions

There are a number of computer-managed instruction (CMI) functions that depend on either the support provided by the operating system or software within the CMI package. Three of these are discussed below.

Man-Machine Interface Function

Within the instructional setting the CMI system interfaces with students, instructors, and administrators through a number of on-line terminals. Considerable data are collected via OMR equipment, which is on-line and often operated by the students. The CRT terminals are used to obtain certain reports quickly and act as data entry terminals. Low- and medium-speed, hard-copy terminals are also employed. As a result, the operating system must provide the software to interface easily a variety of standard and often nonstandard peripheral devices such as simulators and laboratory equipment. In addition, the communication with these nonstandard peripherals should be handled via language constructs within the compiler-level language used for the CMI software. To do otherwise is to invite a host of intractable, long-term, software-configuration management and maintenance problems.

Data-Base Management Function

The success or failure of a CMI system from both an operational and a software design point of view rests on the data-base management function. This function should be implemented as a separate software entity that is used by the remainder of the CMI software as a support package. The CMI data base is characterized by the existence of various classes of files. Certain files are very large and are accessed frequently, but have contents that are reasonably stable during a school term. Other files are large, have heavy use, and dynamic contents. Finally, there are small files with usage characteristics unique to their content.

When the CMI system is employed in an individualized Training School environment, the file update and maintenance procedures are performed on almost a continuous basis in support of instruction and administration. In addition, both on-line and off-line data-base procedures will be performed via the CMI system. Thus, the data-base management (DBM) package must contain features and capabilities to support the maintenance of the data base.

Software access to the DBM package must be such that the persons writing the CMI software can implement the data base and its use in a simple and effective manner. The more powerful these mechanisms, the better the overall CMI software.

System-Generation Function

A basic assumption underlying the design of a CMI system for Training Schools is that these schools are going to vary with respect to many characteristics. They will vary with respect to size-related variables such as the number of students, number of courses, the staff, and the available resources. They will vary with respect to flow-related variables such as student flow, length of courses, courses per program, and staff turnover. They will also vary with regard to which features of a generalized CMI system are in concert with their view of instructional management. Finally, a variety of different computer capabilities will be available for implementation of the CMI system. As a result the CMI system must be capable of being adapted to a wide range of settings but to do so in a way that can be both configuration managed and software maintained by a single organization over the life cycle of the CMI system. This need will be met by providing a system-generation function as part of the CMI system.

CMI SOFTWARE SYSTEM CONCEPT

Introduction

Inspection of the six instructionally related functions makes it clear that CMI is fundamentally an on-line management information system. As such it must rest on a well-conceived data-base design that is exploited by a powerful and flexible DBM package. It is also clear that the man–machine interface must be designed and human-factored to allow students, instructors, and administrators to use the system with only minimal training and no computer-related expertise. The intersection of these two observations should form the basis for the design philosophy underlying the CMI software concept.

The operational environment of a Training School CMI system places the following requirements upon the software concept:

1. The software should be independent of the content of the data. This requirement arises from the need to employ the CMI system in Training Schools with different curricula, different student bodies, and a variety of approaches to instructional management. Thus, the CMI software should be generalized sufficiently to perform its functions independently of the local meaning of the data.

2. Computer-Managed Instruction: A Context for CBI 39

2. The software concept must be independent of the capacity of the system in terms of numbers of students, number of courses, and related variables. Except for some high-level restrictions imposed by the state-of-the-art and economic considerations, the CMI software should not be designed to specific capacities. The data-base design and the CMI software design should be such that they function equally well at their minimum and maximum capacities.

3. The software concept must provide for a high degree of tailorability of the system to adapt to a wide variety of Training School situations. This tailorability involves two types of trade-offs. First, in particular settings, not all features of the CMI system may be needed. Thus, at system-generation time, it should be possible to delete the related software without degrading the rest of the system. Obviously, functions should not be deleted at will, but specific features should be designated as optional. Second, it should be possible to perform a trade-off between data-base capacity and level of detail at which the instructional program is managed. If managed at the behavioral-objective level, large masses of very detailed information are generated during the instructional process. Consequently, the number of students so managed must be smaller because of fixed data-storage resources. Conversely, if managed at the course level, relatively little data are generated per student and large numbers of students could be managed. Both of these trade-offs should be part of the study work done by a given Training School prior to the tailoring of the basic CMI software package to their own situation. Once the trade-offs are made and system generation performed, the operational software is frozen.

4. The operational costs attributable to the CMI system must be minimized. Because a CMI system is added onto an existing instructional process, it represents an additional cost. It is also a cost that is difficult to relate directly to observable benefits such as increased rate of progress, student achievement, and so on. As a result, the CMI software design should be efficient and have a low per student contribution to the overall operational costs.

5. The software should protect the system from errors. Because the CMI system will be operated by novice users, the software should provide features to protect the users from their own errors as well as protect the system from user error. The computer operating system should be such that when hardware and software failures occur, there is a simple and effective recovery procedure. When feasible, degraded modes of operating should be provided to allow for continuous operation.

6. The software design must be extensible. After gaining operational experience with a CMI system, the users often suggest additional features. The software must be designed so that new features and enhancements to existing features can be accomplished with a minimum of programming. Extensibility is particularly important in the area of reporting.

Data-Base Concept

In this section, the data base will be described at a conceptual level. During the system-design process these conceptual files may be allocated to a number of different actual files and particular features of several conceptual files may be combined to create a single file. In this section the logic of the files and the types of data they contain will be discussed.

To facilitate discussion of the data base it is necessary to define the levels in the curriculum hierarchy. Unfortunately, there is no standardized nomenclature. Hence we shall define the elements within the curriculum as follows:

1. *Program:* the largest identifiable curricular element. In the Training School it is commonly associated with a particular trade or skill. For example, a student would enroll in a program leading to certification as a dental assistant. The typical Training School offers many different programs.
2. *Course:* a separate curricular segment dealing with some major aspect of a program. Courses such as basic electronics or advanced circuits would exist. A program is composed of several such courses arranged in a particular structure.
3. *Unit:* a segment of a course that represents a subtask or other identifiable curricular entity. Typically, units are the focus of a student during the instructional process. A unit may be a chapter in a book, or other such segments that the curricular designer feels should maintain a separate identity. Often the unit constitutes the minimum managerial element of the CMI system from the student's and instructor's point of view.
4. *Objectives:* the lowest level of curricular fractionalization possible in the CMI system. Typically these are the behavioral objectives.

It is important to recognize the concept of the miminum managerial element within the CMI context. Both instructors and students tend to view the curriculum at some convenient conceptual level. The choice of this level facilitates discussion and communication in regard to the curriculum and is reflected in the contents of the reports. Thus, the curricular elements at this level become identified as the minimum managerial elements. For example, most individualized curricula are based upon behavioral objectives, but they are managed at the unit of instruction level. As a result the POS, the progress reports, and so on are stated in terms of units rather than behavioral objectives. This is true even though the diagnosis and prescription information given a student is at the behavioral-objectives level. Within a CMI system the minimum managerial element can be based on any curricular level, but the choice has implications for the total system.

Curricular File Contents

The types of data stored in the curricular file will be described in terms of classes of data that would be associated with each of the four curricular levels.

Structural Data

Data will be stored that define the total curricular structure for each program managed by the Training School. The name of the curricular segment, the prerequisite relationships, and other data will enable the school to specify any of the common curricular structures (linear, strand, block, and tree) as well as unique combinations of features of these. The structural information will be used to implement features, such as the POS, where it is necessary to trace prerequisites and interrelationships among and within segments of the curriculum.

Assessment Data

Each assessment procedure employed in the program will be defined in terms of the following:

ID—the external name of the procedure
Type—multiple choice test, checklist, and so on
Input medium—scan sheet, keyboard entry, computer data transfer, other devices
Data generated—total score, subscale scores, ratings, profile, and so on
Scoring procedure—answer key, number ranges, counts of entities
Error checks—number range, number values, and other validity checks used
Curricular location—the places within the curricular structure where the assessment procedure is used
Dependencies—any information needed to link the procedure to other related assessment procedures

Diagnostic Data

When an assessment procedure has been used, the diagnostic capabilities of the CMI system will be applied. Thus, each assessment point will be described in terms of the data used in the diagnostic procedure. The curriculum file contains only a definition of the appropriate data on which to base the diagnosis. The actual data are stored elsewhere. The diagnostic data defined fall into three classes:

1. Assessment procedure and its outcome variables
2. Curricular-related data
3. Student-related data

The assessment-related data indicate what procedure was used, what data is associated with it, and any linkages to related procedures or outcomes. The curricular data specify any data about the curricular structure that are needed for diagnosis at this point. The student-related data may include past performance on the same or related assessment, information from the student's POS, as well as other student history data.

Prescription Data

At curriculum development time the instructional designer must create the prescriptions associated with each diagnosis. These prescriptions are stored in the curricular file along with descriptors needed to access the prescriptions. The data set would consist of the following:

1. The prescription rule applied
2. Any modifying or filtering data
3. The actual prescription messages
4. The underlying diagnostic procedure

Resource Data

Each entity defined in the curricular structure of a program will be accompanied by a definition of the instructional resources it requires. The resource defined will be appropriate to the curricular level involved. The types of resources involved would be as follows:

1. Materials—those instructional materials needed by the student to engage in the instruction
2. Physical facilities—those school facilities needed
3. Personnel—those staff members who are needed to conduct or assist in the instruction

The manner in which these resources are associated with the curriculum is a matter for detailed design. However, it may be appropriate to link resources associated with groups of students, such as classrooms, with an instructional unit or course. Resources such as technical manuals or simulators may well be linked to a behavioral objective.

Curriculum Evaluation Data

Data needed for the curriculum evaluation process should be stored. Included would be the following:

1. Data relating to student flow such as total number completing and the time-to-complete

2. Information as to the number of loops through a segment needed before completion
3. Assessment-related data such as running-item difficulty, test means and ranges

Some design considerations are: How much of the evaluation data should be derived from the student administrative and history files and how much should be stored there? It is preferable to keep the curricular file a static file, but the importance of the curricular evaluation data may outweigh this desire.

Student Instructional History File

As each student proceeds through his or her program of studies, data are generated by the instructional process itself and data, such as prescriptions or test scores, are generated by the CMI system. The dynamic instructionally related data are stored in the student history file. Past experience has shown that more efficient CMI software can be developed if the student history file is divided into two parts having identical formats. The active part stores data for only the curricular segments in which the student is actually engaged. The archival part stores all the data for a completed curricular segment. Typically this would be at the level of the minimum managerial element. The following classes of data would be stored for each student:

Curricular data: a definition of the curricular segment(s) for which data are stored. In addition, any data defining unique instructional characteristics of the segment will be provided.

Assessment data: a definition of the assessment instrument currently assigned such as a pretest, embedded-test, or posttest. For those assessment procedures completed, the procedure identification, the date accomplished, and the actual response data will be stored. If the assessment procedure resulted in a prescription, the identification code of the prescription will be stored. When it is needed, the person completing the assessment procedure, such as an observational schedule, will be identified.

Progress data: whereas much of the progress-related information can be derived from the data stored in this file, certain progress data can be stored to reduce the overall computing requirements. Data such as the number of days the student has been in a course, running averages like the average number of attempts before completion, and predicted completion date, can be computed and stored on a systematic basis or triggered by events.

The student history file needs to be designed with considerable care because it is involved in a number of trade-offs. It should be possible to raise or lower the minimum managerial element without changing the data-base design. It should also be possible to process but not store the instructionally related data associated with curricular segments below that defined as the minimum managerial element. At system generation time it should be possible to delete whole subsets of data, such as prescriptions assigned or item response vectors.

Student Administration File

One of the assumptions made in an earlier section was that a personnel system exists external to the CMI system. Whereas the personnel system contains extensive information about the students past education, jobs, experience and related data, the student administration file contains the student's transcript and other data relating only to current enrollment in the Training School. This latter file acts as a repository of summarized data describing a students progress and as a linking device for a number of CMI functions. The student administration file contains the following classes of data:

Demographic data: the student's name, job speciality, home address, telephone number, and any handicaps that are of note

Administrative data: the name of the student's training program, entering date, scheduled graduation date, and administrative group

Instructionally related data: the primary data are the student's POS. The individual curricular segments within the POS will be described in terms of the following: (*a*) completed, currently assigned, unassigned; (*b*) date assigned; (*c*) completion date—actual, predicted; (*d*) instructional group membership; (*e*) assessment results where appropriate.

It should be noted that the membership of administrative groups is essentially fixed over time whereas the membership in instructional groups is dynamic and dependent situationally on the instructional process. The instructionally related data will also include attendance data in the form of dates and hours that a student is not at an assigned location.

Instructional Resources File

The curricular file specifies the resources needed by each segment of a training program. The instructional resources file defines the resources that can be allocated for instructional purposes. The classes of resources and their descriptive data are as follows:

Instructional materials and supplies: Technical manuals, books, electronic components and similar items will be listed. The monitoring for the usage level of these items will be performed by the CMI system, but the inventory responsibility for them rests with the logistics system.

2. Computer-Managed Instruction: A Context for CBI

Physical plant and facilities: A list of the classrooms, laboratories, simulators, CAI systems, and large pieces of equipment will be maintained. Each element on this list will be described in terms of its capacity (simultaneous number of students served), and any routine maintenance or other applicable schedules that might affect availability.

Staffing resources: The staff necessary to implement the training program will be defined. The names and specialties of the instructors, equipment operators, maintenance technicians, and other persons will be stored. To predict availability accurately vacation schedules may be stored, if the school operates on a continuous basis.

In the case of physical plant and staff resources the CMI system will maintain data on the current allocation of these resources and their future availability.

Software Block Diagram

A high-level block diagram of the CMI software is provided in Figure 2.2. The software is based upon a hierarchical structure that is controlled by a series of cascaded drivers. The core of each driver implements a man–machine interaction where the various modes of operation or functions are selected from lists. Where a function can be performed in the batch mode, the man–machine interaction is mimicked by control cards. Thus, there is no need to distinguish between batch-oriented and keyboard-oriented software. Each of the major software modules will be described in functional terms.

Major Module Controller

The major module controller (MMC) is the executive program for the CMI system and the routine that obtains control from the computer's operating system. The MMC provides the following capabilities:

1. *User log in and authorization:* When a terminal is activated, the MMC verifies that the terminal and its user are authorized to perform the functions requested.
2. *System initialization:* The MMC is used to "bring up" the CMI system each day.
3. *Major mode selection:* The menu of major capabilities is presented and the user selects the function to be performed. Control is then passed to the appropriate major module.
4. *Error recovery:* When the individual major modules cannot cope with an error situation, they pass control back up to the MMC for resolution. Unrecoverable errors result in control returning to the operating system.
5. *System shutdown:* At the end of the school day, a systematic set of shutdown procedures are performed. These include: creating backup copies of

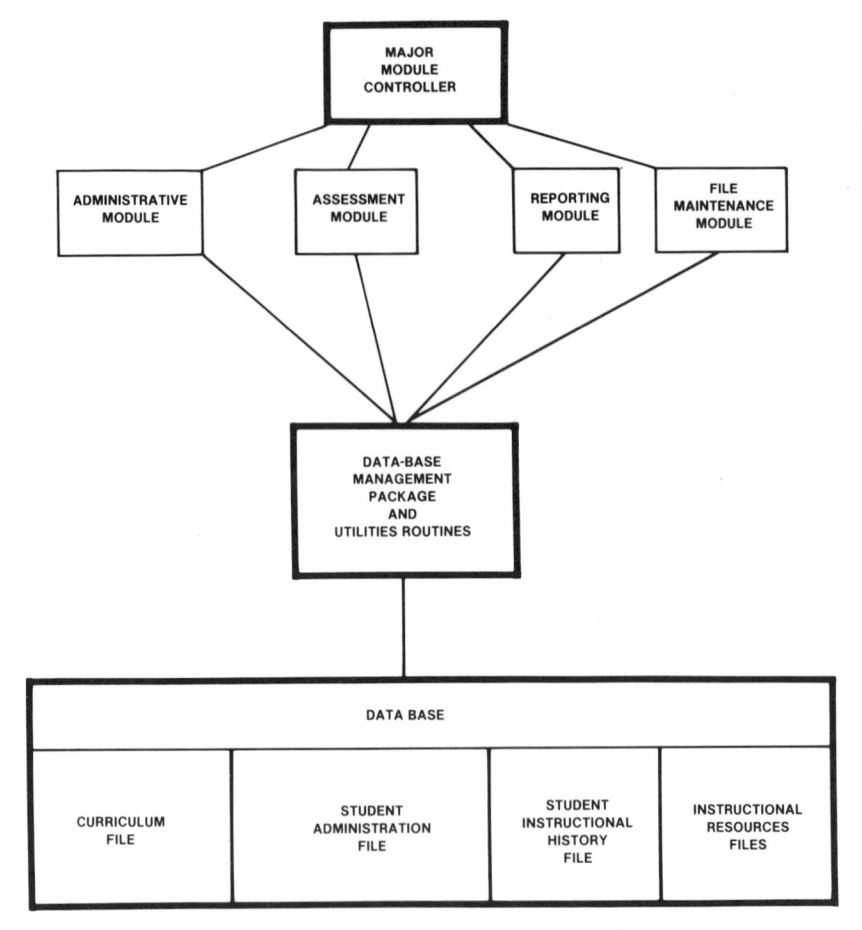

Figure 2.2 Training School CMI software block diagram.

the dynamic files and freeing the transaction logging files or other such error-recovery files. The intent is to ensure system integrity and proper startup the following day.

Administrative Module

The administrative module (ADM) implements those functions associated with instructionally related administrative procedures. Certain of these functions will be performed by the schools administrative staff; others would be done by the instructional staff. The functions implemented are the following:

1. *Individual student registration:* Whereas the bulk of the student registration process is performed via the file maintenance module, there is a need

for a means to register students on an individual basis. The results will be the appropriate data in the student administrative file and the student history file.
2. *Program of studies (POS):* A capability is provided to generate a predetermined POS for each student in a given program or to create a unique POS for each student. The ADM also provides for dynamic modification of the POS by the instructor or other authorized person. In addition, a hard copy of all or selected parts of the POS can be produced on request.
3. *Resource allocation:* The ADM provides the software necessary to allocate the three classes of resources. The process results in storing data in the instructional resource file defining the resource allocation. A capability will also be provided to use information from the student administration and history files to project future resource allocation requirements as well as availability.
4. *Attendance monitoring:* In schools where attendance is taken, the ADM provides the ability to use either OMR scan sheets or keyboard entry to record a student's absence.
5. *Group assignment:* The ADM provides the capability to assign a student to either an administrative group or an instructional group or both. Typically a student's initial group membership is defined at registration time. However, some students will shift administrative groups, and instructional group membership is always dynamic. In addition a student may be a member of a number of different instructional groups at any point in time. The group assignment function allows a student's group membership to be manipulated easily.

Assessment Module

The assessment module (ASM) provides the software needed to process the various measurement instruments used. The assessment results will be entered into the computer primarily via OMR equipment, although keyboard terminal entry is possible for particular instruments. The ASM implements the following functions:

1. *Test scoring:* Information on the answer sheet locates the scoring template, "scores" the responses, and stores the results in the student's instructional history file record. It should be noted that the test-scoring function is capable of handling of wide range of assessment instruments such as observational schedules and checklists.
2. *Diagnosis:* The assessment module contains a subprogram that implements a generalized diagnostic procedure. When the curricular structure specifies that a diagnosis is to occur (usually as the result of scoring an assessment instrument), the definition of the input variables is obtained from the curricular

file. The appropriate data elements are obtained and processed by the diagnostic subprogram. The output of the diagnosis is then stored for use by the prescription process. The diagnosis may be as simple as a test score, result in a profile of standardized scores, or be derived from the student's average performance.

3. *Prescription:* When the curriculum design specifies a prescription is to be assigned, the ASM enters the appropriate diagnostic data into a predetermined prescription procedure and the student's ''tear-off'' sheet is produced. This sheet is given to the student to direct learning activities and contains both the diagnosis and prescription. The identification code of the prescription also is entered into the student's instructional history file record. If the prescription is a forward one, the appropriate adjustments will be made to the student's POS. When a course is completed the active data are transferred to the archival part of the student instructional history file.

Reporting Module

The reporting module (RM) has three major functional modes: a standalone reporting capability, a subroutine accessed by other major modules to produce selected reports, and a report generator used by computer programmers to implement the report software. Because the reports yielded by the RM are later described in detail, only the underlying functions of the RM will be described here.

When the RM is considered a major module it is accessed via the main menu. Subsequently, the RM provides a list of the six major classes of reports. Once a class is selected, the user will use a simple on-line command language to select the particular report and specify any options of interest. The report then will be generated and depending on the options, displayed at a CRT and/or produced as a hard copy. Certain large-volume reports or those requiring extensive data processing will be produced as a background task and delivered via the computer's high-speed printer.

When the software associated with particular report is accessed directly by another major module, the calling module will be perceived as a user. Thus, the command language will be used to initiate the generation of the desired report. It should be noted that the number of reports generated in this manner are limited to those instances where it is necessary to generate a report in the course of performing another function. For example, the printing of a POS when an individual student has been registered via the administrative module.

The report-generator capability is accessible only to the computer programmer who develops and maintains the CMI software. It implements a generalized scheme for specifying both the contents and format of a given report. These specifications are then translated into report generation primitives that are stored for execution when the report is requested. The report-generation scheme eliminates the need for the programmer to create an explicit source code for each report. It also provides a vehicle for easily modifying existing reports as well as the definition of new reports as the need arises. There are a number of alternative ways to implement a report generator, and the minimum overhead technique would keep operational costs low.

In keeping with the tailorability requirement, the reports that will not be implemented can be designated at system-generation time. It should be noted also that the report-generator capability is eliminated from the CMI software at system-generation time.

File Maintenance Module

The file maintenance module (FMM) is used to perform those functions needed to create and maintain the data base. It has been assumed that a support staff exists that has been tasked to maintain the data base. Thus, the primary functions implemented by the FMM generally are not associated with the other major modules. The secondary functions perform particular tasks that are instructionally related but are not part of the instructional process. Both the primary and secondary functions are based upon the capabilities of the data-base management package. The primary functions implemented by the FMM are

1. *File creation:* Procedures will be implemented to enable the creation of each of the major files from input data. The data entry can be either via batch or as on-line processes.
2. *File maintenance:* A variety of functional capabilities will be provided to enable addition, deletion, and replacment of various segments of a file including individual data elements. The FMM will maintain an audit trail of the actions taken against the files.
3. *File clean-up:* A capability will be implemented that provides for the cleaning up of files. The intent of these procedures is to optimize the use of the mass storage as a function of time. Procedures such as reallocation of logical records to physical records will be accomplished via the data-base management package and the operating systems under request from the FMM. Removal of obsolete curricular segments, eliminating students no longer enrolled but not previously dropped, and similar tasks will be implemented.

The secondary file-maintenance functions are those performed by the support staff on a rather regular basis because of the magnitude of the task. These functions are as follows:

1. *Student registration:* Students fill out optically scanned forms, which are processed at registration time by the FMM. The processing results in the creation of a record for each student in the administrative file and in the student instructional history file. Where automatic, the student is assigned to administrative and instructional groups and initial POS is generated in hard-copy form for each student.

2. *Prescription algorithm generation:* Part of the process of creating the curriculum file is the specification of the prescription rule applied to the diagnostic data. The FMM will provide a function similar to that in the Teacher Information Processing System (Kelley, 1973), which allows the specification of the prescription rule associated with a given diagnosis and prescriptive message. Although this feature would be used at the time of creating the file, it is also useful when curriculum are improved dynamically during the course of instruction.

3. *Resource allocation maintenance:* The instructional resources available to a Training School can vary markedly as a function of time. Thus, a separate FMM function is associated with keeping the resource file up to date and accurate. Typically, a staff person would use a CRT to perform this function, and the FMM would maintain an audit trail of the actions against the file.

4. *Curriculum evaluation support:* The file maintenance module supports the curriculum developer–evaluator by providing a highly structured access to the data base. The intent is not to provide a generalized data-base query capability, but to allow access to those files and data segments relevant to development and evaluation. Thus, whole records or file segments would be displayed at a CRT terminal, and the user has the ability to shift from place to place within a file or across files. When the data of interest are found, they could be captured by printing the contents of the CRT screen.

Data-Base Management Package

The whole CMI-software concept is predicated on the use of a sophisticated data-base management package. This package must provide the capability for defining the data-base structure, the data elements, and their interrelationships. In addition, it must contain the tools for exploiting the data base in the ways required by the CMI system. Because the data-base management package is considered support software, it also must provide an effective and efficient host–language interface. Thus, the DBM services will be provided via "calls" from the CMI software. Several characteristics of CMI data need to be considered when selecting or designing a DBM. First, the total number of uniquely defined types of data elements within a particular file is rather small. Second, because a student's path through a training program is uneven, the total amount of data stored for each student vary across a considerable range. As a result there is repetition of basic chunks of data within a student's record. Finally, the basic CMI procedures employ data from several files; thus, cross-file linkages and simple file access are required.

There is a considerable area of trade-off between the design of the DBM package and the FMM. Only the primitives in the DBM could be implemented and the functionally related procedures could be put in the FMM. Alternatively, the FMM simply could pass control to the DBM package when a functional

2. Computer-Managed Instruction: A Context for CBI

procedure was to be performed. In either case the underlying process is hidden from the person using the CMI system.

Utility Routines

Whenever a large software system is developed the software yields a number of functions that appear in many different routines. The utility routines are the collection of these functions in subroutine format. The utility routines fall into the following classes:

1. *Data extraction.* This is a set of generalized subroutines for obtaining data elements from their storage arrays.
2. *Data insertion.* This is a set of generalized subroutines for inserting data into the proper location(s) in the data base.
3. *Data format conversion.* These are routines for converting data from one internal representation to another, routines for converting from internal to external representation and vice versa.
4. *Statistical functions.* These are subroutines for calculating running averages, means, variances, and implementing prediction equations.
5. *Interface routines.* These are routines used in conjunction with the operating system to interface to computer-based and other equipment external to the CMI system. These routines are used to obtain data from simulators, laboratory equipment, and CAI systems as well as to send them control information. Interface routines will also be provided to obtain data from the handheld devices used by instructors to collect observational data in instructional settings.

Reports

The actual layout of the reports yielded by the CMI system will be determined in the next level of design work. In the present section, the contents and purpose of each report within the six major classes of reports will be described.

Performance Profile Reports

These reports are intended to describe the present, past, and future performance of individual students, groups of students, and of the instructors who teach them.

1. *Student performance profile:* Describes the individual student in terms of instructional activities. The present profile is basically the data in the active portion of the instructional history file. The past profile is the data from the archival portion of the instruction history file, delimited by a range of dates of interest. Options will be provided to limit the level of detail reported to that of managerial interest. The future profile uses past

and present progress and achievement data in conjunction with the student POS to predict a students status at a given date in the future. The prediction will indicate where the student will stand relative to his or her POS.
2. *Instructional group performance profile:* describes the selected instructional group in instructional terms. The present profile reports the current curricular status of each student in the group. Data such as current curricular assignment, assessment instruments assigned, and resource allocation would be reported. The past profile summarizes the instructional group in terms of units completed, levels of achievement, rate-of-progress, and other such data. The future profile contains the predicted data for individual students as well as a summarization of this data.
3. *Administrative group performance profile:* identical in content to the instructional group profiles, except that the students are arranged by administrative groups.
4. *Instructor performance profile:* summarizes the achievement levels and the rate of progress of the students who come in contact with a given instructor. The present report indicates the number of students in each course or activity under the instructor, the mean and variance of the number of days on task, as well as the summary statistics for any assessment procedures associated with current activities. The past report presents the summary statistics for a selected time interval. The data reported will correspond to that of the present report. The future report contains projections as to the number of students completing the portions of their POS related to the particular instructor, their achievement levels, and progress paths (number of attempts, etc.) up to the date specified.

Curriculum-Related Reports

These three reports fall into two sets: The first report is concerned with student status relative to the curricular structure, and the second two reports support the curriculum-evaluation process.

1. *Unit report:* lists the names of the students assigned each currently active minimum managerial element. For each student the date the element was assigned, the number of days on task, the number of assessment procedures completed, and the projected completion date will be reported. The report is intended to assist in management at the course and program level.
2. *Assessment-procedure report:* provides a set of summary statistics for the assessment procedures such as item statistics, mean and standard deviations of total and subscale scores, and data relating to the number of attempts prior to reaching mastery levels. This report can be selected for a given assessment procedure and all procedures associated with a particular curricular unit, course, or program. The intent of the report is to provide the evaluator with data to study the effectiveness and appropriateness of the assessment procedures.

3. *Curriculum-segment evaluation report:* summarizes the student achievement, student progress, and resource-use data by curricular entity. This report can be obtained for curricular elements at all levels at or above the minimum managerial element. The data can be restricted further by specifying a range of dates that are applicable. Of particular interest are the data relating to the number of times students loop through the unit of instruction cycle.

Diagnosis and Prescription Report

This is the hard-copy, tear-off sheet given each student when an assessment procedure is processed by the CMI system. It contains the results of the diagnosis, the computer-generated prescription, and indicates any schedule or resource-allocation information needed by the student to fulfill the prescription. When a major segment of the curriculum such as a unit or course has been completed, the student is provided with an additional section on the report summarizing the student's progress and achievement for that segment. This section is similar to a student's present performance profile but is limited to the curricular segment just completed.

Administrative Reports

These sets of reports are designed to support the administrative activities of the school.

1. *Attendance reports:* The name and locator information of students absent from scheduled activities are listed by administrative groups. The reports would be used by the school administration and instructors to monitor attendance.
2. *Grade reports:* In courses where letter or other grades are assigned, two reports are produced. Administrative group rosters listing student names, ID numbers, grades, and a student grade slip for each student.
3. *Transcripts and student competency reports:* A report listing all of the courses constituting a student's program, the time needed to complete each course, the achievement level obtained, and any competencies the student has acquired by completing the program. In many Training School settings the transcript consists entirely of the student's acquired competencies.
4. *Exception reports:* A series of reports detailing exception conditions that would require administrative attention, for example, a list of physical plant and facilities that were not available for instruction and the consequences of this lack. Also included would be identification of courses or other curricular segments where a large proportion of the students have not reached completion in a reasonable time. One of the primary exception reports used by instructors is the contact report, which it lists the names of students, their current assignment, and related data within an instructional group who have had no contact with the CMI system within a specified

time period. The intent of the report is to identify students that are "hiding" within the instructional system.
5. *Logistic reports:* When the level of usage of instructional expendables reaches predetermined levels, a requisition form is produced. This form can be sent to the logistics component to initiate the resupply process if the actual inventory also is low.
6. *Enrollment report:* A report summarizing the status of all students in the school. The report is by administrative group and indicates the number of students in each enrollment category (assigned to a curricular segment, program completed, held back, etc.). The report request allows the report to be generated for a range of past dates, the present, or for a projected future date.

Scheduling-Related Reports

These reports are used to schedule students and resources.

1. *Program of studies:* A student's complete POS or any segment of it can be produced. The student typically receives a hard copy, while instructors simply may view it via a CRT. The POS contains a specification of each curricular segment in a student's program, the associated resources, and where the student is to be at given times to participate in the instruction. The POS could be generated on a weekly or other basis to provide the student with a class schedule, or it could be generated on demand. Report options would be available to limit the POS to say the next week, next curricular segments and their prerequisites, or to a student's class schedule. Where groups of students have identical POS an option will yield a POS for all students in the groups without the requestor identifying each student.

2. *Resource-allocation reports:* These reports describe the three categories of resources in terms of their past, present, and future allocations. Through report options, listings can be obtained of the allocation of individual resources, categories of resources, or only those resources that have been used. The report of past allocations summarizes the level and duration of usage. The current report also shows the curricular segment associated with the resources. The future report uses the POS data to project future allocations and identifies allocation conflicts and availability problems. A capability is also provided that enables the user of a CRT to experiment with trial allocations as a vehicle to resolve predicted allocation difficulties. Such trial allocations will not have any impact on the data base.

System-Related Reports

These reports are used to evaluate the performance and use of the CMI system. They are based on internal event monitors within the CMI software.

2. Computer-Managed Instruction: A Context for CBI

1. *CMI feature use:* The number of times each item in the selection menus of the major modules and their subprograms are used will be reported. In the case of the reporting module, the report option usage will also be indicated. An option of the present report is to partition the report by the on-line terminal that employed the system feature.
2. *Data-base activity report:* The number of times each file was accessed and a categorization of the access by administrative, instructional, or file maintenance usage will be reported.
3. *Terminal usage:* The report describes each on-line terminal in terms of its usage, duration of usage, and availability.

All three of these reports will cover a user-specified time period up to the present.

CMI HARDWARE SYSTEM

Hardware Configuration

The hardware configuration used to implement a CMI system depends on a number of considerations; hence this chapter describes the hardware in generic terms first. The factors involved in selecting a particular hardware suite are discussed second. Figure 2.3. shows a typical CMI-hardware suite, based on the assumption that all its interfaces are computer-based.

Mainframe

The capabilities of the computer mainframe reflects the characteristics of a CMI system. Because CMI is basically a management information system there is a very light scientific computing load. However, there is a significant data storage and manipulation load as well as a need to support a large number of on-line interactive terminals. Consequently, the main frame should possess considerable memory that is reasonably fast, under 1 msec. The instruction repertoire should be I/O and data manipulation-oriented rather than calculation-oriented. Finally, the hardware design should be optimized for implementing a time-sharing environment.

Mass Storage

CMI requires a large amount of mass storage and the total amount is a function of the number of programs, their curricular structure, and the student flow. Fortunately the state-of-the-art in this area is excellent, ranging from floppy disks to trillion bit memories. Thus, the system designer has considerable flexibility in meeting the mass storage needs.

Figure 2.3 CMI hardware configuration.

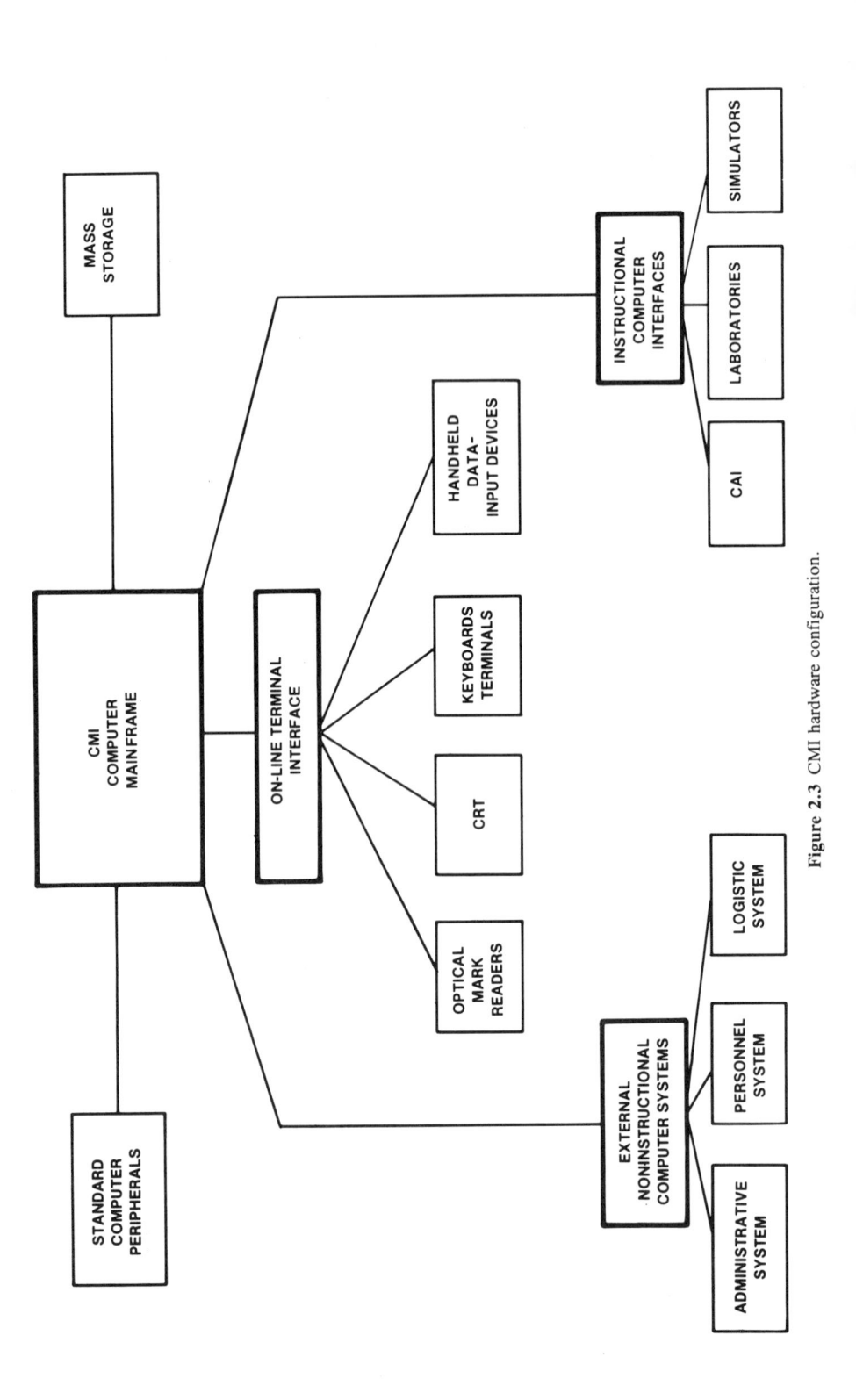

2. Computer-Managed Instruction: A Context for CBI

Standard Peripherals

At a minimum, the CMI system requires a high-speed printer to produce the larger reports. Although card readers and card punches could be employed, they have very limited use and are not recommended for an operational CMI system.

On-line Terminal Interface

The CMI system is characterized by the use of a wide variety of on-line terminals that must be interfaced. Depending on the mainframe design, these terminals could be interfaced via the computer's I/O channel capabilities or by use of a "front-end" to relieve the mainframe of the low-level technical process of communicating with terminals—most of which employ RS-232 interfaces.

On-line Terminals

The following list contains the more obvious types of on-line terminals but does not preclude the inclusion of others.

1. *Optical mark readers:* These devices allow the use of pencil marks on a card or sheet of paper to be used as computer input. There are a number of these devices on the market, ranging from desk-top to high-capacity machines. In the asynchronous environment of individualized instruction, the sheet-at-a-time, desk-top machine is to be preferred. These are inexpensive and can be used by students and placed where the instruction occurs.

2. *CRT displays:* The CRT terminal with its keyboard is very useful when there is a need to interact with the CMI system for informational purposes. For example, when an instructor needs some data about a student's progress. In such applications the "dumb" terminal is adequate. When the CRT terminal is used for administrative purposes and for on-line file maintenance, the new breed of "smart" terminals can be used. These terminals can be programmed to facilitate the execution of data-input procedures and reduce the load on the main frame when large numbers of terminals are used. Both types of CRT terminals can be backed up by a hard-copy device to print the contents of the screen.

3. *Keyboard terminals:* These terminals are very useful for generating the small, hard-copy reports, such as the student tear-off sheet needed to manage instruction. Typically they are paired with the OMR equipment. They are also useful for administrative and file maintenance purposes when the result of the process leads to a report.

4. *Handheld terminals:* These small devices were designed originally for recording inventory and order entry. They allow data to be entered into a hand calculator sized device and subsequently transmit it to the computer. Such devices have wide applicability for collecting observational data or instructor ratings as the student performs a task. Once the class or activity is completed, the instructor carries his or her terminal to the nearest coupler, dumps the memory contents into the computer, and is free to use it again.

Instructional Computer Interfaces

A major trend in Training Schools is the increased use of training equipment that is computer based. This equipment should be interfaced with the CMI computer to collect instructionally relevant data and sent instructional control commands to specify the student's learning experience on the equipment. From a hardware point of view, these equipments pose a difficult interfacing problem because of the widespread use of nonstandard, data-communication conventions. Again, placing a front-end between the CMI system and them often can reduce the problems.

Computer-Based Instructional Systems

There are three classes of such systems that can be interfaced to the CMI system.

1. *CAI:* These systems are used to actually conduct instruction and can be implemented in computers ranging from micro- to supercomputers. In regard to hardware the interfacing is usually straight forward.
2. *Laboratories and classroom:* It is possible to create special classrooms or laboratories where students use response devices or computer terminals to participate in the instruction process, but not in the same manner as under CAI. During the process, instructionally relevant data can be generated and sent to the CMI system.
3. *Simulators:* It is often less expensive and safer to train a student via a simulator rather than an expensive piece of equipment, such as an aircraft. Again instructionally relevant data can be extracted and sent to the CMI system.

The latter two classes present the most difficult interfacing problems because they are designed independently of any CMI considerations.

Noninstructional Computer Systems

It was shown in an earlier section, that the CMI system exists within a larger context. When the external systems are computer-based, interfaces with them can be established to facilitate the operation of the overall environment.

INSTRUCTIONAL MANAGEMENT UNDER THE CMI CONCEPT

To explore fully the management of instruction via the CMI system conceptualized in the preceding sections is a very large task. Therefore, the purpose of the present section is to look at the operation of the CMI system from the point of

2. Computer-Managed Instruction: A Context for CBI

view of the student, the instructor, the school administrator, and the curriculum developer–evaluator. The intent is to present the flavor of the system in a concise manner.

The Student

Upon entering the Training School the student uses a mark-sense form to register. The computer assigns him or her to an administration group and gives out a printed copy of the program of studies and assigns the first lesson. The lesson may be individual study or a session at a CAI terminal; in a laboratory or a field exercise. The computer generates an instructional assignment that not only defines the learning activity but also tells the student where to go and at what time, lists the books, materials, and other resources needed, as well as telling the student how the work will be evaluated. Upon completion of the first segment, a test is taken and the student uses the OMR terminal to process the results. A computer terminal generates a tear-off sheet that describes how well the student has done and what is next. As the students progress through the training program at their own pace, they become distributed over the curriculum. They can check their progress and present status, and estimate their completion data by using a terminal to obtain an individual performance profile. When a number of students reach a common point, an instructional group may be formed in which they work together. When the activity is completed, the group disbands. At major milestones within the program, the student receives an updated copy of the POS, a present performance profile, and a conference assignment with the training staff. This is done to ensure that the student's status is known and is being supported by the staff. Upon completion of the program, the student receives a computer-generated transcript describing the competencies acquired in the training program.

From a student's point of view, the CMI system provides continuous feedback as to his or her status within the training program. It also makes individualization meaningful by diagnosing instructional deficiencies as well as progress, and prescribing learning activities that are unique to the student. Through the use of the OMR, CRT and keyboard terminals, and reports, the students are able to participate in the management of their own programs. The end result is a better informed student, who is proceeding responsibly through a curriculum tailored to ensure that the training goals are met.

The Instructor

Because the level of instructional management related to behavioral objectives has been automated by the CMI system, the instructor can focus on higher levels of management. The computer terminals put at the instructor's fingertips a large number of reports, which can be used in many ways. Although the instructional process is highly individualized, the instructor can monitor individual students and groups of students. He or she can use the unit report to see where the students stand relative to the curriculum. The performance profiles can be used to check progress. When the learning situation requires it, the instructor can assign students to instructional groups for remedial or other purposes. The future performance profile can be used to plan activities. Exception reports can be used to alert the instructor to conditions that need attention, for example, the nonavailability of a critical resource for an upcoming activity. Through the use of the handheld terminals the instructor can record observational data, rate student performance under on-the-job conditions, and easily enter the results into the computer data base. By using a terminal to generate their own performance profile, the instructors may discover areas in which they might change to improve their effectiveness.

From the instructor's point of view CMI is truly a management information system. Both the range of reports and their contents enable an instructor to manage effectively what is fundamentally a very fluid situation. The system also frees the instructors from large amounts of clerical-level work and provides greater opportunity to participate in the instructional process.

The School Administrator

A Training School employing individualization of instruction poses a considerable administrative challenge. Because of the asynchronous flow and progress of the student, planning, coordinating, and monitoring are performed continuously. As was the case with the instructor, the reporting component is the administrator's tool. Through a computer terminal, the past and present status of individual students or administrative groups of students can be monitored. Through the use of the CMI's projection capabilities the future need for resources can be determined and trial allocations made to resolve potential conflicts. It is also possible to estimate the number of students available for placement at future dates from each of the several programs. The instructor performance profile allows the administrator to identify strong instructors as well as those who may be having difficulty in the instructional setting.

From an administrator's point of view, the CMI system provides a wide range of services. It automates many of the routine administrative functions such as registration, attendance, scheduling, and resource allocation. Yet, it also allows access to summarization of instructionally related data needed to manage the student body and to relate to the marketplace. The school administrator's contact with the process and outcome of instruction is severely limited without the CMI system.

Curriculum Developer

In the Training School environment curricular change is a way of life. Training programs must be created, implemented, evaluated, and optimized within a very short time frame. The CMI system provides considerable support for this process. The responses of individual students to tests and other assessment instruments are available in both raw and summarized form. The patterns of student progress through possible paths in the curriculum structure can be followed and summarized. The integration of data from a wide variety of instructional subsystems, such as CAI and simulators, resides in the CMI data base. Finally, through the FMM, the curriculum specialist has access to the total data base. Using this computer-based data and the powerful capabilities, the formative and summative evaluation of all aspects of a training program can be performed readily.

Basically, the CMI system provides the curriculum developer-evaluator access to raw data and data summaries, such as item analyses and distributions of attempts-until-mastery, that cannot be obtained economically via other means. The provision of generalized diagnostic and prescription software greatly facilitates the development of individualized curricula. Because these procedures are rule- rather than data-value-oriented, the curriculum specialist has considerable flexibility when creating and maintaining a program. The end result is that the curriculum specialist is more effective in the Training School role.

EVALUATION CAPABILITIES

Because CMI typically is superimposed on an existing instructional setting, it represents an incremental cost. The obvious question is whether this additional cost can be justified. The answer to this question has two bases, philosophical and pragmatic. It is well known, that it is very difficult to alter dramatically student achievement within a given instructional program. This is a consequence of the fact that an existing curriculum and its instructional paradigm have been designed to enable students to acquire the underlying skills, knowledge, and so on. Given that such schemes usually yield a reasonable level of student achievement, any increase in student performance will be in small increments, obtained via refinement rather than in quantum steps. Consequently, the addition of CMI to an instructional setting would not be expected to alter significantly the level of student achievement. What, then, is the benefit of the additional costs associated with CMI. Basically, what CMI does is to make an unmanageable educational paradigm—individualized instruction—manageable. Without CMI, individualized instruction for large numbers of students is impossible to implement. What CMI does is to provide the automated data collection, data processing, and reporting capabilities underlying the successful management of individualized instruction. In the Training School setting, where the basis of individualization is rate of progress, CMI has direct benefits in terms of increased productivity of the school and the student. Because individualization can be achieved, the expectation is that the average length of time a student spends in a given program would be reduced. This in turn reduces the per pupil training cost and increases the amount of time a student can perform the job for which they were trained. Because CMI enables individualization to be coped with managerially there are a number of subtle but important benefits. There is a smoother running school and a dynamic situation, which retains its fluidity yet becomes orderly in its procedures. At the same time everyone involved is kept informed and adaptation to changing conditions becomes a routine process. Because CMI has interfaces to all the components of the Training School it acts in an integrating capacity. Because much of the data related to operational aspects of the school, such as schedules, resource allocation, and soon are in the CMI system, all components are linked more closely. Whereas this increases their interdependence, it also forces the components of the school to function as a whole rather than as separate entities. Thus, in addition to making individualized instruction a reality, CMI significantly improves the overall functioning of the Training School in both its instruction and administration. The basic philosophic question then is: What value does one place upon these outcomes? The cost–benefit issue reduces to whether or not this value exceeds the additional cost of the CMI system.

Pragmatically, CMI provides the capabilities to perform a wide range of evaluation functions that can be related to the cost–benefit question. The performance-monitoring component enables the evaluation of students, instructors, the curriculum, and the CMI system itself, while the reporting component provides the relevant information in an appropriate format. Student achievement and progress can be evaluated relative to the characteristics of the students and their instructional goals. Instructor performance can be monitored and potential problems identified early enough to take managerial action. The curriculum developer can monitor the instructional program on a continuous basis. In the early stages of curriculum development, such data can be used for formative evaluation. At a later point, it can be used for summative evaluation. In both cases, the data can be used to identify the refinements necessary to keeping a curriculum current and effective. Finally, the CMI system itself can be monitored. Again, the data obtained can be used to refine continually the system and optimize it for a given Training School setting. Whereas much of evaluation deals with the past, the performance-monitoring component has the unique feature of providing projections. These can be used to evaluate future conditions and take the management actions necessary to ensure the proper outcomes. The real beauty of the use of the performance-monitoring and reporting component for evaluation purposes is that it is a second use for fundamental CMI capabilities.

2. Computer-Managed Instruction: A Context for CBI

As such it represents a powerful tool to be used in achieving a cost-effective Training School at no additional cost.

Although the performance-monitoring component, the data base, and the reporting component do not answer directly the cost–benefit question, they do provide the vehicle for answering it. The data provided are of such breadth and depth that a comprehensive view of major aspects of the Training School can be obtained. Properly employed, this evaluation data should result in a better managed, better quality, and a more effective Training School than that which exists without CMI. Thus, pragmatically CMI enables the educator to be an effective manager. Again, the basic question is, what value does one ascribe to these outcomes?

Summary

The CMI system conceptualized here embodies what is understood currently about instructional management. Perhaps its greatest departure from previous CMI systems is the inclusion of administrative procedures within the domain of CMI. This reflects the considerable intertwining of instructional management and administration that results from the individualization of instruction in a Training School and in military schools in particular. Also, in other school settings the evaluation of instructor effectiveness is fraught with problems; however, in many Training Schools it is a necessary function if the long-term quality of the school is to be maintained. The final result is that the definition of CMI has been broadened considerably. The overall intent was to conceptualize CMI as an integral component within an educational system rather than as a unique entity. To do so makes the CMI system larger in terms of the hardware and software needed to implement it. The fundamental advantage is that a truly integrated instructional management system is achieved. Such a CMI system supports instructional management at the instructional, course, and program levels. In addition, it supports administrative processes that are instructionally related.

Although this chapter does not design explicitly a specific CMI system, it does provide the conceptual basis for such a design. Thus, the next step in the implementation process is to translate these concepts into a CMI system design. At this next stage, the data base will need to be specified as to structure and contents; the operating modes and functions performed via the on-line terminals will have to be defined and human factored. The format and contents of the full set of reports will need to be finalized. Finally, the software structure and modules will need to be designed and the utility routines identified. When the design phase is completed, this chapter will serve as the controlling document for the evaluation and approval of the design of the CMI system. It will be possible to ensure that the resultant design reflects both the intent and the philosophy of the system-concept document.

Development of the CMI system defined in this chapter is well within the hardware–software state-of-the-art; it poses no unusual problems. Such a CMI system can become an integral part of existing Training Schools without disrupting their administration or threatening the job security of instructors. Properly developed, managed, and implemented it supports instructors and administrators by solving very real and pressing instructional management problems. In doing so it also provides a receptive context for subsequent computer-based instructional systems.

REFERENCES

Baker, F. B. Computer-based instructional systems: A first look. *Review of Educational Research,* 1971, *41*(1), 51–70.

Baker, F. B. Computer managed instruction: Theory and practice. Englewood Cliffs, N.J.; Educational Technology Publications, 1978.

Kelley, A. C. Individualizing instruction through the use of technology in higher education. *Journal of Economic Education,* 1973, *4,* 77–89.

McIsaac, D. N., & Baker, F. B. Microcomputer CMI: Performance specifications. Madison: University of Wisconsin, September, 1978.

3

Hardware–Software[1]

CRAIG FIELDS
JUDITH PARIS

INTRODUCTION

We have chosen to define the boundaries of this chapter by dissecting informally the concept of a computer-based instruction (CBI) system into some fundamental components. These components are hardware technology, software technology, and instructional strategies.

The hardware of a CBI system may be considered a reliable, fast machine that follows any "orders" it is given. The orders are the instructional strategies—the strategies, tactics, rules, and heuristics of teaching or encouraging learning by other means. The orders are represented and communicated to the hardware using software technology, for example, computer-programming languages.

Comparing the state-of-the-art for the hardware technology, software technology, and instructional strategies is fraught with uncertainty. However, we believe that hardware and software technology development is far in advance of instructional strategies development. Hardware and software technology, which largely determine the cost of CBI systems, are constantly improving (hardware prices are dropping by a factor of two every 2 years). In contrast, instructional strategies, which determine the educational effectiveness of CBI systems, have shown no comparable dramatic improvement over the last two decades.

[1]The work reported in this chapter was supported in part by the Army Research Institute for the Behavioral and Social Sciences, contract number MDA 903-79-C-0558. Views and conclusions contained in this document are those of the authors and should not be interpreted as necessarily representing the official policies, either expressed or implied, of the Army Research Institute for the Behavioral and Social Sciences, the Defense Advanced Research Projects Agency, or the United States Government.

This chapter summarizes the state-of-the-art for hardware and software technology. (The reader is referred to the Chapter 4 by Bunderson for a state-of-the-art assessment of instructional strategies.) In addition, we will try to forecast the status of hardware and software technology 3 years from now and 10 years from now.

It is fairly easy to summarize the state-of-the-art of hardware technology. Hardware performance is not difficult to measure quantitatively. Furthermore, forecasting the status of hardware technology can be based on the performance of prototype systems currently working in industrial laboratories. It is much more difficult to summarize the state-of-the-art and make forecasts for software technology. One basic difficulty is the lack of agreement on how to measure the performance of software technology. For example, with respect to programming languages, how much better is LISP than FORTRAN? There have been tremendous advances in software technology over the last three decades, but no one knows exactly how to measure those advances. Because of this difficulty we will make use of examples of current applications, usually described in qualitative terms. It is even more difficult to forecast software technology, and we will have to rely on reasonable guesses about what "might be true," assuming that levels of research, largely controlled by government rather than industry funding, continue to be about the same.

Moreover, we are restricting ourselves to summarizing and forecasting hardware and software technology that provide the CBI system designer with off-the-shelf capabilities. This is why forecasts for hardware technology can be reasonably accurate—almost anything in the marketplace in 1990 is already in the laboratory in 1980. By and large we will summarize and forecast hardware and software technology building blocks rather than dealing with the architecture of CBI systems, that is, how the building blocks are selected and combined. The design of CBI systems is still an art. The range of possible CBI systems architectures is truly vast. There is no one "best" architecture, and there are no specific rules for matching alternative CBI system architectures to applications. A few examples will illustrate the tremendous range of CBI system-architectures.

At one end of the scale, CBI system architectures are small, portable, and inexpensive, for example, standalone systems like the Texas Instruments Little Professor. The Little Professor uses primitive instructional strategies and stores almost no data. At the other end of the scale is a system like The University of Illinois PLATO IV, a large (900 student-terminals), centralized system that is capable of executing complex instructional strategies and storing large amounts of data. Intermediary values on the scale would be a "miniature" version of PLATO IV, for example, a typical minicomputer-based CBI system that provides instruction for 10 or 20 students at a time; or an expanded version of the Little Professor (e.g., a standalone microprocessor-based CBI system with, say, a videodisk used to store a large amount of subject matter). Such a system would be used by one student at a time, but ownership might be shared among a number of students or held by a training organization.

With the technology of 1980, a system like a Little Professor can store one or a few pages of subject matter; a standalone microprocessor-based system can store a few books of subject matter; a shared minicomputer-based system might store a small library of subject matter; and a large PLATO IV-like remote system might store a very large library of subject matter.

There is a definite trend toward the development of smaller, standalone CBI systems that may be used, or even owned, by individual students. These systems may be connected to communication networks for purposes other than instruction, such as reporting on student progress, communication between students and (human) teachers, and updating of subject matter in the student's CBI system.

There are a number of reasons for this trend. First, there is a trade-off between producing one, or a few, very large CBI systems and enjoying the economics of mass production. With current and future hardware technologies lower production costs and prices are realized for large numbers of small systems. Second, communications prices are subject to government regulation, whereas computer prices are (so far) unregulated. The peculiar cost–price structure favors standalone systems that do not rely too heavily on communications. Third, there appears to be a very real and strong consumer-preference for CBI and other computer systems that are more personal, controllable, ownable, and physically available.

The remainder of this chapter is organized into four sections. The second section is a discussion of the kinds of data and information stored in CBI systems. The third section describes the hardware and software technologies and forecasts future developments. These technologies are primarily concerned with the basic capabilities of CBI systems, and not with the design variables that determine acceptance of computers. These issues of man–machine relations are discussed in the fourth section. The last section suggests several projects that might be undertaken that have the potential for significantly influencing the development of CBI systems. These projects would complement, rather than compete with, industrial developments.

KNOWLEDGE, DATA, AND INFORMATION IN CBI SYSTEMS

The choice of how to represent knowledge, data, and information in CBI systems strongly determines the overall cost, computer technology, communications technology, software technology, and may even influence the educational effectiveness of the system. There is as yet no good theory of how knowledge should be represented for different purposes. Some practical experience has been gained, however, and will be described briefly in this section.

It is important to distinguish between knowledge and data in CBI systems. "George Washington was the first president" is knowledge represented as a particular kind of data, namely, English text. The same knowledge could be represented in different ways, for example, as an animated cartoon or a voice speaking the same sentence in a foreign language. A knowledge representation may be chosen to optimize storage, communication, or display to students.

By and large, knowledge representations that are good for information processing by people are bad for information processing by computer. Knowledge representations such as semantic nets, production rules, frames, and scripts have been developed for representing knowledge in a way that makes it easy for computers to, say, make inferences, find facts, and produce summaries. These same knowledge representations are unsuited for people. In contrast, knowledge representations such as text, speech, and pictures are well matched to human experience and capabilities, but present significant difficulties for processing by current computer programs.

Although there is no theory to aid the system designer in choosing among knowledge representations, there are significant cost considerations: The cost of a representation increases with the amount of storage required for that representation; the least expensive are structured data, for example, tables of numbers, lists of words, and so on. In order of increasing cost are text, speech and cartoons, photographs and animated films, and movies. Speech and cartoons appear to be two bargains among alternative knowledge representations. They represent a favorable balance between cost and apparent quality.

Speech is a bargain because techniques are available now for compressing it to a tremendous degree (about 1000 bits per second) and then reconstructing intelligible speech at low cost using inexpensive Large-Scale Integration (LSI) devices. Speech terminals (i.e., microphones, speakers, and inexpensive electronics) are extremely inexpensive.

Methods are available for representing cartoons and animated stills with many fewer bits than still photographs and movies, thus reducing storage and communication costs. Cartoons and animated films can be produced easily on television at low cost because of mass production; so too line drawings, sketches, and simple graphs, as special cases of cartoons. Photographs and moving pictures are between 100 and 1000 times as expensive as cartoons and animated films (Hunter, 1977).

These guidelines regarding the advantages and disadvantages of knowledge representations will not change significantly over the next 10 years with the exception of one remarkable perturbation that began in 1979. The videodisk makes it possible to store photographs and movies at very low cost; optic fibers

3. Hardware-Software

make it possible to communicate photographs and movies over short distances at very low cost. These technical developments have an impact on those CBI systems for which all pictures are prepared as a library, and actions of the system and student cause a *selection* of pictures rather than a *calculation* of pictures.

HARDWARE AND SOFTWARE TECHNOLOGIES

This section summarizes the state-of-the-art and forecasts the future of technologies for inputting and outputting, communications, data storage, information processing, and aspects of software technology (Withington, 1975).

Inputting and Outputting

Keyboards

At this time, the most popular technology for inputting to CBI systems is the keyboard. This is unlikely to change in the next 3-10 years. Although everyone agrees that the layout of current keyboards is inadequate, the number of existing keyboards is overwhelming and provide an obstacle to change. Attempts at producing and using specialized keyboards, such as the Stanford Research Institute (SRI) Five Finger Keyboard, have been interesting, but not revolutionary for economic and social reasons.

One important development that might overcome economic and social barriers to change are keyboards where the meaning and label of each key is under dynamic, real-time computer control. That is, each key is effectively a display, and so function keys can be produced and changed by the computer to reflect the immediate needs of the student user. For example, the last, say, five commands typed by the student could always be available and continuously updated as function keys, based on the premise that what the student is going to be doing next is the same as what he or she has just been doing.

One new inexpensive keyboard opportunity is the use of the touch-tone telephone for a keyboard input device. Touch-tone telephones are commonly available, and dial telephones can be converted to touch-tone use with ease and minimum cost. It might appear that touch-tone telephones can be used as a keyboard only for numeric information, because there are too few keys for full alphanumeric use. Fortunately, typed sequences are somewhat predictable, especially within the context of subject domains. The prediction may be based on assumptions regarding the use of English, specific words, and specific contents in the student-CBI system interactions. In such a system, interpretation of the touch-tone key stroke is a process of continuous hypothesis generation and disambiguation. To the best of our knowledge, only one such system has been built—one which interprets peoples' names typed on a touch-tone telephone to provide an automated telephone-number information service.

Optical Character Recognition

Another technique for inputting text to CBI systems is optical character recognition (OCR). The goal is for the CBI system to have the ability to read books, periodicals, and newspapers as well, perhaps, as the printing or handwriting of students. A decade ago the OCR problem was viewed as one of simple pattern matching, and performance of OCR machines was poor. One solution to the problem would require intelligent understanding of the text, for example, guessing words and sentences in context—a solution similar to that suggested for a touch-tone terminal system. Despite the insight, it is unlikely that OCR devices will be able to read most text (with acceptably few errors) in the next 3-10 years. Fortunately, an increasing number of text publications are available in computer-readable form because of the use of computerized typesetting and office automation; and the amortized cost of retyping masses of text is remarkably low for any medium serving large student populations.

Drawing, Sketching, and Pointing

Hardware technology for drawing, sketching, and pointing is well developed and available to any CBI system designer. The technology can be used for a number of purposes. If the student is faced with few choices, these can be presented as a menu and one can be selected by pointing. Training in some subject domains, like architecture, requires drawing as input to the CBI system. There is a special problem in making sense of drawing input, which looks to the computer like a series of disconnected "points" or dots rather than as the revolutionary building design, which the student sees. The CBI system must have algorithms for making sense of the dots that it records, understanding straight and curved lines, boundaries, regions, surfaces, solids, and so on. Such algorithms now exist at a useful level of quality (Negroponte, 1973).

The predominant technologies for pointing and drawing are digitizing *tablets, light pens, joysticks,* and the *mouse.* Tablets are two-dimensional surfaces or areas. With a finger or special stylus the student touches a position in the plane, and the x and y coordinates of the position are transmitted "instantly" to the computer. Many tablets are transparent and can be mounted on the surface of a display. This is particularly convenient because, with a little calibration, the student can point easily to something displayed by the computer. If, for example, the computer displays the image of a keyboard, a touch-sensitive tablet attached to the front of a display becomes a keyboard. This is a way of producing the dynamic keyboards previously described.

A mouse and a joystick function in a manner similar to a tablet by allowing the

3. Hardware-Software   71

student to transmit x and y coordinates to the computer. In contrast, a light pen transmits a time to the computer. The typical light pen touches the surface of a computer display; the computer rapidly (too rapidly for humans to see) produces vertical and horizontal lines on the display at many x and y positions. When a line appears (to the light pen) at the position of the light pen, the light pen detects the light and sends an electrical pulse to the computer; the computer sensing the pulse, in turn, "knows" the x and y position of the line just displayed, and thus (initially) locates the position of the light pen. When the light pen moves from its initial position, the computer, cleverly, tracks it by producing intersecting vertical and horizontal lines in the region around which the light pen was last detected—the tracking cross. This reduces the search time and makes it possible to move the light pen at a faster rate across the surface of the display without the computer losing track of the light pen position.

Tablets are available increasingly and becoming less and less expensive; they are likely to predominate in the next decade. They will be used for an increasing number of jobs in CBI systems, including inputting of animated sequences to describe dynamic processes.

Image Inputting

Photographs and facsimiles can be inputted to CBI systems using television cameras or slow, mechanical scanners. Movies are input to CBI systems using television cameras. Most mechanical scanners slowly measure reflectance of a very small spot moved over the entire surface (a few million points) of a document or photograph. The lightness or darkness of each point is transmitted to and stored by a CBI system for presentation later. A television camera optically produces an image on an electronically sensitive plane within the camera and, at very high speed, measures and transmits the brightness of each point. Mechanical scanners are slower and more precise than television cameras. Because television cameras can scan a plane rapidly, they can transmit images 30 times a second, and thus communicate movies to computers.

Printing Paper

There is a common misconception that paper and paper-handling technology will soon disappear from computer systems, including CBI systems. This misconception is based on an exaggerated view of the worth of new capabilities for electronic data storage, communication and, particularly, electronic information display. In fact, paper has tremendous advantages over most electronic displays and much electronic data storage, although it does lag behind substantially for data communications.

There is little doubt that paper is worse for data communications than is electronic transmission. Large amounts of data are best stored electronically, but small amounts of data, say, a book, are best stored on paper. There is no electronic storage technology that can compete economically with paper for small amounts of information. The difficulty is that computer systems inevitably require data communications as well as data storage. If data are stored on paper, they must be converted to electronic form for communication. In principle, the conversion to electronic form is accomplished using television or mechanical scanners; but the practical difficulties of dealing mechanically and automatically with paper are almost insurmountable (e.g., automatic mechanical book-selection and page turning).

Paper really comes into its own when it is used for data display. It provides high resolution, color, portability, low volume, low weight, ease of adaptation, group viewing, and a number of other advantages. The major disadvantage is the impossibility of dynamic displays. In short, a CBI system incorporating electronic data-storage, electronic data-communication, and paper data-display is a very credible option.

Data-display on paper, of course, requires a hardware technology of printers and plotters. Plotters are basically mechanical arms, under computer control, that produce line drawings. Impact printers type a character at a time or a line at a time. Both plotters and impact printers are being eclipsed now by the latest technology of laser-based, nonimpact, raster printers. The use of a raster printer that produces a line of dots as its basic operation provides instant compatibility with television displays—the predominant electronic displays. Raster printing allows the easy combination of graphics and text in a single document or display. Today (1980) laser-based, nonimpact raster printers are expensive devices. The cost per operation is low, but a large number of operations are required to justify the investment. Probably within the next 3 years and certainly within the next 10 years, the cost of these devices will be reduced and paper as a terminal data-display will remain a viable and, in fact, attractive option for CBI system designers.

Electronic Displays

The smallest electronic displays are the liquid crystal displays and light-emitting diodes found in personal calculators. A few years ago, these displays were limited to numbers and a few special characters, but now complete alphanumerics are available in a portable package. The implication is that it is practical to produce a CBI system for which text is an important data type and that is packaged like the Texas Instruments Little Professor, an arithmetic machine. A few such devices have been constructed, but they are not designed for instruction and have very limited capacity.

Most electronic displays are cathode ray tubes (CRT), and most are in televisions. Primarily because of large-scale manufacturing, television displays now predominate and will predominate over the next decade. Their major problems

3. Hardware-Software

are with volume, power (but note the small, portable SINCLAIR 2-inch television), and low resolution. Five-hundred-line resolution in television limits the amount of text that can be displayed. The basic television technology allows a higher resolution (e.g., 1000-line resolution), but then the economies of mass production are lost. The low resolution of television displays is particularly vexing with large, projection television-displays like the Advent Television Projector. These devices, costing several thousand dollars, are by far the cheapest way of achieving large computer-displays. Because the quality of the Advent and similar displays is not sufficiently high for certain applications, television projector displays of one-thousand-line resolution are now available to CBI system designers.

Cathode ray tubes need not be used in television displays. A credible alternative is the so-called vector or callographic display. In a television display, the path of the electron beam over the surface of the cathode ray tube is not under computer control, but the intensity of beam is under computer control. In a vector display, both the intensity and beam path are under computer control.

Several companies in the Unites States and Japan are working on large, flat, solid state displays of television resolution and bandwidth. The goal is a wall or picture-size, flat display for home entertainment use. Practical laboratory prototypes now exist that represent a number of technologies, and it is highly likely that such devices will be on the market and available for CBI systems within a decade, but probably not within 3 years.

Of course, the first of the flat, solid state displays is the plasma panel, which has neither television bandwidth nor television resolution. The plasma panel does not have the low cost of television (viewed from the perspective of a component rather than a system), the range of color of television, or the availability of repair and maintenance of television. Thus, we believe plasma panels will not play an important role in CBI systems of the future for reasons of marketing, availability of maintenance, mass production, visibility, and so on.

Speech Input-Output

Information presentation need not be information display. Very inexpensive electronic devices for the computer synthesis of speech now exist, and the technology for transmission (the telephone system) and presentation (amplifiers, speakers, and earphones) of speech are well developed and very inexpensive. As for speech input, microphones, particularly in telephones, are readily available for transmitting speech from people to computers. The difficulty is that computers readily can receive, store, communicate, and retrieve speech but cannot understand speech very well. For many CBI system applications, speech understanding is simply not needed; and for those circumstances, the telephone should be considered an inexpensive, available, and familiar terminal for interacting with computers. Supplemented with the touch-tone keyboard discussed previously, it is an underexploited, missed opportunity that should be pursued.

Forecast Summary

To summarize the forecast for inputting and outputting technology:

1. Technology for dynamic keyboards; for using the telephone as an inputting and outputting device; and for drawing, sketching, and pointing with a tablet are here now and will be used increasingly in CBI systems.
2. Within 3 years, speech output from CBI systems will be common because of inexpensive electronic technology for synthesizing speech.
3. Low-cost, raster printers; large, flat, television displays; and limited-quality speech input and understanding will be incorporated in CBI systems within 10 years.

Communications

This section is about communications technology, although the most important subject is communications regulation. Computers, storage devices, software, input and output devices, and so on are not government regulated. Communications is government regulated and the regulations change frequently and in unpredictable ways. From the viewpoint of the CBI system designer, communications regulations of the moment spell the difference between a very distributed or very centralized system; a legal system or an illegal system; an expensive system or an inexpensive system. For example, one good method for transmitting large amounts of text to a large student population is to encode the text in the signal (e.g., during the retrace period) of standard television broadcasts). This high bandwidth, low-cost alternative is of questionable legality as of 1978. As another example, the Federal Communications Commission (FCC) has contemplated opening a number of new bands for personal radio services (e.g., expanded citizens band). If this occurs the new communications opportunities can be exploited by CBI-system designers. One direction for possible development is radio-based electronic mail, which, however, may be illegal. The conclusion is that CBI systems that avoid or minimize communications (like stand-alone, microprocessor-based systems) eliminate a source of legal headaches, ambiguities, and difficulties that may overwhelm the technical issues. Despite this conclusion, I have organized a number of credible communications technologies along two dimensions. First, some technologies are most suitable for short-distance communications (e.g., within a building or building complex), whereas other technologies can be used for short or long distances but will most commonly be used for long distances. Second, some communications

3. Hardware-Software

technologies have bandwidths high enough to communicate practically photographs or movies, whereas others do not.

Short Distance, Low Bandwidth

One technology for low bandwidth, short-distance communication are power lines. Power lines within buildings presently carry a signal—60-cycle hum. They can be used to carry more meaningful and important signals. For years, home intercom systems have been available that operate over power lines. More recently, electronic devices, which communicate over powerlines with appliances and other gadgets in the home can be purchased for turning these machines on and off. The major advantage of power lines is that they are present in all buildings. There is no need to rewire the building for data communications as, for example, with cable-based systems. In many cases, rewiring costs, because of labor unions and building codes, are more expensive than computer systems.

Short Distance, High Bandwidth

High-bandwidth communication over short distances is provided now by cable-television technology and, in the future, will be supplied by optical cable technology. The distances involved can extend to miles. Cable-television technology provides enormous bandwidth and is available now for data communications. It is possible that optical cables will be available particularly for the CBI system designer within 3 years and certain that they will be available within 10 years. Cable-based systems, optic or not, are typically broadcast systems. As such, all terminals attached to the system "hear" all communications. Communications protocols, interpreted by software, are required (and available) for seeing that the right message goes from source to destination. Because CBI systems are, in part, data-base management systems containing personnel information, privacy is a critical issue and encryption in broadcast cable-based systems is surely necessary.

It is worth mentioning that infrared and laser links are now available for line-of-sight interbuilding communication. They can be set up quickly and cheaply and for many purposes avoid the wiring costs of cable-based communications.

Long Distance, Low Bandwidth

A number of technologies are available for long-distance, low-bandwidth data communications. Perhaps the most commonly used are dial-up telephone lines. It is practical to transmit several thousand bits per second on dial-up telephone lines. This is a credible rate for, say, typing, compressed speech, or cartoons. It also has the unique advantages of being available inexpensively in small quantities and, more importantly, available almost anywhere.

If higher bandwidth is required, leased lines of a megabit or, more commonly, 50 kilobit rates can be rented. The major problem with such high-speed leased lines is that they are too expensive for many purposes unless they are used continuously. Communications packet switching solves this problem. The basic idea is based on the observation that most people use high-speed communications in bursts. If a number of people have requirements for such bursts and if those bursts are sufficiently asynchronous that they can be interleaved without much difficulty; many people can share a single communications line. This is the same idea as the time-sharing of processing capacity of large computers.

The ARPANET is a typical packet-switched, communications network. It consists of a number of minicomputers called Interface Message Processors (IMPS) connected by shared high-speed (50 kilobit) communications lines. The ARPANET provides communications from computer to computer. Typically, a computer will be connected to the ARPANET by being connected to an IMP. Such a computer connected to an IMP is called a *host*. A host will communicate information with another host by transmitting a "message" to the IMP. This message has a header containing the numerical address of the receiving host. The IMP connected to the sending host will transmit the message to the IMP connected to the receiving host, and the IMP connected to the receiving host will transmit in turn the message to the receiving host. From IMP to IMP the message may be broken up into packets. The path of communication from the first IMP to the last IMP need not be direct, and the packets could be passed from IMP to IMP in the communications network. Each IMP knows the location of each host, and so can calculate the right way to send a packet to the next IMP. Because the communications are divided into bursts—packets—time-sharing of the high-speed communications lines is possible, and a line may be transferring information successively among many independent hosts. Because each packet is addressed, proper delivery takes place almost all the time. In the ARPANET, the IMPS choose a route for transmission from sending host to receiving host that takes into account not only distance but also the number of packets being transmitted by the network. It may be faster to transmit a packet from New York to Los Angeles and then to Boston than to transmit directly from New York to Boston if that line is "clogged." Further, ARPANET IMPS check the contents of packets to make sure that, say, electrical noise has not caused an error. This may seem complicated—it is—but it provides very reliable, very inexpensive data communications over long distance with modest bandwidth. Until recently IMPS were fairly expensive minicomputers, but now microcomputer-based IMPS are possible, facilitating low-cost, packet-switch networking.

Another recent development is the PLEURIBUS IMP, which is a special IMP containing a number of processors for added reliability and bandwidth. Specifically, it is possible to remove pieces from a PLEURIBUS IMP while it is

3. Hardware-Software

operating, and it will keep operating at slightly lower capacity. This provides a high-reliability communications option for CBI-system designers.

Packet radio is a radio broadcast version of the ARPANET (Kahn, 1977). A packet-radio network consists of three kinds of radio stations—sending stations, receiving stations, and repeating stations. Each does what its name implies. The broadcasts of each sending station are received by a number of repeating stations, and repeating stations retransmit—repeat—in the direction of the eventual receiving station, as indicated in the numerical address of the receiving station at the beginning of each broadcast packet. Packet-radio transmissions are so called spread-spectrum transmission. That is, rather than transmitting a signal at a high-energy level at a specific frequency, the signal is transmitted at a low-energy level on a large number of frequencies. As a consequence, packet-radio transmissions can exist in the same frequency bands as, say, commercial radio or citizens band, without significant interference.

Long Distance, High Bandwidth

Long-distance, high-bandwidth communication technology is provided by broadband satellite channels and television broadcast equipment. For both of these technical options, the cost of transmitting a bit of information is low but, typically, very large capacity has to be purchased at high cost for reasons of communications policy. In the case of broadband satellite channels, the problems of selling "pieces" of a satellite channel have been solved by applying packet technology. The idea is that the broadband channel is viewed as carrying a succession of identified packets of information rather than a continuous stream of information. Charges may be made on a packet basis, and the identification of each packet assures that messages go from proper sender to proper receiver. Unfortunately, packet broadband-satellite service is not yet available widely on a commercial basis, but it is highly likely that it will be available during the next decade.

Forecast Summary

In summary, change in communications for CBI systems over the next decade will be increasing use of technologies that are currently available. Specifically, these include data transmission over cable television, radio, and broadcast television. The major technical innovation making this possible is packet communications.

Electronic Storage Technology

There have been a number of papers summarizing the state-of-the art and forecasting storage technology. Rather than repeating those summaries and forecasts, we want to organize storage technologies into categories and highlight a couple of technologies that are commonly overlooked (Theis, 1978).

Semiconductor and Core Memories

The first set of technologies are those for which it is impractical to store much voice. These are semiconductor and core memories. Core memory is not going to disappear within the next decade, although it will play a decreasing role despite technical improvements. Semiconductor memory will continue to get faster, so that the limiting factor in future computers will be communication between devices—such as computer processor and memory—rather than limits on the speeds of components themselves. In the limiting case, the significant factor is the slow speed of light, only overcome by producing smaller computers or those with an architecture that geographically integrate processing and memory.

Bubble Memories, Charge-Coupled Devices, and Small Magnetic Disks

Several storage technologies are adequate for some voice but inadequate for photographs and movies. These include charge-coupled devices (CCD); bubble memories that have the advantage of easily integrating processing and memory, as in associative memories; and small digital, magnetic disks.

Large Magnetic Disks and Tapes

Some moving magnetic-storage devices are adequate for a few photographs. These include analog magnetic disks, now useful for storing a few hundred videoframes; magnetic tapes, ranging from cassettes to nine-track; high-density tapes and large magnetic digital disks. Because of inertia, magnetic tapes will not disappear during the next decade. Digital magnetic disks, ranging from small floppy disks to large moving head-disks, will continue to improve, and within the next decade moving magnetic media will not be replaced by solid-state, bubble, or CCD memories.

Mass Memories

In the last few years, there has been an emphasis on the production of very large-capacity memories that are adequate for numbers of photographs and movies. Mass memories such as the IBM 3850 use wide magnetic tape and achieve a measure of random (rather than serial) access by using large numbers of very short, wide magnetic tapes mechanically accessed by robotic arms. However, these mass memories can only store one or a few trillion bits. Electron-beam memory, now under development, may be available in a decade and will store about a trillion bits in each electron-beam tube with a large system containing a thousand tubes. Such an electron-beam memory makes it practical

3. Hardware-Software

to store large numbers of movies for instructional purposes and access individual movies or frames of movies in a few microseconds.

Optical disks are an important competitor for trillion-bit mass memories. There are both analog and digital optical disks, and these are either quickly writable or slowly writable. One kind of videodisk contains a number of shallow pits arranged in circular tracks, with one video frame stored in each track. The picture is coded by the length of the pits, and thus this is an analog device rather than a digital device. Fifty-four thousand individual pictures or one half hour of video can be stored on each of two sides of such a videodisk. We consider such a disk slowly written because it is produced by a mechanical pressing process that takes hours. In contrast, it is possible to produce disks of sensitive media that can be "instantly" written using a laser to both burn the pits into the surface of the disk, and later read the pits (at a lower light intensity) to reproduce the signal. Such a quick writing (but nonerasable) analog videodisk will be available within the next 3 years for commercial if not home applications.

It is important to contrast analog optical disks, where the signal is stored by the shape (length) of depressions on the surface, with digital optical disks where the signal is coded by the existence or nonexistence of pits at specific places on the surface of the disk. Both slow writing and fast writing digital optical disks will be available within 3 years. They will store between 10 billion and 1 trillion bits on each disk. Because of sharing components with videodisks for the home entertainment market, mass production will keep the cost of these devices low. With a low media cost, they should replace conventional trillion bit mass memories. Even if a 1-trillion-bit capacity for individual optical disks is not achieved practically in the near future, 10-billion-bit capacity is possible easily, suggesting a trillion-bit storage system consisting of one hundred 10-billion-bit disks, each controlled by a microprocessor and connected to an optical cable. Such a system would have vastly more bandwidth, reliability, and lower cost than a conventional mass memory.

Incidentally, one of the major advantages of quickly writable optical disks, both analog video and digital, is the feasibility of producing large-capacity disks in low quantities. Using the mechanical pressing technology for the home market, it is necessary to produce large quantities to amortize costs, but this is not suitable for a number of educational applications.

There are a number of more conventional large capacity nondigital memories that should be considered for CBI system use. These include random access videotape and random access film—both slides and microfiche. Finally, books provide a very high-quality storage medium for information if there is no requirement for communication, that is, if the books are located near the student. Under those circumstances, a CBI system need do nothing more than provide pointers to books, leaving it to the student to read the relevant material.

Information Processing

Information processing is at the heart of CBI systems. Information processing functions can be organized on a scale from the least intelligent jobs, controlled primarily by hardware, through the most intelligent jobs, controlled primarily by software. These include low-level arithmetic calculation; functions of the CBI system operating system, such as resource scheduling, control of data files, control of communications and input–output; data-base management, modeling and simulation, speech and picture compression and speech synthesis; English, speech, and image and drawing understanding; and teaching that uses some instructional strategies.

Hardware

The major revolution defining CBI systems during the next decade is large-scale integration (LSI). In the context of information processing, rather than information storage or communication, LSI provides a technology for producing very low-cost microprocessors that have modest capabilities, small volume, and low power consumption. Whereas microprocessors are very cost effective, they are not very effective for processing information. They address relatively small amounts of information and are fairly slow at computation. The need to address large amounts of information is critical for CBI systems, and is gradually being solved through the introduction of microprocessors with longer and longer word lengths. Microprocessors of 16-bit word length are now available and, within 5 years, microprocessors of 32-bit word length will probably be available. The problem of slow speed is being solved in a number of ways. Basic technological advances in the electronics should produce order of magnitude improvements within the next 5 years.

That improvement is not enough, however, to cope with the massive computational demands of very large intelligent programs required for truly advanced CBI systems. Another approach is to develop microprocessor multiprocessors that exploit parallelism to provide very large-speed improvements. Multiprocessor microprocessors are now practical for very special, limited applications, but a new invention is required to produce a technology that will have more general utility for CBI systems. Such an insight may or may not appear within the next decade.

A number of exotic technological developments may have an impact on CBI systems within the next decade, but they are probably of longer-term interest. These include single chip processor architecture specialized for higher-level languages; new single chip computer architectures that integrate processing and memory; new single chip architectures that provide dramatically improved reliability by exploiting the features of error-correcting communications protocols for connection of small electronic components; very large-scale integration that will provide one or two orders of magnitude improvement in cost, speed, volume, and power consumption; techniques for producing three-dimensional LSI chips instead of the current two-dimensional LSI chips; and commercialization of Josephson junction technology to produce nanosecond computation, but at very low temperatures.

Operating Systems

The boundary between computer operating systems and computer hardware is blurred increasingly because of microprogramming, ROMS (Read Only Memory), and PROMS (Programmable Read Only Memory). Therefore, we will discuss operating systems without drawing an overly sharp and artificial boundary between hardware and software.

The operating systems of choice for 1980 CBI systems are multistudent interactive time-sharing systems. Such a design should be contrasted with batch-oriented systems (practical only for certain management tasks in education) and single-user interactive operating systems. Most CBI systems now rely on hardware that is too expensive to devote to a single student. That will surely change, and single-student interactive operating systems are likely to predominate within 10 years. Surprisingly, the underlying software is about the same whether the CBI system is interacting with one student or a number of students. The reason is that even with a single student the CBI system is likely to be doing a number of jobs "simultaneously" and thus needs to execute some algorithm to manage its resource allocation among competitive demands.

The jargon used to describe interactive CBI systems is not particularly specific or informative. "On-line," "real-time," and "interactive" all imply an ill-defined level of psychological comfort associated with interaction with the system, without providing any specific definitions or guarantees. Some interactive time-sharing systems have been developed that provide more than vague promises regarding the quality of interaction. These guaranteed-response, time-sharing systems provide a minimum, guaranteed quality of service for each student, computer program, or process demanding attention. Predictably, because only 100% of the computer resource is available, not all possible combinations of demands can be satisfied. There is a requirement to be able to calculate what combinations of demands can be satisfied before allowing any combination of programs and users to access the system resources, and then to allocate resources intelligently among the demands.

One difference between single-user interactive systems and multiuser interactive systems is a greater emphasis on privacy, security, and secrecy in multiuser systems. The CBI system builder must realize that the computer system contains personnel information. As such, separation among users must be maintained and access restraints must be enforced. With a few exceptions, multiuser time-sharing systems provide low levels of security—anyone with a little imagination can "break" the system. Recently, a few systems have been developed that promise considerably greater levels of privacy, but the software technologies have not been applied to CBI systems. Perhaps the most promising technology will be the construction of the multiuser operating system based on a small piece of software, the "kernel"; it is responsible for much program interaction and control, and is highly likely to work properly because it is so small.

Languages

Most operating systems upon which CBI systems are built provide capabilities for writing programs in a number of computer languages. Because there are at least a thousand different computer languages that are now used, I will make no attempt to summarize existing languages but only point out some categories of programming languages and some examples, chosen for their popularity.

The earliest computer languages were specialized for doing arithmetic calculation. By far, the most popular example is FORTRAN. Other languages are specialized for manipulation of symbols, lists, and strings rather than the manipulation of numbers. Languages like LISP and SNOBOL fall into this category. Since most "intelligent" computer programs are based on symbolic manipulations, a language such as LISP is most popular for those applications (Bobrow and Raphael, 1974).

A number of modeling languages exist for constructing simulations of real world processes. These can be divided into those languages that are best for writing simulations of processes composed of discrete events (e.g., GPSS), and those languages designed for simulating processes that are continuous in time (e.g., Simula).

Overall Design

By and large, CBI systems of the past have been designed to teach, to present information in small digestable amounts, ask penetrating questions both for assessment and teaching, give hints to the student, assess student difficulties to adapt teaching, and so on.

It is important to remember that the goal of the interaction between a student and a CBI system is learning, not teaching. In fact, CBI systems can "do" things other than teach to provoke learning. They are probably worst at teaching, because underlying algorithms for teaching are unknown essentially. Two alternatives to consider are (*a*) that a CBI system can provide the student with a modeling and simulation facility, and (*b*) that the CBI system can provide the student with an expert question-answer system and electronic library for exploring a world of information.

A modeling system would allow the student to interact with a simulated real world under particularly advantageous circumstances—the student could see the inner workings of things, could change natural laws (e.g., the law of gravity),

3. Hardware-Software 83

and could create inexpensively and quickly situations and see their consequences.

A good electronic library would allow the student to explore a multimedia (e.g., text, sounds, movies) world of information with an intelligent partner that could make credible inferences about what information the student wanted despite what he said. Both the concept of a modeling system and a library system to provoke learning depend on a significant amount of student motivation and probably require some initial guidance to help the student get started.

Multimedia Processing

Linear predictive coding is an algorithm for compressing speech. It is possible to get intelligible speech at only a thousand bits per second. Equally important, the algorithm can be built into an LSI device, thus significantly reducing the cost of speech compression. It is important to remember that the compressed speech is not understood by the computer. Algorithms for speech production are available that transform English text stored in the computer into intelligible speech. As with speech compression, significant cost savings can be realized by incarnating important parts of the algorithm as an LSI device.

Pictures—halftone photographs and movies—can also be compressed to about one bit for each picture element. For example, a modest-quality, page-size photograph can be compressed to 1 million bits, a significant savings of at least one order of magnitude. Algorithms for picture production (e.g., calculating perspective, shading, shadows, reflections, and hidden surface removal) require so much arithmetic that special hardware has been built for practical execution. Unfortunately, such picture generators are extremely expensive, ranging from about $70,000 for equipment to generate three-dimensional line drawings to several million dollars for equipment to generate three-dimensional colored halftone pictures at high speed. Because most of the cost of these devices is electronics, there may be significant reductions over the next decade if there is sufficient and sufficiently obvious customer demand to stimulate the development effort for producing the most modern generation of devices. Nevertheless, it is unlikely that sophisticated image generators will provide real-time picture production for every student. More likely, non-real-time picture production (with pictures stored on videodisks) or simplified, cartoon-like picture production will be available commonly. The software to support cartooning and animation systems is available now but not used as an integral part of current CBI systems.

A number processing jobs demand that the computer system really understand the contents of the information that it is manipulating.[2] Techniques of intelligent information processing are required for English understanding, speech understanding, image understanding, and sketch recognition by the computer. In

[2]See especially Negroponte (1973), Hanson and Riesman (1978), and Reddy (1975).

each case, it is impossible for computers to understand a knowledge representation convenient for people (speech, English, and so on) by simply trying to match the data to prestored templates describing the appearance but not the meaning. To understand the English, it is not enough simply to try to recognize words—the context of sentences and paragraphs must be understood. The same considerations apply to speech, images, and sketches. It is easier to understand an image of a horse if the computer knows that it is likely to be a picture of an animal; it is easier to understand a sketch of an automobile if the computer knows that it is likely to be a mechanical object. Because of the importance of context, intelligent understanding systems traditionally have been built for particular domains—particular classes of utterances, statements, or pictures.

English understanding systems have been built as part of intelligent question-answer systems (e.g., asking questions about the position of ships in the ocean). How well do such systems now work? There have been no informative measurements, but they are comfortable for use by novices for limited applications. Speech understanding systems have been built for a variety of subject domains, including interfacing to bibliographic data bases. A typical state-of-the-art system will understand sentences in a domain if the vocabulary is limited to about a thousand words. The development of image understanding and sketch recognition systems is more limited, and it is difficult to describe how well current laboratory prototypes work.

What about the future? English and speech understanding programs are probably good enough for some CBI system applications now, but they still require hardware that is overly expensive. It is highly likely that both English and speech understanding will be practical for use in CBI systems within a decade, and just possible that they will be practical for use in CBI systems within 3 years. It is important for the CBI system builder to remember that novices are very intolerant of errors in English and speech understanding systems. Error rates that are acceptable with people are unacceptable with computers. It is unlikely that image or sketch understanding systems will be useful for CBI system designers within the next decade, primarily because of the low level of research and development (R&D) investment devoted to finding new algorithms.

Intelligent processing of information is needed for *production* as well as *understanding* of data types convenient for people. Perhaps the most interesting example is the field of idiographics—the automatic production of pictures from knowledge. At this time, there are only two circumstances under which it is possible to produce pictures from knowledge automatically. One is if the knowledge can be represented statistically as graphs, scatter diagrams, pie charts, and so on. The other is if information is geographic and can be represented as maps. In other cases (e.g., politics) pictures have to be produced by hand rather than by computer. Techniques and heuristics might be developed for the automatic production of pictures from information perhaps by capturing the rules used by "hack" illustrators to do their job. For example, an important kind of knowledge representation are sets of partial differential equations, which describe models of weather, economics, and so on. One way for a computer system to produce pictures illustrating such models would be to prepare and store a library of visual metaphors drawn from hydraulics and mechanics (e.g., gears, faucets, levers, and so on). The computer could examine the component parts of the partial differential equation models and select analogs from the library of visual metaphors, labeling and connecting the analogs by reference to the partial differential equations.

Intelligent Systems

Software technology for intelligent information processing extends beyond techniques for intelligent understanding of English, speech, pictures, or sketches. Intelligent systems for questions answering, teaching, and problem solving exist in prototype form. It is impossible to provide a summary of the state-of-the-art except through a qualitative description of some examples of intelligent computer programs. Further, forecasting the state of artificial intelligence over the next 3-10 years is little more than a process of qualitative conjecture. There are many reasons for this difficulty. First, there is no useful definition that separates the concept of an intelligent program from the concept of unintelligent program. Second, there has not been performance measurement of intelligent programs (e.g., how intelligent they really are). No techniques have been developed for measuring how intelligent programs are. Third, progress in the field of artificial intelligence has been based on a set of unpredictable and independent insights—"eureka" events—rather than an orderly progression of technology. Fourth, with respect to teaching, there has never been any comparative measurement of performance of intelligent teaching programs with unintelligent teaching program (Winston, 1977).

Accurate forecasting's difficult, but for the building of CBI systems the situation is promising. There is general agreement that new and better software techniques for producing intelligent programs emerge, unpredictably, at a reasonable rate and that intelligent computer programs today are much "smarter" than they were a decade ago.

Probably the most obviously intelligent programs are the so-called expert systems that have been developed based on production rule software technology (Anderson & Gillogly, 1976). A number of such systems have been developed, including one for the prescription of antimicrobial therapy (Mycin) and another for the interpretation of nuclear magnetic spectra (Dendral). The advantages of these systems are that they combine the knowledge of a number of human experts; they are exhaustive in the application of that knowledge to the interpretation of real-world data (symptoms of a patient or characteristics of nuclear magnetic spectra); when they draw a conclusion, they can communicate the reasons behind that conclusion to the human operator in clear terms; and their rules of reasoning are easy to change and improve based on new circumstances or knowledge. The disadvantage is that the construction of such systems is usually expensive because a large number of rules have to be developed using many hours of time of human experts, and the large size of the rule sets mean that execution of the program is either very slow on a small, inexpensive computer or slow on a large, expensive computer.

There are a number of potential applications for production rule "intelligent" systems in CBI systems. First, a CBI system can be a production rule system that contains rules for teaching—what information to show, what questions to ask, and how to react to students' replies and inquiries. As such, the rule set would be a theory of teaching and only as good as that theory. Second, a CBI system can be an expert system answering questions that involve complicated reasoning and inference making. As such, they would serve not only to provide answers, but also to explicate the reasoning that would provide further benefit for the student. Third, and perhaps most important, a CBI system could provide facilities for students to create their own rule sets—their own intelligent computer programs—in a subset of English. In effect, students would be able to describe their own theory of, say, economics, and to calculate in fairly precise terms the implications of their theory.

Summary

The developments in the area of inputting and outputting include dynamic keyboards, touch-tone telephones as computer terminals, and technology for drawing and sketching to computers, all of which are available now but underused in CBI systems. In the 3-10-year time frame, low-cost high-quality laser printers, large flat television displays, and small portable displays will be available to CBI system designers.

In the area of communications, the major new technology impacting on CBI system design will be optical cables allowing low-cost picture transmission, and shared satellite channels allowing low-cost digital communication, essentially independent of distance.

The major new storage technology to be seen in the next 3 years is the digital optical disk allowing both economical picture storage and economical high-capacity storage—the latter implying that it is possible to store the same information many times, organized in different ways to ease access by the user. In the 10-year time frame, electron-beam memories may make possible much higher speeds of access to much larger amounts of information than is possible with optical disks.

In the area of information processing, the main implication of LSI in the 3-year time frame will be inexpensive speech compression and techniques for low-cost computing based on multiprocessor microprocessors. There will be a

3. Hardware-Software

gradual trend toward single-user standalone systems, away from many-user, remote time-sharing systems. In the 10-year time frame, useful speech understanding systems and English understanding systems will be available to the CBI system-designer. The most important part of information processing technology—generally intelligent programs for teaching—await new and unpredictable developments in the field of artificial intelligence and instructional strategies.

MAN–MACHINE RELATIONS

This chapter has been concerned with reviewing and forecasting computer hardware and software technology that can provide basic capabilities for CBI systems. Unfortunately, capability is not enough to ensure success for a CBI system—it must also be accepted and used by students, teachers, and managers. By and large, computers are not well accepted in our society. People find computers not credible—or too credible. People blame computers too much when things go wrong—or blame them too little. People do not use computers when they could really help with a job—or they use them for the wrong things. People find computers are threatening and too smart—or too dumb. People do not enjoy or like computers. People think computers always help others, but never themselves. The most common consequences of these problems are that computers are unused. As a result, there is a missed opportunity for increased effectiveness; there are no cost savings and frequently costs go up because of the necessity of maintaining parallel manual (used) and computer (unused) systems.

We view this as a social problem and, in fact, it can be considered a "race relations" problem between people and computers. In reality, it far outweighs technical limitations of capabilities of computer systems for CBI applications. It can be argued that this problem of poor man–machine relations will remedy with time. That may be true in the far future, but in the near future of the next decade—for many reasons—the problem is going to increase in magnitude. For example, there is going to be an increase in the degree and breadth of economic threat that computers represent as their capabilities increase. Because there appears to be an irresistible temptation to apply computers to problems before systems are fully debugged and perfected, there should be an increasing number of (premature) introduction failures that are blamed on computer technology rather than human impatience. Now, a large percentage of users of computer systems are technocrats. In the future, a decreasing proportion of users will be predisposed toward technology. As computers are used for more and more tasks, there will be an increasing reliance on their proper functioning and, inevitably, a larger number of failures, which will lead to an intense backlash. As computers become increasingly capable and, perhaps, simpler to use, their internal working is becoming increasingly complex and difficult to understand. Finally, a number of social conflicts will be blamed unjustly on computers (e.g., old guard versus new turks; artists and humanists versus technocrats; poor versus rich, and so on).

If this is truly a race relations problem, we should be somewhat discouraged because people have not been able to solve race relations problems that only include human beings. Fortunately, we have an advantage in dealing with man–machine relations problems, namely, that one of the partners—machines—can be redesigned at will.

Traditionally, the design of computer systems is aimed at increased capability with the view of leading to better attitudes toward computers. The combination of good attitudes and capabilities can lead to effective performance. However, there are a number of design variables associated with computer systems that are not aimed at increased capability but that can affect attitudes directly. In other words, some proper design choices can lead to improved attitudes without really improving capability. Rules and heuristics for the design of computer systems to improve attitudes only is a largely unexplored field of man–machine relations, with more global concerns than considerations of man–machine interaction (concerned with matching human cognitive function with computer design) or human factors (aimed at good physical matching of computers and people).

Some of the neglected design variables that largely may govern acceptance and effective use of computers are: (1) appearance; (2) *apparent* intelligence; (3) responsiveness; (4) understandability; (5) learnability; (6) transparency; (7) simplicity; (8) quietness; (9) quality; (10) authoritativeness; (11) interaction style; (12) awareness of user; (13) impressiveness; (14) ownership; (15) prestige; (16) acceptance by others; (17) acceptance by one's organization; (18) novelty; (19) extensibility by user; (20) programmability; (21) scope of access to data, information, and other people; (22) portability; (23) pocketability; (24) disposibility; (25) personality; (26) vocabulary; (27) personalization; (28) privacy; (29) correctness; (30) ignorance; (31) fragility; (32) verbosity; and (33) location. Some of the variables on this list overlap, and some combine effects on both capability and attitude. Nevertheless, they give an idea of the kinds of variables that can be manipulated in computer systems.

Based on common sense, we can invent a number of credible but unproven and sometimes contradictory designs that can be applied to computer systems to improve attitudes. For example, it is possible that computers should look large and impressive so that people will pay attention to them, and it is equally possible that computers should look small and "underwhelming" so that they appear controllable.

One of the consequences of LSI is that it is a feasible and an inevitable trend for computers—microprocessors—to find their way into many objects producing, say, "smart" telephones, smart televisions, smart desks, smart chairs, and

3. Hardware-Software

so on. As such, computers are going "underground" and will end up looking like familiar objects. Will that improve attitudes or hurt attitudes?

It is now impossible to purchase a computer terminal that has a feel of very high quality, like some automobiles. Perhaps computers should look expensive and of high quality so that they will be valued.

Most computers hide their inner workings from the user rather than showing what is happening. Perhaps they should use graphics, sounds, and messages to keep the user informed of what is going on and to provide the user with some model, inevitably incorrect, of how they work.

It is possible that computers should be made with customizable interaction languages so that people can make their computers act in the way they want, similar to training a subordinate.

Computers are available only infrequently, unlike the telephone, which is constantly available despite not usually being portable. Perhaps computers should, through a variety of technologies, be made constantly available.

Although it is very difficult to make computers that understand English or speech, it is easy to make computers that produce English and speech. Nevertheless, most of the output of computers is in a bizarre language, frequently offensive to the user.

Most of these principles are ignored in the design of computer systems. The designer of CBI systems, relying on common sense (because no science is available), must take these principles into account in building a new facility.

RECOMMENDATIONS FOR RESEARCH

1. Among the means by which CBI systems can provoke learning is the unexplored option of interactive modeling. A modeling system can be developed for some subject domain (e.g., vehicle maintenance), and student learning can be assessed after interaction and use of that modeling system.
2. Interaction with a large-scale library and an expert question–answer system can provoke learning. Such a system can be developed for some subject domain, such as international political relations, and student learning can be assessed after interaction with that system.
3. A CBI system can be developed that uses a telephone as the terminal, with control supplied by typing on the touch-tone keys and information supplied by recorded or computer-synthesized voice. Such a system would be very inexpensive, be available anywhere, and be embodied as a familiar device. One possible area for such a program would be remedial mathematics.
4. A powerful, ownable, portable, small, and advanced version of the Texas

Instruments Little Professor can be developed for some subject domain. An example might be navigation.
5. An idiographic system can be developed to facilitate teaching through graphics for a subject domain, such as international economics.
6. At this stage the entire field of man–machine relations is based on intuition rather than laboratory experiments and data. A number of experiments are possible to test and validate or invalidate credible hypothesis such as those listed.

REFERENCES

Anderson, R. H., & Gillogly, J. J. *The RAND Intelligent Terminal Agent (RITA) as a network access aid.* Proceedings of the American Federation of Information Processes Societies, 1976.

Bobrow, D. G., & Raphael, B. New programming languages for artificial intelligence research. *ACM Computing Surveys,* (September 3), 1974, *6* 155-174.

Hanson, A., & Riesman, E. (Eds.). *Computer vision systems.* New York: Academic Press, 1978.

Hunter, G. Computer animation survey. In *Computer and graphics,* 1977 (Vol. 2), 225-229.

Kahn, R. E. The organization of computer resources into a packet radio network. In *IEEE transactions on communications,* 1977, *25*(1), 169-178.

Negroponte, N. *Recent advances in sketch recognition,* National Computer Conference, 1973.

Reddy, D. R. (Ed.). *Speech recognition: Invited papers presented at the 1974 IEEE Symposium.* New York: Academic Press, 1975.

Theis, D. J. Overview of memory technologies. *Datamation,* January, 1978, 113-131.

Winston, P. H. (Ed.). *Artificial intelligence.* Massachusetts: Addison-Wesley, 1977.

Withington, F. G. Beyond 1984: A technology forecast. *Datamation,* January, 1975, 54-73.

4

Courseware[1]

C. VICTOR BUNDERSON

COURSEWARE: CONCEPTIONS AND DEFINITIONS

With the growth of the computer industry over the past 40 years came the convenient terms *hardware* and *software*. The term *hardware* refers to the electronic and electromechanical devices, usually in blue, red, or gray boxes constituting the computers, their peripherals, and interfaces. The term *software* refers to the programs that control the hardware devices. These programs are made visible on paper tape, punched cards, magnetic tape, or computer disks. The development and marketing of software promises to exceed in dollar volume the magnitude of the hardware business.

Seeing the analogy between audiotapes, films and videotapes, and computer software, audiovisual specialists began to call their products software as well. After all, their products were programs that were run through hardware devices to provide a variety of services. It was inevitable, however, as computer-assisted instruction (CAI) grew, for a distinction to be made between the computer software that supports the general functions of the hardware and the software that is tailored for providing instructional interactions. Thus, the term *courseware* came into use. It is not clear where it started. I first heard if from Frank Haas in about 1967. Haas passed briefly through the leadership of one of

---

[1]The work reported in this chapter was supported in part by the Army Research Institute for the Behavioral and Social Sciences, contract number MDA 903-79-C-0558. Views and conclusions contained in this document are those of the author and should not be interpreted as necessarily representing the official policies, either expressed or implied, of the Army Research Institute for the Behavioral and Social Sciences, or the United States Government.

IBM's active CAI groups. Through some process of natural selection the term *courseware* emerged triumphant over such competing terms as *teachware* and *lessonware* and has now come into fairly common use, although persons who work primarily in the media and print fields stubbornly cling to the undifferentiated term *software*.

Courseware: Product Definitions

As it has come to be used, the term *courseware* implies a product definition: It refers to the materials of instruction that constitute applications programs administered by computer delivery systems, but include the off-line adjunctive materials that round out the courseware package. Thus, a courseware package visibly might include a magnetic tape or floppy disk; but, it might also include a filmstrip or tray of color slides for use on a computer-controlled device; an audio tape or disk; a videotape or videodisk; a set of microfiche cards; and, most commonly, a set of printed materials. The printed material might only be a few pages of general instructions for the use of the computer programs or it might be workbook material with extensive graphics and text referenced by the computer program. In some cases, it appears as a complete textbook; in other cases it might consist only of a job aid or job performance guide a few pages long.

The term *courseware* then has come to refer to the materials of instruction constituting the consumable products that operate on and with technologically mediated instructional delivery systems. It is distinguished from software in that computer software is more generalized; software is used to deliver and to author any kind of courseware. Thus, we have editing software, data collection and reporting software, software that provides registration for any course and provides teacher and researcher reports. A distinction may be made between *delivery system software* and *authoring system software*. Delivery system software controls interactions between the computer and the student, for example, instructions for what to do when the student pushes the "help" button. Authoring systems software controls interactions between the system and authors, for example, instructions and displays to enable the author to locate any frame and edit it. By contrast, the computer program portions of courseware constitute data that are interpreted and executed by the delivery system software, for example, the content of a particular *help* message. It is originally produced and edited using the authoring system software.

Process Conceptions

The growth of modular, self-paced, individualized packages of instruction has been another major influence in the development of the concept of courseware. The effort required to produce materials that will stand alone with learners

4. Courseware

working on their own is a very different matter than the development of materials of instruction to be used within the conventional classroom and integrated into a teaching framework provided by a human teacher. To produce materials which will stand alone it has been necessary to develop and refine an instructional systems development (ISD) process. This includes at least the following steps:

1. *Analysis* of the needs of a job, the tasks that must be taught, and the existing courses.
2. *Design* of the overall structure of lessons and objectives that will be taught, along with tests to assess mastery of the objectives.
3. *Development* of the materials of instruction that will achieve the design objectives, including validation of the materials of instruction.
4. *Implementation* into real-world settings. Implementation is a part of any systematic ISD model and an attempt has even been made to define additional terms *skinware* or *peopleware* to refer to the essential roles of human beings in implementing the materials of instruction in real settings (fortunately, these terms have not come into common usage.)
5. *Control* of the implemented instruction system, to include field evaluation and subsequent revisions.

In the programmed instruction movement, a process definition has been preferred to a product definition (Bunderson & Faust, 1976). Systematic design and validation are emphasized (Markle, 1967). Even as the economic volume of the computer software industry is exceeding that of the computer hardware, the costs of developing and distributing courseware will definitely exceed that of the delivery systems on which these products are administered. Thus, the process of developing courseware becomes extremely important.

Courseware as Replicated Work

Despite the importance of the ISD process it will not form a part of the definition used in this chapter, although the ISD process must be considered in any discussion of courseware. The definition of courseware that will be used in this chapter is: an economically replicable and easily portable package which, when used in combination with a technologically mediated instructional delivery system, is capable of performing work related to training and performance improvement. This definition introduces some concepts that have not been a part of either product or process definitions in the past. These concepts are (*a*) economical replication; (*b*) delivery system; and (*c*) education work. These concepts are seen to be of such fundamental importance that courseware as a concept cannot be assessed properly without including them in the definition. They are discussed in the next section.

THE IMPORTANCE OF COURSEWARE IN A TOTAL DELIVERY SYSTEM

The Powerful Concept of Delivery System

A delivery system consists of physical objects and structures designed to perform or facilitate the work necessary to achieve education and training goals. In addition to the physical objects and structures, an effective delivery system incorporates a human culture: a set of traditions, values, and habits that inform and constrain the use of the physical artifacts. The powerful physical presence of a delivery system and the powerful intangible force of its culture are able to promote radical change in the way training and education are conducted. This power comes through the differential potential to do work of physical artifacts in alternative delivery systems. Thus, we can contrast the German tanks with the Polish cavalry in World War II in their ability to deliver projectiles to enemy positions. No matter how skillfully trained and disciplined, polished and prepared the Polish cavalry may have been, it was annihilated by the German tanks. There used to be centuries between the development of new weapon systems, so for a long time the military could ignore concentration on hardware and instead rely on working on more generally effective training techniques and strategies. In this century, however, the military services have had to learn how to conduct research and development (R&D) in weapons and to implement new weapons systems through a complex life cycle. The delivery systems in education have been fairly fixed for many centuries. We stand today, however, on the verge of major breakthroughs in educational hardware.

An example of a nonmilitary delivery system, McDonald's hamburger stands, illustrates the role of human traditions and values in a delivery system. The physical objects and structures consist of a drive-in restaurant located strategically on a busy highway and designed and arranged around very rapid delivery of standardized food products. Machines are used to produce the french fries, the milkshakes, drinks, and so on, but in addition to the skillful design of all of the physical artifacts, a set of traditions and habits has been standardized, which makes McDonald's very popular. There is even a "McDonald's University" for training managers, who then establish the traditions, skills, and habits in their local staffs so that speedy and courteous delivery of the consumable products is accomplished within the skillfully designed structures. Thus, the definition of the delivery system includes attention both to the physical objects and structures and the culture: the traditions, habits, values, and skills that grow up around them.[2]

---

[2]These concepts and examples of delivery systems were first propounded by Wicar's chairman, Dustin Heuston, in unpublished sources.

4. Courseware

I learned the lesson of delivery system cultures the hard way. Responsible for the implementation of the TICCIT system, a major mini computer-based CAI system of the early 1970s, I saw TICCIT as "a Trojan horse laden with values," that could be infiltrated into a traditional junior college. The learner-centered values of self-pacing; coaching instead of didactic instruction; focus on individual needs instead of teacher schedules; and so on were supposed to creep out at night and alter the culture of the school. Four years later, the teacher-centered culture had not been altered appreciably, but TICCIT and the way it was designed to be used had been altered substantially.

It is almost impossible to change the existing classroom delivery system because of the strength of the culture associated with it. The culture that has grown up around the classroom is a teacher-centered one, whereas the delivery of indivualized instruction in modular courseware packages requires a learner-centered culture.

The hardware portions of a delivery system, however, and intelligent software that can carry with it a way of "conversing with" the humans who use it offer major potential for change. A new delivery system can be designed to carry with it (through disciples—like the McDonald's managers—not just through automated material) a way of teaching the new traditions, habits, and skills necessary for introducing learner-centered cultures. It is possible to design complete learning centers in the military, in nontraditional settings, and eventually in schools. These centers, designed to deliver a total training or education function, may be free to deliver enough of the total offerings that pertain to particular students so that an effective student-centered culture can be established. In the military the definition of learner-centered will emphasize learner productivity, not necessarily learner control. The noncommissioned officers will have to be trained to carry the new culture. In all settings, learner productivity will be important, and, in some, learner choice as well.

Learning psychologists and instructional design experts generally ignore any comprehensive analysis of the type of hardware delivery system that will be dominant in the future. They feel that hardware is not a substantive issue and that learning theories and instructional theories will make all the difference. Many learning theorists tend to be biased in favor of a research model that treats the delivery system as something to be specified by the objectives, not a force in its own right. Because changes in delivery systems traditionally have been so slow, they may not have understood the implications and importance of the delivery system. This observation can be interpreted as a direct consequence of information theory. Where there is no uncertainty to reduce, there is no information. Because the teacher-centered classroom models have been so dominant, it has been difficult to think in terms of other total delivery systems. The increasing availability of excellent validated courseware that can be delivered in student-centered environments on equipment that performs educational work more effectively than ever before is going to change this perception, because alternatives will introduce uncertainty again.

The Concept of Educational Work

Implicit to the concept of courseware as the deliverable product of a powerful new technologically mediated delivery system is the notion of individualization. At the CAI learning station, we see a single student working at tasks appropriate for and adaptive to the momentary needs of the student. Delivery of this kind of individualized instruction without computer-based delivery systems has proved to be too much work for individual human beings, even if they are equipped with conventional linear media such as print and audiovisuals. Efforts at individualization usually have died out after the originators left because other teachers accustomed to the teacher-centered culture are not willing or able to perform all of the necessary work. Another way of saying this is that the present system has reached the limits of its improvability (Heuston, 1977). When education is analyzed into the work that is required, technology is seen to be the *only way* to make a fundamental difference.

Think of the amount of work that is required to present accurate information at an appropriate level for an individual person and the even greater amount of work that is required to give the person repeated trials with appropriate feedback for each discrete trial. Think of the work required to provide registration on an individual basis and records that keep track of individuals at different positions in the learning curriculum. The work of producing and replicating the materials and coaching and counseling the students in the use of them also proves to be greater than can be accomplished at acceptable levels of staffing. Table 4.1 lists seven categories of educational work that must be performed in an individualized learning setting. In the right-hand column Table 4.1 lists the most common means of delivery of each kind of work. It can be seen that in conventional classrooms and even in classrooms that have tried to adapt to individualized instruction the most common means of delivery is the teacher. However, in category 1 (presenting accurate information) a technological delivery tool—the book—has obviously taken over a crucial role. It is clear that a teacher without books cannot compete with a teacher with books because of the work potential inherent in the print medium. It is also seen in category 4 that affective appeal and interest can be greatly enhanced through the use of motion pictures. Most critical elements of educational work, however, remain almost entirely in the hands of teachers. Both courseware and software must be developed to perform major portions of the work listed in Table 4.1 and to replicate this work potential economically.

4. Courseware

TABLE 4.1
Some Kinds of Educational Work and Delivery

Work category	Most common means of delivery (order)
1. Presenting accurate information	Print media, teachers
2. Modeling of process	Teacher or master–apprentice
3. Providing trials with feedback	Teacher with workbook or blackboard
4. Diagnosis of individual needs	
At the "task" level	Teacher with printed tests
At the "cognitive procedure" level	(rarely occurs)
5. Affective appeal and interest to motivate learning	Teacher, sometimes using motion pictures and audiovisual aids
6. Coaching and counseling in the use of the delivery system	Teacher or counselor
7. Management information, registration, attendance, testing, grading, credentialling	Teachers and administrators

The Concept of Replication

Replication means that the potential for educational work can be rapidly and inexpensively duplicated and disseminated, and that the replicated product reproduces the work reliably. The book is the great example in the history of educational technology. It freed the dissemination of accurate information from the constraints of the oral tradition. Not a great deal has been written about the concept of replication because this event happened so long ago, and we do not have common examples of other forms of replicated work.

The invention of the printing press is instructive to us in this age, with new delivery system potential. Not only is the passing of information verbally from person to person an extremely burdensome task, but it was and is an approach that introduces many errors in transmission. The book usurped the oral tradition; it allowed information to be written and replicated accurately for distribution to a great many people. The low cost of paper was a big factor in this phenomenon.

Aside from the replication of static information, how can we replicate parts of the work required in all seven categories of Table 4.1? To replicate content, we can use densely packed optical storage of video, text, and computer programs. To model process, we now have a very labor-intensive system using teachers or masters with apprentices. There is a great deal of variation in the accuracy of transmission of the process being modeled because of individual differences in the teachers. Video presentations and simulation can help. To provide individual trails with feedback is similarly too much work. Individual tutors are too expensive. In addition, it is hard to maintain quality control over the interactive trials in an effective manner. Similar points can be made about the other categories.

The point of this discussion is that it is now possible to replicate *interactions* as well as *information*. Thus, the interaction between a student and a model of process can be replicated by video and simulation. The interaction involved in providing trials with feedback can be replicated by CAI practice with feedback. Motion pictures and television are replicable packages that have affective appeal and interest and can be integrated more intimately into courseware packages than has been possible in the past. Parts of the coaching and counseling function that pertain to known information can be replicated by artificially intelligent programs, as will be described later. The management and administrative work of category 7 is being aided now by computers in computer-managed instruction (CMI) and computer aids to administration. By analogy to the invention of the book, we can see that a revolution is at our doors. What is required is excellent courseware and software packages capable of replicating different varieties of educational work, and deliverable on new low-cost CBI delivery and management systems.

The Limits of Nonhuman Replication

The definition of delivery system in a previous section incorporated human traditions, values, and skills. Although it is possible to replicate much of the educational work in the various categories of Table 4.1, this work potential cannot be delivered to large numbers of people without providing a suitable human environment. The replication of accurate information is usually imperfect because of changes in the information between printings or replications. Excellent teachers can correct this. The modeling of process by motion pictures and simulations often leaves out subtle steps, which an excellant teacher can bring out for individual students. Even with an excellent *help* function, which illustrates an expert algorithm with the students current practice example, a student may not be able to perform a particular trial and will need human assistance. Whereas movies can provide motivation and affective appeal, the hardware and courseware of a delivery system just sits idle, unless humans organize themselves into groups and create value in the act of working with the hardware and courseware. Computerized coaching and counseling cannot encompass all of the counseling needs of individual students. Interpretation of tests and records must remain a human function, although computers can provide tentative interpretations. These too were lessons of the ambitious CAI projects of the past 15 years.

Social Impact Potential

One implication that can be drawn from the Coleman Report (1966) is that the American educational system has been improved to the point where no major inequalities remain. One way to interpret this finding is that the system has about

4. Courseware

reached the limits of its improvability. The fact that millions of dollars have been poured into educational improvement and research and yet few findings have been able to "stick" or be implemented in schools, lends credence to this conclusion. It appears necessary to change the whole delivery system and in so doing, change the traditions and habit patterns that make it so resistant to the introduction of change. It may be necessary, however, to introduce learner-centered subcultures in the military, in industrial training, in nontraditional schools, in foreign countries, and even in the home, before sufficient alternatives to the present school system are visible, fostering change in public education.

In military training, the introduction of more powerful delivery systems seems necessary. Weapon systems are increasing in complexity each year. The amount of print materials needed to convey the concepts and skills related to these weapon systems and to other miliary training matters is increasing greatly. For example, the amount of documentation needed to describe and train on the new XM-1 tank is reported to be larger than the carrying capacity of the tank itself. With training budgets being cut every year, it does not appear possible for the Department of Defense to maintain conventional methods oriented to stand-up instructors and print materials. New courseware forms and new delivery systems must emerge.

WHERE ARE WE NOW?

In this section, it is necessary to discuss both product and process aspects of courseware.

What Courseware Product Forms Have Achieved Success?

Through the 1960s we were treated with a great outpouring of federal monies related to modularized self-paced instruction, including CAI. Most of these projects bloomed briefly and then died; but not all. It is instructive therefore, to ask the question, "What product forms have become successful enough to have continued in use through this day despite the decline in federal funding?" The answers to this question can be organized into four groups: conventional presentational packages, packages that replicate interactions, packaged performance aids, and testing systems.

Conventional Presentational Packages

In this category are included all kinds of books, workbooks, programmed instructional texts, and linear audiovisual packages. By far, various forms of printed packages constitute the dominant courseware product form in use today. Print media usage builds on hundreds of years of traditions and habits. Users of print have experienced many years of schooling in which habits and skills for using books have been inculcated. Moreover, print media have the unique advantage among other media forms that they do not require hardware for delivery—only for production. Thus, a book is a friendly thing that can be taken almost anywhere, with or without an electrical outlet or a battery. It has always been among the least expensive media product forms for production as well. It has the benefit of costing quite a bit to produce one copy of a book. This has been an advantage in making it possible to copyright, replicate, and market books. Some new media product forms such as optical videodisks have this same property.

Some of the historical advantages of books are changing. The cost of paper and printing is going up rapidly so that it is conceivable within the next decade for the costs of other kinds of product forms to cross under the cost curve for books, especially when large volumes of information must be encoded on a single product form. Another factor that may change the long-time dominance of print is the increasing availability of certain electrical and electronic delivery systems such as television receivers and tape recorders. The major force, however, is that the book enables us to replicate only information *content* in a truly effective manner. (Although programmed instruction texts replicate a certain form and level of trials with fixed feedback, they leave much to be desired.) The graphics that are possible in books are not interactive nor do they include motion, but they can be motivating and provide affective excitment and interest. The more they are able to do this through color plates; however, the more expensive is the book as a courseware product form and the less it is able to compete in terms of cost with other audiovisual media.

Many forms of audiovisual media such as filmstrips, slide-sound presentations, videotapes, and movies have found sustained and regular use. In addition to providing motivation and visual interest not always present in books (especially for the young people who have grown up in the television era), these media can model the processes occuring over time and can convey information through the auditory channel while the eyes are fixed on visual displays.

The greatest weakness of books and audiovisual media is that they are not able to replicate the interactions and so cannot convey the tutorial aspects of the modeling of process; cannot provide trials with true feedback, scoring, records; and so on. They cannot in and of themselves provide diagnosis of individual needs nor coaching and counseling in their own use. These are forms of work that are becoming increasingly necessary in a delivery system. It would seem, then, that printed materials and audiovisual packages much be incorporated increasingly into total delivery systems capable of performing far more educational work.

4. Courseware

Packages That Replicate Interactions

Table 4.2 illustrates the kinds of computer-assisted instruction strategies that have achieved prominence in the past 20 years of research. Table 4.2 also lists these basic strategies against the kind of performance objectives they are best suited to achieve. The basic objective types are memory or simple skills, concept and rule learning, and the integration of skills and concepts. A memory objective involves presentation of a stimulus term, then a response term is given through recognition or recall. A concept or rule learning objective involves the application of a classification or procedural rule to unencountered instances. An integration objective involves an unencountered problem or "case" that requires selection from and integration of a number of concepts and rules.

There are several degrees of additional intelligence that can be added to the basic strategies. These are listed in the last three columns in Table 4.2. Answer analysis and feedback require more than the recognition of multiple-choice responses. Numbers, words, short phrases, or pointing responses (with finger or cursor) may be entered. Answer analysis routines can recognize these responses as anticipated or not, and give feedback messages prepared in each case. A level above such "canned" feedback messages is a *help* function that will prompt the student in the semantics of the rule being applied, and model an expert algorithm or procedure for applying the rule to the current instance being attempted by the

TABLE 4.2
Learning Objectives and Related Strategies Common through 1975

Kind of objective	Basic strategy	Answer analysis and feedback	Algorithmic and prompting help	Theory-based diagnostics
Memory of simple skills	Drill or generated practice	Yes	Rarely	Rarely
Concepts or rules	Tutorial	Yes	Rarely	Rarely
	Rule–Example–Practice with advisor	Yes	Yes	Rarely
Integration of concepts and simple skills and problem solving	Simulations–games	Special	Rarely	Rarely
	Student programming	No	No	No

(Strategy / Intelligent enhancement)

student. Theory-based diagnostics take *help* to a deeper level. They do this by using a cognitive model of the expert and a representation of the common discrepancies of learners from the expert model. The intelligent. theory-based computer program then tries to diagnose what the student is doing wrong and prescribes remedial action. Such programs were rarely available in courseware through 1975.

There are other intelligent enhancements that go well beyond these three. These will be discussed in connection with Table 4.3. In Table 4.2 we are concerned with strategies common through 1975. Generated practice exercises (or "drill and practice") have achieved perhaps the most widespread use and the greatest success among that class of courseware packages that replicate interactions. Drill and practice packages have been shown to be effective in a variety of settings (Alderman, Swinton, & Braswell, 1978; Suppes & Morningstar, 1972; Vinsonhaler & Bass, 1971). The Computer Curriculum Corporation has found a way of marketing these packages to conventional schools in a manner that helps the school (Clinton, 1978). The school can use Federal Title I monies, funds applicable to help students who are well below grade level. The programs are adjunctive to the teacher and do not require a student-centered environment. The CAI materials help to solve some difficult problems in students whose performances are substantially below grade level. The success of drill and practice is a powerful vindication of the general concept that the educational work of providing individual trials with feedback can produce marked performance gains. Unfortunately, the Adlerman, Swinton, and Braswell study (1978) reveals improved item performance skills but not conceptual understanding.

There are two strategies (listed in the column two of Table 4.2) dealing with the teaching of concept and rule learning objectives. The oldest of these strategies is the tutorial strategy, which can be defined as a branching strategy that may include constructed responses. It is being used widely on a variety of computer systems using older languages such as Coursewriter III, the CAN language at the Ontario Institute for Studies and Education, PLANIT, PILOT, and other CAI languages. The rule–example–practice strategy is explained in Bunderson and Faust (1976). The authors prepare "courseware components" including rules (definitions of concepts or statements of principles), examples of applying the rules, and practice in applying the rules to unencountered instances. In the TICCIT system (Bunderson, 1973; Volk, 1978), the leaners control the selection of components, aided by an "advisor program" that is designed to help them learn to select wisely.

Although rule–example–practice has a stronger theoretical basis than the tutorial strategy, it is not as widespread on computers. Starting with the TICCIT project at Brigham Young University, this model has been spread through several companies that emerged during or shortly after the TICCIT project. The oldest

4. Courseware

and largest of these is Courseware, Incorporated, which has developed in cooperation with military authors literally thousands of hours of modular self-paced instructional packages using this componentized rule-example-practice strategy. These materials can often be adapted readily to computer assistance and, in some cases, are developed initially for this delivery system. The University of Mid-America has a metrics course that uses this strategy; the users of Hazeltine TICCIT systems are also using it. WICAT Incorporated, a nonprofit corporation dealing with educational technology, has developed a software package that not only uses this strategy but also has generalized it to a variety of computer systems other than the TICCIT system.

Rule-example-practice has implications for substantial efficiencies in authoring. These efficiencies are the result of the component structure of the courseware. There exist job aids and training materials to assist authors in developing the components. New authors or authors on short-duty assignment can quickly become proficient in developing a few components, and hence can become productive team members.

Simple simulations and games (column three in Table 4.2 are widespread. Many of them have been developed in the BASIC language available on a large number of computer systems, including the new personal computers. Substantial libraries of materials exist within computer-user groups (e.g., the DECUS group for DEC equipment and the Hewlett Packard users group). Also, published packages of simple simulations and games, primarily academic subjects, are available through popular periodicals such as *Creative Computing, Byte,* and *Interface Age*.

One patterned simulation is the medical diagnosis simulation-tutorial. The situation is analogous to a qualitative chemistry laboratory. An "unknown" is presented and the students may ask for tests until they are able to make a diagnosis. In the medical situation the "unknown" is a patient exhibiting certain symptoms. A branching program structure leads the students down through a series of decisions where they may be allowed to suffer the consequences of their wrong decisions or may be told through tutorial interactions what is wrong and then required to proceed down the right path. This model of simulation is in wide use in medical and dental schools and is published commercially by the Milliken Communications Corporation. This company has recently made these kinds of simulation tutorials available on a small personal computer, the Apple II with mini floppy disks.

Because of the widespread acceptance and use of the four basic strategy classes described in Table 4.2, they must be regarded as the "mainstream strategies" for replicating interactions. Even so, the effective and regular use of the more advanced forms of intelligent enhancements have been infrequent and inconsistent in quality.

Performance Aids

A performance aid is a computer program, usually interactive, that performs calculations or other data processing operations in symbiotic interaction with a person. The dividing line between courseware and software often virtually disappears in the category of performance aids. This category includes problem solving software packages tailored for domains of problems. The most common of these are statistical packages for the analysis of data. Among the most used and disseminated packages studied by Hunter, Kastner, Rubin, and Seidel (1975) was Statistical Package for the Social Sciences (SPSS). Other packages contain data bases from which information may be retrieved and then analyzed to test certain hypotheses or gather data relative to certain propositions.

Another kind of performance aid is finding considerable use in the military and industry but has not often been implemented on computers. This is the job aid. The job aid may be checklist, list of steps, or a flow chart that guides the user through a series of branching decisions related to a task such as maintenance of equipment. Although the print medium has been the dominant means for the production of job aids so far, there is a bright future for rugged, interactive CAI systems that can conceal inside the computer's memory the great bulk of the branching decision tree of a complex job aid and only expose the students to that path they are taking during their diagnostic and maintenance activities. Tutorial and simulation guidance can be available at critical points of the decision tree.

Testing Systems

Packaged computerized testing systems fit the definition of courseware in this chapter. Mark sense or computer-scored testing is now widespread. It is not administered over a computerized delivery system and hence is not considered as courseware, unless adjunctive to instruction that is so administered. Increasingly, however, on-line testing is being used in CAI systems (e.g., the Control Data CMI system and the Digital Equipment Corporation CMI system). This opens a host of new opportunities for diagnosis and prescription systems, and evaluation systems with new courseware product forms. Weiss (1978) provides an overview of some recent work in computerized adaptive testing. Because tests have been one of the few products of behavioral science to penetrate schools and society widely, computerized tests might gain rapid acceptance and use.

Where Are We in Process?

ISD Models

Logan, (1979), recently completed a study entitled *A State-of-the-Art Assessment of Instructional Systems Development*. In the study, Logan defined ISD as follows: "Instructional Systems Development is defined as a general systems approach with multiple components called phases which, operating amongst a certain set of constraints, is used to produce an instructional system. The phases are sequential sets of activities called *analysis, design, development, implementation,* and *control* [p. 1]."

The most widely used ISD model is described in *Interservice Procedures for Instructional Systems Development* (TRADOC, 1975). This model was commissioned by an interservice committee for instructional systems development and was developed at Florida State University under the direction of Robert K. Branson. The difficulties and successes involved in adoption of this model in the Army and Navy were reported in part by Branson (1979), who discussed the lessons learned in attempting to implement the interservice ISD model. He highlights three case studies—one at the Army Signal School, where lack of command priority resulted in an initial failure; one at the Army Infantry School, where high command priority and a carefully executed 14-month implementation plan resulted in substantial success; and one in the Navy where the creation of Instructional Program Development Centers and the implementation of the model in those centers resulted in a substantial degree of success.

The Interservice Procedures ISD model (IPISD) is not very old; TRADOC pamphlet 350-30 is dated August 1975. It is becoming a standard for communication throughout the military training establishment and beyond. This is one of the positive benefits of the model. Indeed Logan (1979) regards ISD as merely "a logic set for talking to one another in order to produce a package of learning whose beauty lies in the eye of the beholder."

The IPISD model is general to any kind of instructional program and is not specialized in terms of particular media delivery systems or courseware package forms. There are other models that have been developed in the civilian sector that are more appropriate for computer courseware. Bunderson (1970) published an early ISD model for the development of computer courseware. Courseware Incorporated has produced some training packages for developing the rule-example-practice strategy on the TICCIT system (Freedman, 1978). Hazeltine, Incorporated has another set of packages for ISD related to the TICCIT system. Taylor (1979) described the CREATE course developed by Control Data Corporation for instructional systems development. This set of courses includes specific instructions on how to develop PLATO lessons. In addition there are a number of books and papers available from talented instructional developers who have worked extensively on the PLATO system. (Ghesquere, Davis, & Thompson, 1976; Sherwood, 1977).

Critique of ISD Models

Considering the IPISD model (TRADOC pamphlet 350-30) as a standard, there are some areas where improvement is definitely needed.

1. The ISD model tells what to do and the order in which it should be done but not "how to do it." This criticism has been noted frequently (e.g., Schulz, 1979; Bunderson, 1977a). One response to this problem for certain steps of the IPISD procedure is an author training course developed under contract to ARPA by Courseware, Incorporated (O'Neal, Faust, & O'Neal, 1979; Freedman, Bresee, Hermanns, & O'Neal, 1978. See also Merrill, 1979). This author training system uses a component courseware approach that breaks the authoring of courseware materials into seven components: objective, generality, generality help, examples, practice on test items, feedback, and introduction with wraparound. Authors can be trained in the production and sequencing of the courseware components by step-by-step, how-to procedures. Other procedures are available for other kinds of strategies, for example, conventional programmed instruction strategies (see Thiagarajan, 1971).

2. The IPISD model has a great amount of complexity, which could be greatly simplified. Wilson (1977) has developed the ISD approach and training system now in use at Fort Sill, Oklahoma. Wilson's procedure is consistent with the major phases and steps of IPISD but is much simpler. Because of this, training developers throughout Fort Sill have been able to learn to use it quickly. One potential way to simplify the procedure dramatically is to begin "in the middle," as it were, by developing pilot lessons and exposing them to test students. Then they can be iterated backward, touching all of the bases in the IPISD procedure, but not insisting on a rigid top-down sequence now demanded by the model. This potential ISD variation will be referred to as "iteration theory" in this chapter. One difficulty with the top-down sequence is that alternatives are carried along that need not be considered all the way through. A good example is the media selection model described in steps 3.1 and 3.2 of the IPISD model. This top-down procedure makes decisions about media selection at the objectives level of analysis. In reality, media decisions are constrained by political and economic considerations at a much earlier stage than objectives. For example, at one military instructional development center visited by the author, a guideline has been given that the materials will be 80% text and about 20% audiovisual (usually interpreted as 10% slide tape and 10% videotape). Bennik, Hoyt, and Butler (1978) have described a media selection procedure that incorporates early constraining considerations in a simpler manner.

3. The IPISD model lacks generality for the new delivery systems and courseware product forms. When the IPISD model was written, videodisks were ruled out as not having been developed sufficiently. CAI was included as an alternative, but the specific kind of CAI product forms that (it appears) will become dominant in the next few years were not considered in depth by the IPISD model. The videodisk has the power to combine and store on one inexpensive disk most of the capabilities of any print and audiovisual medium and must be considered carefully in any ISD approach.

Technological Aids to ISD

The ISD models provide us with a way of looking at the ISD process analytically to "divide and conquer" by finding ways to produce each component product more economically. This can often be accomplished through the use of technological aids. Interactive computer programs promise to offer the greatest aid. In accordance with earlier analysis (Bunderson, 1979) there appear to be four major categories of technological aids to authoring.

1. *Author prompting systems* teach the author or developer how to perform each step of the ISD procedure.
2. *Text and graphics editing systems* are built around componentized patterns (which keep the text and graphics components in digital form while they are going through revisions).
3. *Formative evaluation systems* obtain data geared at the rapid improvement of the lesson materials.
4. *Author management systems* monitor the progress being made by development teams toward project goals and flag bottlenecks and problems.

It would appear that new delivery systems and courseware product forms can simultaneously improve the cost effectiveness of instruction and simplify the process of development. This is because inherent in these new systems are the combined capabilities of television, books, and computers. This great flexibility could lead to greater simplicity in media selection and in other ISD steps. Simultaneously, author aids, with author prompting systems to teach people "how to," can increase the speed with which materials can be developed and thus reduce their cost.

At a seminar sponsored by the ARPA Cybernetics Technology Office in 1977, a unique and positive attitude was noted for the first time: instead of arguing about this or that aspect of ISD or this or that approach to making it more cost effective, it became apparent that instructional developers invited to that conference now had a common frame of reference about the ISD process and were able to focus on the problems of bringing technology to bear on making each of the phases and steps of ISD easier and more cost effective. A number of papers were presented discussing early attempts at using technology to aid particular steps of ISD. Some of these were published in a book entitled *Procedures for Instructional Systems Development* (O'Neil, 1979b). The chapters include a discussion of computer aids for developing tests and instruction, computerized adaptive achievement testing and test development, tools for evaluating the quality of instructional materials, and intelligent CAI. In another book, *Issues in Instructional Systems Development* (O'Neil, 1979a), additional technological aids are discussed including an authoring system for the Lincoln Terminal facility, (Harris, 1979); an author management system (O'Neal & O'Neal, 1979);

and proposed data bases for obtaining intermediate design products or actual completed courseware components (Brackett, 1979).

Logan (1977) conducted a survey and analysis of aids to ISD but did not restrict them to technological aids. For the most part, the Logan survey is an annotated review of various how-to training packages for authors and task analyzers. Logan did note a few technological aids to ISD, but these were highly restricted and specialized to small aspects of ISD.

The field of technological aids to ISD is in its infancy, yet it could be extremely promising. The most promising tool would appear to be component-oriented author entry and edit systems that have all of the capabilities of word processing and text processing systems but have author prompting systems associated with them. The latter can bring the "how to" information to the exact moment of creation of a particular courseware component or ISD subproduct. The next most important technological aid would appear to be hardware and software tools for the rapid collection of formative evaluation data. A lot of false starts and costs can be avoided if revision is assumed to be a major ISD technique from the beginning and if less effort is committed to the first lean version. Formative evaluation tools can bring data to bear on the areas where "glitches" or bugs exist, structure is wrong, more instruction is necessary, or its construction is defective.

An author management system such as that described by O'Neal and O'Neal (1979) could go a long way toward documenting what the actual costs of the different steps of ISD are. These data are not available at the present time so no thorough and systematic analysis of the process is possible, despite the improvement brought about in thinking and talking about the ISD process because of the existence of IPISD. As data become available on what the true costs are of each ISD step, then additional technological and human management aids can be used to reduce the time and costs. This is perhaps the major benefit of an author management system, although it has immediate use for helping managers keep projects on schedule, notice slippages early, and correct the slippages.

It is also possible that substantial savings can be made by establishing data banks that describe existing jobs and existing courseware packages. Such data bases are related less intimately to the ongoing process of instructional systems development than to the tools just mentioned but could nonetheless produce advances in cost effectiveness.

It should be stressed that existing CAI authoring languages like TUTOR, Coursewriter, PLATO, PILOT, and so on do not provide the properties discussed previously with the exception of formative evaluation data (especially with TUTOR) and editing. These are programming languages, not authoring systems or authoring aids in a real sense. Users must become skilled programmers and supply their own instructional semantics, for these languages do not have the semantics related to ISD. The semantics of CAI languages really deal with the controlling of computer displays, the accepting of responses from student interface devices, the processing of these responses, branching, data collection, and analysis.

The Need to Blend Artistic, Analytical, and Empirical Traditions

Bunderson and Faust (1976) and Reigeluth, Merrill, and Bunderson (1978), discuss the artistic, analytical, and empirical traditions. The artistic tradition is that practiced by the television and motion picture developers and to some extent those in the audiovisual field. The emphasis is often on the visual, artistic aspects of a presentation; the dramatic content; and the action and movement—in short, those things that will cause a motion picture or television production to win a large audience and awards from industry groups. The artistic emphasis has considerable merit. The outcomes of the emphasis on visual interest, drama, and involvement are the viewers' approach toward, and engagement in, the media production; persistence because of interest; and positive attitudes. These affective objectives influence completion rate and thus, costs of delivery. Actually, motion picture sequences are quite limited in the cognitive instructional content that they can convey because most of the information must come through the audiotrack or through a very slow pacing of the visual presentations. Slow pacing has a tendency to lose some of the interest and drama that lead to engagement and involvement.

The analytical approach deals with applying instructional theorems to the production of courseware components (Merrill, Olsen, & Coldeway, 1976). The theorems should have been validated and shown to lead to a high probability that the instruction produced following these theorems will be effective. Instructional theorems have been validated primarily on cognitive and psychomotor objectives. It is only indirectly that they lead to persistence and positive attitudes (success in learning is motivating). The instructional theorems are also related to reducing the costs because the first version is more likely to be effective and will need less revision. In addition, the first revisions are more likely to correct any instructional problems than if no instructional theorems are used.

The major strength of the empirical tradition is to validate the claim that courseware produced using either the artistic or analytical approach does achieve its desired outcomes. Empirical testing can validate the instructional theorems used to produce cognitive and psychomotor outcomes. It can also validate the affective outcomes of the artistic approach. What historically has characterized the empirical tradition, however, has not been this sophisticated. Mostly, it has been used to remove the need for theory. The idea was to put a product out quickly and then keep changing it until it worked. Changes may be based on whimsy, caprice, or logic (Markle, 1967). It has also been shown that empirical testing and validation may not lead to a program that is any good (Markle, 1973). It depends on the objectives against which the program was validated.

One extremely pervasive and important aspect of the empirical tradition is the discovery of idiosyncratic bugs. No matter how good the analytical model or the artistic talent of the developers, there are always bugs in courseware packages. Usually these are detected very quickly by students or teachers in the target population in learning settings. These "gliches" are usually totally idiosyncratic to the particular content and presentation format. They must simply be exposed until they are found. The debugging process is a long and difficult one in courseware development even as it is in software development. Internal reviewers cannot be expected to notice all of the bugs in a cost-effective manner. They are too close to the situation and their environment is not attuned to make the bugs appear obvious.

It is possible to take extreme positions in any one of these traditions and many instructional developers still do so. However, in the preceding discussion, it has been shown that each tradition leads toward certain outcomes: the artistic tradition toward affective outcomes, but with high cost implications; the analytical tradition toward cognitive outcomes and reduced cost; and empirical tradition toward the removal of bugs, the validation of the goals of the other traditions, and reduced costs by early iteration. A blending of the three traditions with intelligent use of technological tools—a new "iteration theory" for ISD—is more promising than stubborn reliance on one tradition.

Lessons Learned about the ISD Process for Computer Courseware

It has been difficult at many computer-assisted instruction centers to make broad generalizations about the ISD process for CAI materials. It has been hard to maintain an effort over a long enough period of time involving enough people who are able to use equipment that is sufficiently general and powerful. Instruction in schools and established military training centers is so complex and interrelated with social factors that small studies with short pieces of courseware do not yield valid generalizations. Fortunately, some brave people at the National Science Foundation put their careers on the line and raised $10 million for the PLATO and TICCIT projects, providing at least a 5-year run with two thorough and complete CAI delivery systems. At the time of this writing, TICCIT had 7 or 8 years of experience to its credit. PLATO had that and 10 years more.

TICCIT and PLATO provide a valuable contrast in their respective approaches to authoring. The PLATO approach can be described as a merger between the artistic and empirical traditions. TCCIT tried to merge analytical and empirical, with a modest effort to blend artistic. Because of the time pressures

4. Courseware

and a lack of working software on the TICCIT project, the courseware can be seen primarily as a reflection of the analytical approach.

Lessons Learned from the TICCIT Project

The analytical model espoused by the TICCIT courseware developers at Brigham Young University (Bunderson 1973; Bunderson & Faust, 1976) was based on instructional theorems and hypotheses primarily in the domains of concept and rule learning (Merrill & Boutwell, 1973). This analysis led to the specification of courseware components. The *rule, example, practice,* and *help* components have been described. In addition *maps* at the course, unit, and lesson levels guided students in accessing segments containing the components. *Objectives* showed the students what they would be able to do after mastering the material in a unit, lesson, and segment. "Minilessons" provided an overview (a linear series of pages with text and graphics) of each unit and lesson. Tests were provided for each lesson (three tests for three attempts). Advisor messages were provided both on request and automatically when certain conditions were met.

Rather than sequencing these courseware components by means of computer algorithms, few restraints were placed on the sequence and the students were given a "learner control keyboard," which allowed them to put the components together in terms of their own moment-by-moment perceived strategy and tactics. The learner control approach was viewed as advantageous not only to the student but also to the authoring groups who would not have to contend with numerous "go-to" statements, conditional branches, and the inherent complexity and nonstructured nature of the resulting program. The TICCIT courseware approach was a true top-down structured programming approach.

The functions that each TICCIT component was to perform were studied carefully and specified to the authoring teams. Division of labor was used so that different staff members developed and reviewed different courseware components. By means of this component approach, and management procedures that were established, a large body of courseware in first-year and remedial mathematics and English was developed in time for testing at two community colleges.

Learner-Controlled Componentized Courseware Is Effective

The TICCIT courseware had to be evaluated publicly before it had been subjected to internal formative evaluation and revision. It was thus exposed to evaluation by Educational Testing Service (ETS) when it had barely been debugged. Its quality was primarily a function of the analytical theorems and artistic talents of the courseware development teams at Brigham Young University, assisted by the faculty members at Phoenix College and Northern Virginia Community College, who reviewed the materials and assisted in making revisions. The results were that students who completed the TICCIT lessons did significantly better than the students in conventional classes in both mathematics and English (Alderman, 1978).

The Need for Additional Courseware Patterns and Flexibility

Although the rule-example-practice pattern proved highly effective for the production of instruction related to concepts and rule-learning objectives, a courseware development group should have access to other kinds of patterns. There are a variety of drill and practice strategies that are now patterned and could be used. There are some patterned simulations and games such as the qualitative analysis or medical diagnosis model. Finally, a flexible language should be available for the creation of totally new sequences, whether patterned or not. Hazeltine Incorporated, the company that now distributes TICCIT has responded to this need by the development of a TICCIT Authoring Language (TAL) that provides this needed flexibility.

The Power of the Advisor in Learner-Controlled CAI

TICCIT posited a "second level of discourse" wherein student and machine could "converse" about strategy and tactics. The advisor program kept records on the student and made this information available to help tell the students how they were doing and give them suggestions as to what strategies and tactics might be useful to them. When students are given learner-controlled courseware they need help in becoming proficient learners. The extent to which the students pressed the advice button or saw advisor displays (up to 25% of the displays seen) shows the heavy use of this orientation feature. Because of the importance of the advisor, it is clear now in the development of modular, structured CAI systems like TICCIT that designers should consider at least two levels of instructional strategy. At the lower level, presentation strategies deal with the *rule, example, practice,* and *help* components. At the higher level, orientation strategies deal with the advisor, the maps, the objectives, and the overviews. Orientation strategies also promote synthesis.

The Need for Synthesis

When instruction is broken up into small components organized hierarchically, students are able to learn each segment quickly if the instruction is good, but may have difficulty in synthesizing it into its larger wholes. There was a variety of incidental evidence from TICCIT use pointing to the fact that many students had difficulty synthesizing their TICCIT instruction. A similar phenomenon has been reported for a hierarchically organized modular PLATO reading course. This observation led to a line of research in "structural strategies" or "orientation strategies" that deal with the problems of synthesis and review (Riegeluth et al., 1978).

Differentiation Requires Heroic Efforts at Integration

To get large amounts of materials ready in time for the ETS evaluation, the TICCIT teams grew fairly large and the staffing was highly differentiated. Componentized instruction lends itself to differentiated staffing. One problem is that it is difficult to integrate all of the components into lessons that hang together well. One response to this problem was to write very careful lesson-specification documents that spelled out in precise terms the rules, examples, and practice items, feedback messages, and helps to be developed. Once these lesson-specification documents were written, the lessons almost wrote themselves, production was rapid, and integration problems were easier. The writing of lesson-specification documents, however, was itself a difficult task and sometimes one or two iterations between the lesson and the specifications were required.

Teacher-Centered versus Student-Centered Cultures

TICCIT posited a mainline instructional approach in which a total student-centered culture was introduced. This was an individualized system where the machine, the books, and even the teachers serve in a resource role to the students. In a teacher-centered culture, the teacher retains the control of the schedule, the grading, and the pacing. PLATO maintained a teacher-centered culture, but TICCIT tried to introduce the student-centered culture into two community colleges. Like almost all community colleges, they were teacher-centered. The ETS evaluation showed rather low completion rates for TICCIT—lower than in the conventional classes. For example, mathematics completion rates, already low (about 55%), ranged around 25% with TICCIT. There are many possible reasons for this but high among them must be included the penalties and driving factors that force work in the conventional classes scheduled and controlled by the teachers. These factors were not present in the TICCIT classes, although some deadlines with penalties were added later. Perhaps more importantly, the traditions and habits that the students have become accustomed to over 12–14 years of schooling were not present with TICCIT. At Brigham Young University, a series of studies were conducted to build new human environments that would promote higher completion rates by building new traditions, habits, and human support. Completion rates above 90%, higher than in conventional classrooms (76% at Brigham Young University), were obtained through the construction of such human environments (Bunderson, 1977b).

Lessons from PLATO

Avner (1979) has provided a major service by documenting some of the practical problems of time, cost, and other matters related to the production of computer-based educational (CBE) materials on PLATO. He describes two studies. One study involved inexperienced authors who, after at least 1 year of experience with the PLATO system, were measured in terms of the production rates they were able to generate for CBE lessons during a 1-year period. Their average rate was 291 hours of work per hour of PLATO instruction. In the second study, highly experienced CBE authors worked under nearly ideal conditions, that is, they were programmers for teachers or the teachers themselves. Experienced with PLATO, these teachers had specified clearly the number and nature of the lessons to be produced. This group produced CBE lessons in an average of 26 author hours per student hour. Many generalizations could be drawn from the material Avner draws together in his paper. Some that seem relevant to this paper are the following:

1. Heavy start-up costs: There are heavy start-up costs for authors who must learn an authoring language like TUTOR. Avner did not begin to measure production until the authors had been working with PLATO for at least 1 year. Their learning was informal. They learned from existing programming manuals and from the excellent "computer culture" that exists at the University of Illinois and to a lesser extent at its satellite centers. At the end of the year, they had not reached asymptote in their programming skill. Avner pointed out that during the period of acquiring the CBE language, there was little interest in pedagogical techniques appropriate to the new medium. When authors began to expose their materials extensively to students, some of them became quite interested in pedagogical issues, but other authors "became so involved in the use of the CBE language that production of impressive sequences of animation or simulation became almost an end in itself [1979]." Thus, when authors are given no pedagogical patterns in advance, but are given a general purpose language with semantics for controlling displays, anticipating responses, branching, and so on, it takes them a long time to acquire programming skills and then to move to the vital instructional design questions that will produce performance gains in their students.

2. The power of "patterns": In the second study, the production rates of 18 experienced TUTOR programmers were examined. Each programmer worked with (or was) a subject matter expert and apparently (it must be inferred from the article) at least an informal front-end analysis must have been done because they knew exactly what lessons needed to be produced. They also had a repertoire of pedagogical strategies (patterns) that they could follow in generating the new materials. As was mentioned above, their production rate was more than 10 times better than the relatively inexperienced authors. In addition, Avner noted different styles in the authors—a production style that was oriented toward getting it

done quickly and an "effectiveness" orientation in which the authors had a strong need to expose materials to students to see whether they actually taught.

3. Pitfalls of systems approach: Avner cautioned against the heavy reliance on a systems approach built around an ill-conceived analysis of the subject matter and an ill-conceived specification of standard patterns. Until the patterns evolve and a group of programmers are possessed of a complete knowledge of the patterns, it may be premature to impose the discipline of the systems models like the IPISD and the management pressures that are associated with it.

Avner did not emphasize considerations of the size of the team, but it would appear that the most efficient PLATO teams were quite small, including a few persons who possessed programming skills, pedagogical skills, and the skills to evaluate and revise based on student input.

A Contrast between PLATO and TICCIT

There appears to be a dilemma in the introduction of CAI. The ETS evaluation of the PLATO community college project showed that the teachers and students had very positive attitudes toward PLATO and that there was no effect on completion rates. However, there was no effect on performance either when the achievement of students in PLATO classes was compared to that of students in conventional classes. For TICCIT, on the other hand, in a student-centered culture with analytically developed courseware, there was a significant performance advantage in favor of the TICCIT students. However, their attitudes were not as positive nor were the teachers' attitudes. Also, the completion rate was substantially lower than that in the classrooms. This is the dilemma: It may be necessary to go all the way to introduce student-centered cultures to get achievement gains. However, the teacher resistance, coupled with the students' lack of habits and traditions for learning in this kind of environment may lead to worse attitudes and lower completion rates. These comments apply to the *implementation* phase of instructional systems development and call for much more elaborated procedures for introducing student-centered cultures and sustaining them.

Lessons from Software Engineering

In addition to experience with CAI courseware development we can learn lessons from the field of software engineering, which has had the benefit of experience on many dozens of large-scale software development projects. CAI courseware of any scale is a large, complex application program written in some computer language or data structure. Other computer software faces analogous problems.

Two excellent documents should be read by anyone planning large courseware development projects. One of them is *The Mythical Man-Month* by Fred

Brooks, Jr. (1975). The other is *Perspectives on Software Engineering* by M. V. Zelkowitz (1978).

Pitfalls of Overstaffing

Both Brooks and Zelkowitz confirm the lesson of differentiated staffing taken from TICCIT, which was discussed previously. The problem of integrating many small components produced by separate people would appear to be great. As the size of a programming team grows, problems of communication grow geometrically, so that adding persons to a team actually may delay the completion of a software project rather than speed it up. Other lessons deal with the way teams should be organized, and Brooks describes the "chief programmer team" that has proved effective in software engineering.

Do Not Be Afraid to Start Over

Brooks also recommends that the first effort at programming a large computer system be thrown out. The lessons learned from the first effort can be used to make a much more compact and efficient second effort. The entire system should not be a function of the vision and understanding of the programmer analysts (or courseware authors) at the beginning of the project. This recommendation is in the same spirit as the concept of iteration theory mentioned previously.

Plan Time to Debug

An important summary of experience in software development is the allocation of total effort required for various development activities (excluding maintenance). Thus, requirements analysis takes 10% of the total, specification another 10%, design 15%, coding 20%, module test 25%, and integration test 20%. Module test and integration test, which together comprise 45% of the total effort, can loosely be called debugging or "formative evaluation and revision." These steps are comparable to proofreading and small-group testing of courseware. When compared to courseware development, it is seen that the error or bug-finding and fixing aspect of courseware development often is underestimated greatly by courseware-development project managers. The writing of manuscripts or first drafts on a computer is analogous to coding. This really only comprises 20% of the effort.

PROSPECTS THROUGH THE EARLY 1980s

Delivery System Developments

All of the more interesting courseware product forms discussed in this paper are dependent on the existence and widespread distribution of computer-based delivery systems. Thus, some mention must be made of anticipated progress in

4. Courseware

the availability of delivery system hardware. Electronics periodical literature is filled with information about the rapid advances in the capability of microcomputers and the rapidly declining cost curves. The personal computer manufacturers are reaping in large profits from what is already approaching a market of $200 million per year. Even the $500 Radio Shack personal computer with 4K memory, so far the most widely distributed, has the capability to administer smaller and simpler examples of the courseware product forms described in Table 4.2. With the addition of more memory, this and other personal computers can administer more and more complex courseware product forms.

The availability of substantial processing intelligence in the terminal opens the way for new kinds of distributed systems. Complex time-sharing executives will not be needed. Instead, local storage stations that merely store files and switch them out to intelligent work stations will become increasingly evident through the early 1980s. This will open the door to even further distribution of courseware in offices, schools, government agencies, and homes. In homes, the slower communication provided by telephone lines will restrict rapid downloading of files, until cable television begins to provide this service.

New Forms of Distribution Media

The videodisk or optical videocard will become increasingly evident as a medium for the distribution of courseware. It has many inherent advantages. It can store video, audio, and booklike still frames. A single side of a videodisk can store 54,000 still frames. The distribution cost of this medium will become highly competitive with alternative courseware media forms such as audiocassettes, videocassettes, floppy disks, and printed pages. Videodisks also have the advantage of being expensive to master initially, so that it is uneconomical to make a small number of copies. This property will induce publishers to use this medium of distribution. Increasingly threatened by inexpensive duplication of printed materials, coupled with the rising cost of books. and also the easy duplication of video and motion picture productions, publishers may find the videodisk family of media to be a more profitable vehicle for distribution. Other forms of read-only memories such as the read-only memory (ROM) cartridges now available for a variety of home game computers and personal computers also offer the advantage of being more difficult to copy. These undoubtedly will be used for commercial program distribution. Publishers may be reluctant to put their best materials out on easily copied audiocassettes, but may seize the opportunity to distribute on ROM cartridges and later on videodisks.

Projected Use of Courseware Product Forms

Conventional courseware and the distribution of existing print and audiovisual media definitely will be transferred onto videodisks and microcomputer-based systems. The investment in producing these courseware products and the familiarity of an audience of users with some of these products will force this development. It is true that the transfer of an existing videotape or super 8mm program to a videodisk will not take advantage of interactive capabilities of that medium, with or without microprocessor support. Nevertheless, if an existing courseware product has been validated and is in widespread use, it will be cost effective for an organization to replace several different pieces of existing audiovisual equipment with a single audiovisual delivery system such as a videodisk player and replicate the old materials on disks. Some small degree of interaction can be added at low cost such as practice items, test items or modest branching structures.

Common Forms of CAI

As for the more common forms of computer courseware listed in Table 4.2, it is likely that we will see these product forms increasingly as computer-based delivery systems become widespread. Of the product forms listed in Table 4.2, (plus performance aids and testing systems), we will probably see games and personal programming occupying the greatest number of contact hours on the personal computer systems, when these systems are installed in schools and homes. We will probably see drill-and-practice and testing systems; and secondarily tutorial and rule-example-practice systems used, in order, after games and programming. In military and industry, the order will probably differ and we will see performance aids, tutorial or rule-example-practice systems, and testing systems predominating.

Emergence of Intelligent Courseware

During the early 1980s, intelligent courseware will begin to emerge rapidly. It will probably appear initially as an outgrowth of the more conventional courseware category of simulations and games. However, it will also extend into academic subjects. Intelligent courseware [or intelligent computer-assisted instruction (ICAI) as it is usually called by its practitioners] is rapidly gaining prominence. A good case for it was made before Congress by Brown and Goldstein (1978). The January 1979 issue of the *International Journal of Man-Machine Studies* was devoted entirely to ICAI.

In Table 4.2 "intelligent" enhancements to standard courseware strategies were listed for some common courseware strategies. The ICAI people would not regard these as being intelligent in any fundamental sense, because the intelligent enhancements in Table 4.2 rarely get to a deep structure level. At best they remain at what Brown, Collins, and Harris (1978) have called a "surface trace." One way to characterize the kind of deep structure models that the ICAI prac-

4. Courseware

titioners would acknowledge as intelligent is found in Table 4.3. Four classes of models are described in the first column and some examples listed in the second column. Every ICAI program (and, indeed, it can be argued, every CAI program) must have a model to simulate a performance environment. Generally, this model is a simulation model such as the SOPHIE model (Brown & Bobrow, 1975) of a circuit trouble-shooting environment. But, actually, even drill-and-practice programs simulate a performance environment—that of working arithmetic problems in a workbook. Thus, drill-and-practice conceals a simulation of one aspect of the classroom environment. Tutorial programs simulate an aspect of the classroom environment as well. It seems more interesting to simulate some performance environment that is more real-world (e.g., joblike or gamelike settings). There is motivation inherent in such simulations. There is integration of subtasks. There is greater potential transfer to joblike tasks.

The model most commonly associated with ICAI is that of an expert performer in the simulated performance environment. This expert should have conceptual domain knowledge that lets him or her understand the concepts and relationship between concepts in the domain. He or she should also have procedural knowledge that guides performance of relevant tasks in the domain. The authors of the TICCIT courseware tried to "can" the expert algorithm and present it to the student in a *help*. This did not seem to be successful for some of the less able students (Axtell, 1978), indicating that a deeper analysis and probably a diagnostic model will be necessary. The scholar system (Carbonell, 1970; Collins & Grignetti, 1975) was an early system with domain knowledge. The SOPHIE program (Brown, Burton & Bell, 1975) had both domain and procedural knowledge. The EXCHECK program had a built-in expert proofchecker (Goldberg & Suppes, 1979).

The third model, a diagnostic model of the learner status, is of utmost impor-

TABLE 4.3
Models Required in a Complete Intelligent System

Model	Examples
1. Model to simulate a performance environment	Working arithmetic problems
	Trouble-shooting a circuit
2. Model of an "expert" performer	"Expert algorithm" in a good TICCIT help
Conceptual domain knowledge	SCHOLAR
Procedural knowledge	SOPHIE
	EXCHECK
3. Diagnostic model of the learner's status	BUGGY
	WEST
4. Prescriptive model for how to tutor a given individual	TICCIT advisor
	WEST "Coach or Kibitzer"
	SOPHIE-III

tance in instruction. A learner's status can be compared to the procedural model of the expert's performance and discrepancies can be noted. The BUGGY program of Brown and Burton (1977) is an excellent and clear example. The discrepancies in a student's procedural knowledge of the subtraction algorithm is identified by the BUGGY program, and explained (by the cognitive scientist) in reference to the subprocedures that are being executed improperly, yet consistently by the student. The WEST program (Burton & Brown, 1976) provides a model of the students' strategic knowledge in playing the game, "How the West Was Won" and introduces suggestions on strategy at appropriate strategic moments.

A fourth type of model in ICAI is a prescriptive model for how to tutor a given individual. The WEST "Coach" or "Kibbitzer" is one example. The procedures in SOPHIE-III that provide hints to the person engaged in the troubleshooting exercise is another example. At another level, the earlier TICCIT advisor was an attempt to collect data on how the student was doing in the strategy and tactics of learning from a rule-example-practice system. The TICCIT advisor was designed to monitor aspects of the learner's strategies and tactics and feed it back to him or her on request; or, when certain conditions were met to prompt the use of those learning components that might be most helpful. Although this program was not based on a semantic network or other representation of deep structure commonly associated with ICAI, its intent was similar to that of a WEST Coach or Kibbitzer concept later stressed by Brown and Goldstein (1978) and others. The TICCIT advisor, however, dealt with a learning strategy that encompassed the on-line behavior of students in several semesters of mathematics or English. The algorithms in advisors like the TICCIT advisor can benefit greatly from advances in ICAI.

It is probable the ICAI courseware packages will make their first appearance in games for the personal computer market. Games with all of the four models listed in Table 4.3, introduced into homes, conceivably could have a significant impact on the intellectual skills development of children and adults. In government (especially the military) and industry, intelligent CAI probably will emerge during the early 1980s in the variety of performance aids and also in the form of generic simulators. (By generic simulator is meant a device that can represent a whole class or family of different equipments rather than one specific device.)

PROSPECTS FOR THE LATE 1980s AND BEYOND

Delivery Systems

Total distributed instructional systems will be available and will begin to be distributed quite widely in society, especially in industry and government. Dur-

4. Courseware

ing this time frame, the systems will not be time-sharing systems. The intelligence will be in the terminal with a storage computer nearby, connected by coaxial cable or fiber optics for rapid down-line loading and storage of personal files in between sessions. The learning station will have display devices with the storage and display capabilities of videodisks. Hence this visual display medium can provide the fidelity of generic simulators and can also display all audiovisual forms of courseware via a single display medium. It may be that two screens will be necessary so that higher resolution graphics can be presented. Around 1985, 32-bit microcomputers on a single chip with a million bits of memory will be available.

The Impact on Educational Work

Table 4.4 is an update of Table 4.1 and presents expected changes in the delivery of educational work. Because of the availability of the new delivery system, the changes are in the most common means of delivery of the work category listed in the first column. For presenting information, the videodisk will have moved into second place behind print media, displacing the function of teachers (at least in governmental and industrial applications). The videodisk with powerful microcomputer as simulator will make strong inroads in the modeling of process. CAI will be the preferred mode for providing trials with feedback; although in schools, paraprofessionals will perform some of this function. In diagnosing individual needs at the task level, DIS's with testing systems will displace teachers in industrial, military, and other applications where cost effectiveness is important, but teachers with pencil-and-paper tests will hold out for a long time in other sectors. Intelligent CAI will be introduced for diagnosis and remediation at the cognitive procedure level. Conventional audiovisual

TABLE 4.4
Expected Changes in the Delivery of Educational Work

Work category	Most common means of delivery
1. Presenting accurate information	Print media, videodisk, teachers
2. Modeling of process	Teacher, master–apprentice, videodisk–simulator
3. Providing trials with feedback	CAI, paraprofessional, teacher
4. Diagnosis of individual needs	
At the "task" level	Teacher with printed tests, DIS testing systems
At the "cognitive procedure" level	
5. Affective appeal and interest to motivate learning	Teacher, videodisk
6. Coaching and counseling in the use of the delivery system	Intelligent advisor, paraprofessional, teacher
7. Management information, registration, attendance, testing, grading, credentialling	Teachers and administrators, DIS

forms including motion pictures and audiovisuals will be distributed increasingly on optical media such as the videodisk. For coaching and counseling, intelligent advisors will become more proficient than humans in advice regarding the use of the delivery system itself, although paraprofessionals, (usually called proctors) will be necessary to help new users become proficient quickly.

Finally, distributed instructional systems will make increasing inroads on the management information functions in training and educational systems. In some industrial, military, and home applications, human teachers will not be available. However, in schools and in most mainline industrial and governmental training activities human teachers will remain an essential element, although their roles will change and differentiate. They will increasingly do things that are uniquely human. These human functions include modeling the kind of professional person that the student can become when he or she masters the objectives of the courses; stimulating enthusiasm, interest, and desire; diagnosing tacit dimensions that have not or cannot be included in intelligent courseware systems; and coordinating productive and creative tasks that synthesize and integrate skills learned with the computer.

New Courseware Industry

A courseware development industry will begin to evolve, built around technological aids to ISD. These, in turn, will be designed around an increasingly standardized set of courseware patterns. This authoring industry will use iteration theory rather than the highly complex, expensive ISD process that is now in vogue. Needs will be identified earlier through the distributed networks that will exist. Target lessons will be developed quickly based on patterns that have good instructional science "built in," and exposed to students very quickly so that rapid iteration can occur. The iteration will occur in the task analysis as well as in the instructional design of the materials.

Unemployment

The power of microcomputers, robotics, and mass storage devices will be applied in many fields other than education, producing a large amount of unemployment. The challenge is that technological innovations in instructional systems development and in training can (*a*) produce new knowledge-industry jobs; and (*b*) be used to upgrade the skills and knowledge of our population rapidly enough to enable the unemployed to fill new roles in knowledge and service industries not appropriate to automation.

REFERENCES

Alderman, D. L. Evaluation of the TICCIT computer-assisted instructional system in the community college, *Final Report,* PR 78-10, Princeton, N.J.: Educational Testing Service. September, 1978.

4. Courseware

Alderman, D. L., Swinton, S. S., & Braswell, J. S. Assessing basic arithmetic skills across curricula, *Computer-assisted instruction in compensatory education: The ETS/LAUST study*, Princeton, N.J.: Educational Testing Service, 1978.

Avner, A. Longitudinal studies in computer-based authoring. In H. F. O'Neil, Jr. (Ed.), *Issues in instructional system development*. New York: Academic Press, 1979.

Axtell, R. H. *Learner controlled instructional strategy options effects for generality help and instance help on a procedure using task*. Unpublished doctoral dissertation, Brigham Young University, Provo, Utah, 1978.

Bennik, F. D., Hoyt, W. G., & Butler, A. K. *Determining TEC media alternatives for field artillery individual-collective training in the FY 78-83 period*. Systems Development Corporation under contract to ARI, Contract DAHC 19-76-C-0027. Santa Monica, Calif., 1978.

Brackett, J. W. TRAIDEX: A proposed system to minimize training duplication. In H. F. O'Neil, Jr. (Ed.), *Issues in instructional systems development*. New York: Academic Press, 1979.

Branson, R. K. Implementation issues in instructional system development. In H. F. O'Neil, Jr. (Ed.), *Issues in instructional system development*. New York: Academic Press, 1979.

Brooks, F. P. *The mythical man-month*. Reading: Mass.: Addison-Wesley, 1975.

Brown, J. S., & Bobrow, R. J. Applications of artificial intelligence techniques in maintenance training. In *New concepts in maintenance trainers and performance aids*. Technical Report: NAVTRAEQUIPCEN IH-255, October, 1975.

Brown, J. S., & Burton, R. R. *Diagnostic models for procedural bugs in basic mathematical skills*. BBN Report No. 3669. ICAI Report No. 8, Bolt, Beranek and Newman, Inc.: Cambridge, Mass., December, 1977.

Brown, J. S., & Goldstein, I. Computers and the learning society: Notes for a hearing before Congress. In U.S. Congress, House, Committee on Science and Technology, *Hearings before the subcommittee on domestic and international scientific planning, analysis, and cooperation*. 95th Cong. First sess., H. Rept. No. 47, 1978, 289-305.

Brown, J. S., Burton, R. R. & Bell, A. SOPHIE: A Step toward creating a reactive learning environment. *International Journal of Man-Machine Studies*, 1975, 7, 675-696.

Brown, J. S., Collins, A., & Harris, G. Artificial Intelligence and learning strategies. In H. F. O'Neil, Jr. (Ed.), *Learning strategies*. New York: Academic Press, 1978.

Bunderson, C. V. The computer and instructional design. In W. H. Holtzman (Ed.), *Computer-assisted instruction, testing and guidance*. New York: Harper & Row, 1970.

Bunderson, C. V. *The TICCIT project: Design strategy for educational innovation: Proceedings of the educational technology symposium*. Stony Brook, New York, September 23-26, 1973. Institute for Computer Uses in Education (ICUE) Technical Report No. 4, Provo, Utah: Brigham Young University, 1973.

Bunderson, C. V. The ARPA prescriptive authoring system project. In *Analysis of needs and goals for Author Training and Production Management Systems*, Technical Report No. 1, Contract MDA-903-76-C-0216, March 18, 1977.(a)

Bunderson, C. V. Rejoinder to the ETS evaluation of TICCIT CTRC Report No. 22. Brigham Young University, Provo, Utah, 1977.(b)

Bunderson, C. V. *Author languages vs. authoring systems in department of defense instructional systems development*. ARI Technical Report, 1979.

Bunderson, C. V., & Faust, G. W. Programmed and computer-assisted instruction, Chapter 3. In *The psychology of teaching methods, 1976, Part I, Seventy-fifth Yearbook of the National Society for the Study of Education*. Chicago, Ill.: University of Chicago Press, 1976, 44-90.

Burton, R., & Brown, J. S. A tutoring and student modelling paradigm for gaming environments. In R. Coleman, & P. Lorton, Jr. (Eds.), *Computer Science and Education*, SIGCSE Bulletin, February, 1976, 8 (1), 236-246.

Carbonell, J. AI in CAI: An artificial-intelligence approach to computer-assisted instruction. *IEEE Transactions on Man-Machine Systems*, December, 1970, MMS-11, (4).

Clinton, J. P. M. Computers and the Learning Society. In U.S. Congress House Committee on Science and Technology, *Hearings before the subcommittee on domestic and international scientific planning, analysis, and cooperation.* 95th Cong. First sess., 1978, H. Rept. No. 47, 77-84.

Coleman, J. S. *Equality of Educational Opportunity.* Summary report, U.S. Department of Health, Education and Welfare. Washington D.C.: U.S. Government Printing Office, 1966.

Collins, A., & Grignetti, M. *Intelligent CAI.* BBN Report No. 3181, Bolt Beranek & Newman, Inc., Cambridge, Mass., 1975.

Freedman, C. R., Bresee, J., Hermanns, J., and O'Neal, H. *Author training course: User manual.* San Diego, Calif.: Courseware Inc., January, 1978.

Ghesquere, J., Davis, C., & Thompson, C. *An introduction to CERL report.* Normal: University of Illinois, 1976.

Goldberg, A., & Suppes, P. A computer-assisted instruction program for exercises on finding axioms. *Educational Studies in Mathematics,* 1972, *4,* 429-499. In H. F. O'Neil, Jr. (Ed.), *Issues in instructional system development.* New York: Academic Press, 1979.

Harris, W. P. An authoring system for on-the-job environments. In H. F. O'Neil, (Ed.), *Issues in instructional system development,* New York: Academic Press, 1979.

Heuston, D. H. The promise and inevitability of the videodisc in education. A paper submitted to the National Institute of Education. Orem, Utah: WICAT Inc., September, 1977.

Hunter, B., Kastner, C., Rubin, M., & Seidel, R. J. *Learning alternatives in U.S. education: Where student and computer meet,* Englewood Cliffs, N.J.: Educational Technology Publications, 1975.

Logan, R. S. A Survey and analysis of military computer-based systems: A two part study, Volume I. In *A Survey and Annotated Bibliography of Aids for Instructional Systems Development., Vol. I,* St. Louis, Mo.: McDonnel Douglas Astronautics Company—East, February, 1977.

Logan, R. S. A state-of-the-art assessment of instructional system development. In H. F. O'Neil, Jr. (Ed.), *Issues in instructional system development.* New York: Academic Press, 1979.

Markle, D. G. In which it is demonstrated that a program that works may well be worthless. *Improving Human Performance,* Fall, 1973, *3,* 175-80.

Markle, S. M. Empirical testing of programs. In Phil C. Lange (Ed.), *Programmed instruction, Part II, sixty-sixth yearbook of the National Society for the Study of Education.* Chicago, Ill.:, University of Chicago Press, 1967, 104.

Merrill, M. D. Analyzing instructional quality: The instructional quality profile, a curriculum evaluation and design tool. In H. F. O'Neil, Jr. (Ed.), *Procedures for instructional systems development.* New York: Academic Press, 1979.

Merrill, M. D., & Boutwell, R. C. Instructional development: Methodology and research. In *Review of research in education.* (Vol. 1). Itasca, Ill.: Peacock, 1973, 15-131.

Merrill, M. D., Olsen, J. B., & Coldeway, N. A. *Research support for the instructional strategy diagnostic profile.* Technical Report No. 3, Courseware, Inc., San Diego, Calif., March, 1976.

O'Neal, A. F., & O'Neal, H. L. Author management systems, in H. F. O'Neil, Jr. (Ed.), *Issues in instructional system development.* New York, Academic Press, 1979.

O'Neal, H. L., Faust, G. W., & O'Neal, A. F. An author training course for resident school environments. In H. F. O'Neil, Jr. (Ed.), *Procedures for instructional systems development.* New York: Academic Press, 1979.

O'Neil, H. F., Jr. (Ed.). *Issues in instructional system development.* New York: Academic Press, 1979.(a)

O'Neil, H. F., Jr. (Ed.). *Procedures for instructional systems development.* New York: Academic Press, 1979.(b)

Reigeluth, C. M., Merrill, M. D., & Bunderson, C. V. The structure of subject-matter content and its instructional design implications. *Instructional Science,* 1978, *1* (2), 11-16.

Schulz, R. E. On-line authoring aids for developing tests and instruction. In H. F. O'Neil, Jr. (Ed.), *Procedures for instructional systems development.* New York: Academic Press, 1979.

Sherwood, B. A. *The tutor language.* Control Data Education Company, 1977.

4. Courseware

Suppes, P., & Morningstar, M. Computer-assisted instruction at Stanford: 1966-68. In *Data, Models, and Evaluation of Arithmetic Programs*. New York: Academic Press, 1972.

Taylor, S. S. CREATE: A computer-based authoring curriculum. In H. F. O'Neil, Jr. (Ed.), *Issues in instructional system development*. New York: Academic Press, 1979.

Thiagarajan, S. *The programming process: A practical guide*. Worthington, Ohio: Charles A. Jones Publishing Co., 1971.

Training and Doctrine Command. *Interservice procedures for instructional systems development* (5 Vols.). TRADOC Pamphlet 350-30. Fort Benning, Ga.: Combat Aims Training Board, August, 1975.

Vinsonhaler, J. F., & Bass, R. K. Ten major studies of the evaluation of CAI drill and practice. East Lansing, Mich.: Information Systems Laboratory, Michigan State University, ISL Report No. 21, August, 1971.

Volk, J. W. Statement to a House Committee on TICCIT. In U.S. Congress House Committee on Science and Technology, Hearings before the subcommittee on domestic and international scientific planning, analysis, and cooperation. 95th Cong. First sess., H. Rept. No. 47, 1978, 195-203.

Weiss, D. J. *Proceedings of the 1977 computerized adaptive testing conference*. Psychometric Methods Program, University of Minnesota, July, 1978.

Wilson, T. *Instructional systems development course text*. U.S. Army Field Artillery School, Office of Faculty Development. Fort Sill, Okla., June, 1977.

Zelkowitz, M. V. Perspectives on software engineering. *ACM Computing Surveys*, June, 1978, *10* (2), 197-216.

5

Learning Strategies[1]

J. W. RIGNEY[2]
ALLEN MUNRO

WHAT ARE LEARNING STRATEGIES?

The pervasiveness of individual differences in achievement in education and training, even within one classroom and one course, demonstrates that there are different ways of going about learning, determined by differences in the processing resources that individuals can or choose to bring to bear on the task of learning. It is likely that individual students develop these idiosyncratic ways of learning over long periods of time, and that they continue to use these strategies, even those that are inefficient, because they are familiar and have predictable outcomes. These ways of going about learning are called *study habits* in educational settings. Many educational institutions now have special programs for developing better study habits for students whose own familiar approaches to learning do prove to be notably less effective than those of their peers.

These idiosyncratic ways of learning will be called *strategies for learning*, or *learning strategies*, in this chapter. A distinction could be made between strategies and tactics, in conformance with the common military usage of the term *strategies* for the long-range, global objectives of winning the war, and of *tactics* for the immediate goal of winning a battle. By analogy, a student's long-term plan of action for learning the subject matter of a profession might be

---

[1] The work reported in this chapter was supported in part by the Army Research Institute for the Behavioral and Social Sciences, Contract number MDA 903-79-C-0558. Views and conclusions contained in this document are those of the authors and should not be interpreted as necessarily representing the official policies, either expressed or implied, of the Army Research Institute for the Behavioral and Social Sciences, or the United States Government.

[2] Deceased.

called a strategy, to distinguish it from the processing operations he or she performs on small chunks, such as a single day's lesson, which might be called learning tactics. However, to simplify the discussion, *strategy* will be used for cognitive processing operations with both short-range and long-range implications for learning. Recent shifts in research interests in psychology toward studying cognitive processes and the birth of cognitive science (of cognitive psychology, computer science, and artificial intelligence parentage) have provided fresh viewpoints toward the processes involved in learning and remembering, and new tools for studying them. Thus, it seems appropriate to address the question of whether humans can be *taught* how to learn and to remember. Can student's idiosyncratic strategies for learning be replaced by more effective techniques? Rigney (1978a) has reviewed these possibilities. Table 5.1, adapted from that review, presents some conceptual geography for relating learning strategies to other relevant concepts and variables in education and training.

According to this conceptual geography, learning strategies are human information-processing activities that facilitate acquisition, retention, and retrieval of representational and procedural knowledge in long-term memory. This processing is directed by orienting tasks, either self-assigned, assigned by an

TABLE 5.1
Some Conceptual Geography for Learning Strategies[a]

Processing resources	Orienting tasks	Subject matter
Representational	Communication	Information
Perceptual	Instructions	Narrative
Imaginal	Questions	Explanation
Verbal	Content structures	Representation
Procedural	Location	Prescription
Processing	Preceding	Performance
Metaprocessing	Embedded	High or low semantic
Selectional	Following	High or low motor
Attention	Generality	
Intention	Scope	
Self-directional	Complexity	
Self-programming		
Self-monitoring		
Technology	Target populations	Environment
High	Children	Schools
Intermediate	Adults	Conventional
Low	Special	CMI
		CBI
		OJT
		Experimental

[a] Adapted from Rigney (1978a), p. 193.

instructional system, or implicit in the description of the subject matter, and uses the different kinds of processing resources in the categories listed in Table 5.1. The domain suggested is indeed a large one, considering the different possible combinations of different kinds of processing resources, orienting tasks, subject matter, technology. and environment. Exploring this domain in any reasonably conclusive way would be a large undertaking, indeed. Nevertheless, this exploration is underway, here and there, in corners of the domain, in terms of the learning-to-learn question, in terms of cognitive processes that constitute the processing resources on which learning strategies must draw, and in terms of the (presumably) general architecture of the human processor, including its short- and long-term memories.

This chapter will survey these beginnings, starting with a review of current sociomilitary pressures to improve learning skills, and continuing with examples of recent frontal assaults on the puzzle of human processor by instructional technologists, and with indirect contributions from cognitive science and educational psychology that may lead to a better understanding of that processor and of the conditions that will influence it. The chapter continues with an attempt to foresee the prospects, in the immediate future, for improving students's learning skills, and concludes with some recommendations for achieving this objective.

WHY DO RESEARCH ON LEARNING STRATEGIES?

Functional Illiteracy in Society

This and the proceding decade have seen a series of studies, most notably the Coleman Report (1966), that have attempted to discover "what is wrong with" the primary and secondary school systems in the United States. These studies may be ripples from the waves generated by Sputnik, which provoked Conant's (1961) analysis of the American high school, or they may be just current examples of the intellectual discontent with the educational system that has always existed. The 1970s also saw a series of well-meaning programs, funded by the federal government, aimed at curing some of the socioeducational ills that have been perceived. Of these ambitious programs, "Project Headstart" and "Project Follow Through" have, perhaps, been most publicized. Other programs, sponsored by the Department of Labor under the heading of Job Training, have the admirable objective of giving disadvantaged persons opportunities to acquire marketable skills, thereby reducing unemployment and, presumably, human misery.

Sputnik stung our national prive and destroyed forever the comforting stereotype, so long nurtured by our press, of Russians as uneducated peasants unable to cope with the mysteries of high technology. The principal resulting action was the dumping of tens of billions of dollars into a program to put man on the moon, which accelerated the development of engineering technologies, gave large numbers of engineers and physical scientists employment, and produced the greatest man-made show yet. All of it culminated in a drive across the desolate moonscape by two astronauts in the world's most costly dune buggy, and the return to earth of a number of small rocks that no one seems to know quite where to put.

Results of the post-Sputnik, federally funded educational and training programs have been less spectacular. In fact, results have been extraordinarily difficult to measure, attempts at evaluation having stimulated more controversy than agreement, regarding beneficial effects on students. Certainly, the results of these programs have not been unequivocal. In retrospect, the reasons seem to be obvious. There were too many different managers and would-be managers, too many independent school districts, too many different people to please; there were no carefully designed and thoroughly tested treatment procedures, no rigorous experimental designs, or the possibility for them; too many ad hoc changes in midstream; there were no universal criterion measures, nor agreement about what they should be. Schools are not, after all, just educational institutions. They are sociopolitical educational institutions, subject to sociopolitical pressures from the federal government to the community level. Schools are expected unreasonably to compensate for individual and social ills that interfere with the acquisition of knowledge, and to be the implementers of politically expedient programs.

As a consequence, it is not at all clear that primary and secondary schooling *is* any better today. In fact, there is a considerable amount of hand-wringing over functional illiteracy, which surfaces most glaringly among recruits in the military. There is some evidence (Figure 5.1) for a decline in scholastic aptitude test scores among high school graduates.

There are 30 million persons on welfare (*Time*, June 12, 1978) and unemployment among teenagers is high. These figures are not a direct indictment of the educational system, but they do suggest that there are large numbers of essentially surplus people that the economic system does not need, and who cannot, although undoubtedly for a variety of reasons, compete for employment. A lack of marketable knowledge and skills must surely be a major reason.

Pressures to Make Military Training More Effective

As long as the Services must depend on first-enlistment men for operating and maintaining their high-technology devices, there will be pressures to make military training more effective within fixed time constraints. One way to do this is to skim the cream of the eligible population. But this is difficult to do under an all-volunteer policy in relatively good economic times and falling birthrates. It is

5. Learning Strategies

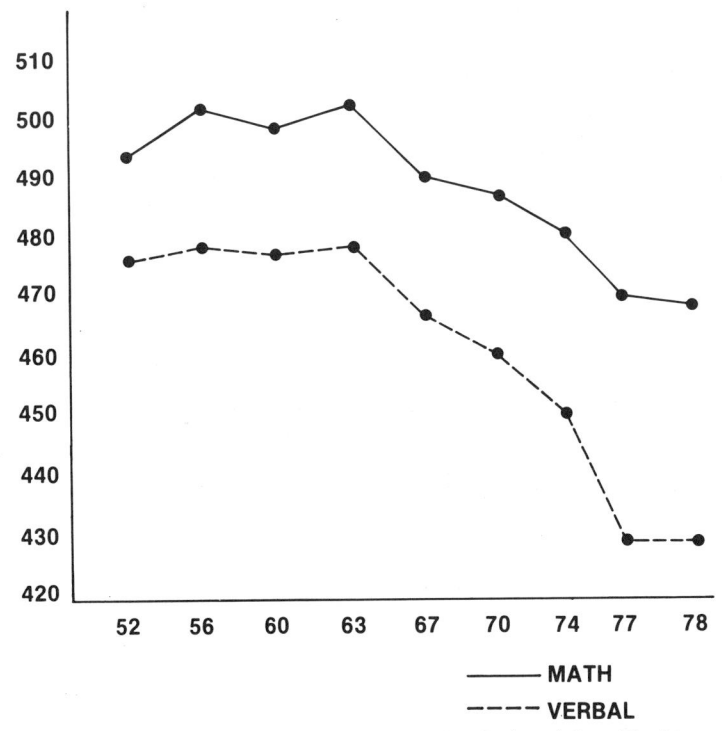

[Figure: line graph showing SAT scores from 1952 to 1978, with Math (solid line) declining from ~495 to ~468 and Verbal (dashed line) declining from ~475 to ~430]

Figure 5.1. SAT scores 1952–1978. (Updated and adapted from *The Literary Hoax* by Paul Copperman, with permission of William Morrow & Company.)

particularly important to recruit prospective technicians who already can read fluently. From recent studies of reading skills among Naval recruits (Aiken, Duffy, & Nugent, 1976; Duffy, 1975), it is apparent that appreciable percentages of these recruits do not have high levels of reading skills. Conversely, until recently, technical manuals were written from engineering design notes and were not among the most comprehensible of documents. Various measures are underway to reduce the mismatch between trainee basic skills and the difficulty level of technical documentation; the principal measures are reduction in the presumed reading grade-level to read technical manuals; discharge of recruits with reading grade-level scores below a certain grade level; and remedial reading courses for recruits just above the cutoff. These measures may help, but the fundamental requirement for the technician—to acquire a mental model of the device or system he or she is supposed to operate or to maintain that is accurate and sufficiently detailed to enable him or her to satisfy job performance specifications—may still be difficult to meet within the time available for training.

The problem is, of course, that one-enlistment personnel are available for only that period (4 years in the Navy) for training and subsequent service in a technician capacity. The Services receive some return on their investment in training only during the period of on-the-job performance, and then only after the technician has learned to function with a sufficient degree of proficiency. Under these time constraints, rate of acquisition of knowledge becomes a parameter of primary importance in training. Working against this objective are those apparently declining aptitudes of the prospective trainee population (illustrated in Figure 5.1), and the often noted increasing complexity of weapon systems and other military hardware.

Advances in Cognitive Psychology

The past 10 years has seen a remarkable shift of the center of interest in psychology from input–output to what goes on in between. In rapid succession, psychologists discovered mental imagery, mnemonics, and long-term memory. It became fashionable to think about thinking. Increasing numbers of psychologists fled the austere bastions of behaviorism, abandoning its fetish of the empty organism for an organism with its head full of busy demons.

As often happens, a major impetus for this paradigm came from outside the discipline, from the flowering of computer science, which is very much concerned with process, and from advances in psycholinguistics. Feigenbaum (1963) pioneered a computer simulation of associative models of human long-term memory. Computer scientists began to construct intelligent processes with computer programs, and there grew up at MIT, Stanford, and elsewhere, a discipline called Aritificial Intelligence (AI), which demonstrated the power of computer programs for implementing processes that, in many respects, produced outcomes similar to products of human thinking. Psychologists and computer scientists were intrigued by post-Chomskian psycholinguistics with its insistence on distinguishing between syntax and semantics; its formalisms for describing deep structure and for getting there from surface structure; and its parsing mechanisms for understanding and for generating natural language. They recognized that language *is* the mediating mechanism in human training and education, and that it is fundamentally involved in the cognitive processing that leads to the acquisition of knowledge, and that it is doubtful that human learning and mental processes can be understood without using psycholinguistic concepts. Certainly, strategies for learning must be formulated and communicated in linguistic terms, whether they are self-generated or imposed by others. Even instructions to use mental imagery as an elaborative or a recall strategy must be communicated verbally! New concepts and new tools in psycholinguistics have put the study of human learning in a new perspective in which the memory drum and the nonsense syllable are, at long last, absent.

In psychology, Sternberg's (1969) studies of short-term memory described a

5. Learning Strategies 133

processing mechanism and identified processes that occurred there. Studies of short-term memory proliferated, but psychologists finally realized that, in their preoccupation with the Sternberg paradigm, they were overlooking the place where the action really was and began to venture into the almost infinite recesses of long-term memory, armed with list-processing languages, predicate calculus, graph theory, and the new psycholinguistics. All of this research work has come together under the heading of "Cognitive Science,"—a self-conscious title that may or may not signal a new branch of science. After all, putting things into the head is still a lot easier than getting them out again. Cognitive science models, rife with interacting autonomous schemata or "demons," are vulnerable to cries of "demonology!" from skeptics (Kendler, 1978). But, for better or for worse, psychology will never be the same again, so it is appropriate to inquire what cognitive science has to offer research on learning strategies. Perhaps, as much as anything else, it is a part of a zeitgeist that is stimulating interdisciplinary aggregations of concepts and tools, which did not exist before, for investigating cognitive processes.

WHERE ARE WE NOW?

Examples of Recent Research on Learning Strategies

The literature of educational research is sprinkled with studies of learning strategies, with subjects from populations ranging from early primary school to university, and subject matter ranging from simple verbal learning to mathematics and problem solving. Undoubtedly, studies of the effects of mental imagery were originally stimulated by Bower's (1972) research on the effects of mental imagery on recall of paried associates. Another stream of research originated from Craik and Lockhart's (1972) conception of depth-of-processing. The most ambitious recent program of research on learning strategies was funded by the Defense Advanced Research Projects Agency. This program included the following projects: *The Development of a Systematic Training Program for Enhancing Learning Strategies and Skills* (Dansereau, 1978); *Improvement in the Speed of Complex Learning Through Reduction in Test Anxiety* (Spielberger, Gonzalez, & Fletcher, 1979); *Investigation of Study Behavior* (Anderson, 1979); *Generalizable Elaboration Skills* (Weinstein, 1978; Weinstein, Underwood, Wicker, & Cubbverly, 1979); *Learning Strategies for Motor Skills* (Singer & Gerson, 1978); *Teaching Students to Manage Their Study Time in a CMI System* (Judd, McCombs, & Dobrovolny, 1979); *Strategies for Self-Directed Learning from Technical Manuals* (Rigney, Munro, & Crook, 1979); *Literacy Training* (Sticht, 1979); *An ISD Approach for Learning Strategies* (Logan, 1978); *Program Evaluation*

(Wagner & Seidel, 1978); *Artificial Intelligence and Learning Strategies* (Brown, Collins, & Harris, 1978); and *Learning Strategies: A Theoretical Perspective* (Rigney, 1978a).

Since descriptions of this program are available in two publications (O'Neil, 1978; O'Neil & Spielberger, 1979), there will be no attempt to review these large projects in the limited space available in this chapter. Instead, two examples of recent research on learning strategies will be described, to illustrate two quite different kinds of strategies and two quite different approaches. In terms of the conceptual geography in Table 5.1, the first of these studies used perceptual (auditory), imaginal, and verbal processing resources, and instructions for orienting tasks. These orienting tasks that preceded the subject matter were general for foreign-language vocabulary learning, and were of broad scope (i.e., one set of instructions covered the entire learning session). The orienting tasks were relatively simple. The instruction took place in an experimental environment, using high technology, and adults as subjects. The subject matter was very simple. The performance required was low semantic, low motor.

In the second study, verbal processing resources were implicated primarily. Instructions, questions, and content structures were used as orienting tasks. These proceedings were embedded in, and followed the subject matter. The orienting tasks had high generality, broad scope, and were complicated. The study was done in a conventional school environment. Low technology was used and adults were subjects. The subject matter was complex explanation and the performance required was high semantic, low motor. The strategy training included not only instructions but also specification of the results of the learning skills, practice with feedback, and testing with feedback.

Simple Verbal Learning

Atkinson's well-known research on strategies for teaching foreign vocabulary stands as a model (Atkinson, 1975; Atkinson & Raugh, 1974). Atkinson was impressed by the variability in learning rates across subjects, and by the difference between good learners and poor learners in the ability to describe what they are doing. His good learners could easily describe their "bag of tricks" for learning vocabulary items. His poor learners were incredibly inept at describing what they were doing. (This observation has important implications: Is this a general difference between good and poor learners? It certainly should be investigated.) Atkinson and Raugh devised a keyword method that divided foreign vocabulary learning into two stages. In the first, the subject was required to associate the spoken foreign word with a similar sounding English word that otherwise had no relationship to the foreign word. The association was formed quickly because of acoustic similarity. In the second stage, the subject was required to form a mental image of the keyword interacting with the English translation of the foreign word. This stage is comparable to a paired–associate procedure for learning unrelated English words, in which Bower (1972) demonstrated the striking effectiveness of mental imagery for improving recall. Differences between experimental and control groups on recall of 120 Russian vocabulary items were large and highly significant statistically. On the immediate posttest, the experimental group recalled 72% of the words versus the control group's 46%. On a delayed posttest given 6 weeks later, percentages recalled were 43% and 28%, respectively. Repetition of the two-stage strategy with Spanish vocabulary confirmed these results. Analysis of the relative effectiveness of the two stages, acoustic link and imagery link, indicated that the two are independent (rank-order correlation, .02) and that the product of the probability of a correct response on each is a good predictor of posttest performance. The acoustic link allowed students to link a known English word, with many semantic relationships already established in long-term Memory, to an unfamiliar Russian or Spanish word on the basis of similar sounds. The mental imagery allowed the translation of a subset of the existing relationships between two well-known English words into a compelling mental image. Atkinson recommended that, in an ideal situation, students should be coached in using the keyword method until they are proficient in the skill, noting that the brief written instructions used in the experiments were not sufficient for this purpose.

Learning from Scientific Text

Larkin and Reif (1976) were interested in teaching learning skills for acquiring useful abilities from text. Quantitative sciences, such as physics, are concerned with developing and exploiting various relations between quantities. A major goal of a science course is to teach students how to use relations flexibly and accurately in solving problems. In the common instructional procedure the student must somehow use the text or lecture to acquire the abilities he or she will need in using a relation to solve a problem. In fact, there is good evidence that many students do *not* have the learning skill needed to acquire these abilities simply through a study of text. Thus, Larkin and Reif were interested in whether or not students could be trained in this learning skill so that they could subsequently acquire from a textual description of any new relation the abilities most essential to applying it. They began by specifying a set of general abilities they considered to be essential to applying any relation, and which they thought could be acquired from text. These are summarized in their Table 5.2. If a student could do the things specified in Table 5.2 with a relation, he or she was considered to understand it.

Larkin and Reif developed a training procedure with the objective of teaching students how to acquire understanding of relations described in textual material in a manner similar to that of an experienced person. This procedure consisted of a specification of the desired learning skill, followed by a systematic program of practice and testing with feedback. This procedure was repeated for 10 relations studied during a period of 4-6 weeks. Larkin and Reif were interested in experimental answers to four questions:

1. Does a physics course plus direct training in the learning skill enhance a student's ability to acquire understanding in comparison with (*a*) students entering an introductory physics course; and (*b*) students who have had comparable training in physics without learning-strategy training?
2. Does a student in the experimental group actually use the skill for acquiring understanding, after strategy training?
3. Does this training diminish a student's need for extensive and explicit instructional material? For example, can he or she acquire understanding as effectively from text as from text plus programmed instruction?
4. Does this skill of acquiring understanding transfer to other subject matter?

In the first experiment, Larkin and Reif used a pretest-posttest design with four groups, and tested different random samples from the experimental and control groups, each sample including from 100 to 150 students. The second experiment was done 2 weeks after the experimental group had completed its training, to answer questions 2 and 3 in the preceding list. The measure chosen to assess success in training students to master the skill of understanding was the parameter M—the fraction of students demonstrating such mastery by making not more than one major error on a test.

The result of this strategy training were generally positive. The training did improve student's skill in acquiring understanding of new relations from text; students did use this skill after training; training did enable students to become

---

TABLE 5.2
Summary of Abilities Included in Understanding a Relation[a]

---

1. State information characterizing the relation
    (*a*) State the relation
    (*b*) Give an example of its application
    (*c*) List properties of quantities in the relation
2. Interpret the relation by using information in various symbolic representations
3. Make discriminations
    (*a*) Applicability
        (1) Discriminate between information relevant and irrelevant to finding each quantity in the relation
        (2) Discriminate between situations to which the relation does and does not apply
    (*b*) Comparison
        (1) Discriminate each quantity in the relation from other quantities
        (2) Discriminate the relation from other relations
4. Use equivalent forms of the relation to find or compare values

---

[a] Adapted from Larkin and Reif, 1976, p. 432.

5. Learning Strategies

less dependent on extensive instruction; this skill did transfer to different subject matter; this skill was retained for at least 2 weeks; and most students implemented this skill without conscious effort, according to postsession interviews.

Contributions from Cognitive Science

A number of lines of research on cognitive processes are flourishing in the zeitgeist that has emerged from the cross-disciplinary parentage of cognitive psychology, computer science, and psycholinguistics. In some instances, the objective is to model essential features of the human processor itself, to explore questions of how well-known processes of learning and memory might be organized (Anderson, 1976). In others, the focus is on resolving controversial topics, such as the nature of mental imagery (Anderson, 1978a; Cooper, 1978; Kosslyn, 1978). In others, the interest is in investigating an important component of the human processor; for example, long-term memory has been modeled with semantic networks (Anderson & Bower, 1973; Norman, Rumelhart, & LNR, 1975). In still others, the objective is to understand processes associated with particular kinds of subject matter; the transportation problem (Atwood & Polson, 1976); analogical reasoning (Sternberg, 1977); and word puzzles (Bond, McGregor, Schmidt, Lattimore, & Rigney, 1978). A large number of cognitive scientists are concerned with the processes of basic skills, primarily reading, from word decoding to lexical decisions and sentence understanding. Fredericksen (1978) has undertaken a chronometric analysis of this whole range. Carpenter and Just (1975) have concentrated on sentence understanding; as have Anderson, Spiro, and Anderson (1977), who have demonstrated the effects of depth of processing and the conceptually driven, data-driven nature of this processing at the suprasentential level. R.C. Anderson (1978b) has shown the influence of different kinds of prior knowledge on what is comprehended from ambiguous passages. Gordon, Munro, Rigney, and Lutz (1978) developed schema-theory based descriptions of the characteristics of deep structures of different kinds of texts, and demonstrated differential effects of these different structures on summaries and recalls.

All these diverse lines of research, along with many others not mentioned here, will lead to closer approximations to an understanding of the human processor and of the different processes that support acquisition, retention, and remembering, as implied by the conceptual geography sketched in Table 5.1. The most immediate contributions are found in a volume on cognitive psychology and instruction edited by Lesgold, Pellegrino, Fokkema, and Glaser (1978). The major sections contain papers on learning, comprehension and information structure; perceptual and memory processes in reading; and problem solving and components of intelligence, cognitive development, and approaches to instruction. In this last section, Case (1978) discussed the implications of developmental psychology for the design of effective instruction; Rothkopf (1978) described the reciprocal relationship between previous experience and processing in determining learning outcomes; Sticht (1978) presented his conception of cognitive research applied to literacy training; and Glaser, Pellegrino, and Lesgold (1978) presented some directions for a cognitive psychology of instruction. In their overview Glaser *et al.* give a perspective on the implications on cognitive psychology for instruction:

> [If] the participants in this conference were asked what the general requirements are for building a theory of instruction, they would probably agree on the following kinds of work: (*a*) analysis of the structures of knowledge and skill that comprise objectives of instruction and that characterize high-knowledge, well-skilled individuals; (*b*) analysis of the intermediate knowledge states that characterize the transition from lack of knowledge to competence; (*c*) specification, in terms of a cognitive process theory, of the aptitudes for learning that individuals bring to an instructional situation; and (*d*) specification of the transformations that take place between various stages of acquisition and of the conditions that can be implemented to bring about change from one stage of knowledge to more advanced stages [p. 515].

Of special interest to this chapter is the paper of Neches and Hayes (1978) in the Lesgold *et al.* volume. Neches and Hayes describe a series of strategy transformations that, they maintain, mark differences in processing strategies between an expert and a novice. The expert takes the strategies taught to him or her, and, through practice, discovers ways to modify them into more efficient and powerful procedures. A theory of strategy transformations might allow the design of easily learned novice strategies that also could be easily transformed into expert strategies. Such a theory could also lead to a system that would promote the transformation process by teaching students explicitly how to improve their strategies. Neches and Hayes observed strategy transformations in a complex sequence–generation task involving arithmetic and symbolic transformations: reduction to results, reduction to a rule, replacement with another method, unit building, deletion of unnecessary parts, saving of partial results, reordering, and method switching.

The eight types of strategy transformations have features in common. *Reduction-to-results* replaces a complex procedure for computing a result with a simple retrieval from memory. This method is, of course, most useful in those cases in which the results are needed often. *Reduction-to-a-rule* replaces a procedure with a simpler rule that predicts the results of the procedure. *Replacement-with-another-method* replaces one procedure with another that is better-learned, faster, or easier to apply. *Unit building* replaces several procedures that must be used in sequence to perform a task with a single unified procedure. It is one means of bringing about automatization of task performance. *Deletion-of-unnecessary-parts* restructures a procedure by eliminating unessen-

5. Learning Strategies

tial operations. It makes the procedure more truly of special purpose. *Saving-of-partial-results* restructures a procedure in such a way that computational portions are replaced with memory–retrieval portions that look up the products of earlier computational portions of the procedure. *Reordering* alters the sequence of operations. This is done either to minimize execution time for the procedure or to reduce transcient memory loads. *Method switching* is sometimes used to handle special processing cases for which there is a faster, more reliable, or easier method of computation. When these types of data are input to the procedure, a test detects the special case and switches control to the alternative procedure.

It should be noted that many of the preceding transformations have the effects of reducing short-term memory loads and reducing computational effort. This is often done at the expense of increased demands on long-term memory. Neches and Hayes identified knowledge-based processes and pattern detection as the bases of making transformations. Research on human problem-solving (Newell & Simon, 1972), and on chess playing (deGroot, 1966) has shown that long-term storage and pattern detection are the strengths of the human information-processing system. The transformations of Neches and Hayes seem to take appropriate advantage of these strengths.

Process Models

Currently, there are four different ways of going about modeling cognitive processes. Semantic network models (such as those by Anderson & Bower, 1973; Rumelhart, Lindsay, & Norman, 1972) are derived from the associationistic background of psychology, and take a relational view of the structure of long-term memory, with hierarchical webs of nodes and internode relational operations.

Componential analysis of cognitive processes (e.g., R. J. Sternberg, 1977) starts with assumptions about a few elementary operations, and seeks to construct all higher processes from these primitive elements, using additional assumptions about how they combine in linear sequences.

Production systems are concerned with modeling the stream of processing activities generated by the human processor when it is engaged in solving a problem, where "problem" is defined broadly. Production systems go by a variety of names, including procedural semantics (Miller & Johnson-Laird, 1976; Norman, *et al.,* 1975; Schank & Abelson, 1977) and frame systems (Minsky, 1975).

Each of these types of models can be (and, in each case, has been) represented in a computer simulation. A computer simulation will, typically, be restricted to limited aspects of the theory and will simulate human information processing in a very limited knowledge domain. There is also, however, another type of mode, which is often realized as an ad hoc computer simulation. This type of model usually takes the form of a number of component processes that can be arranged in a flow chart. Ordinarily, the ad hoc computer-simulation model is developed to represent cognitive performance in a very limited domain, and it is not constrained ordinarily by considerations of generality or applicability to other domains.

Semantic Memory Models and Production Systems. Hybrids of the model types discussed above are possible. Some of the production system models cited previously also include features of semantic memory models. The most recent example of a semantic memory–production system model is described in Anderson (1976). Anderson presents a model of human cognition that combines a propositional network representation of declarative knowledge with a production system model of procedural knowledge. Anderson contends that it is not possible to determine uniquely the representational structures and processes responsible for cognitive performances. He argues that cognitive theories should be evaluated in terms of their capacity for practical applications, thereby not only legitimizing application-oriented cognitive research, but also claiming that applications may be the only means of choosing among competing cognitive theories.

Anderson (1976) embodied a version of his system in a computer simulation, called ACT. This was done, not only to demonstrate the adequacy of some of the features of the model to account for certain cognitive performances, but also in the hope that new consequences (and, in particular, new applications) of the theory would emerge. This hope was largely unrealized:

> The obvious focus for practical applications of a theory like ACT is on education. As the reader of this book has no doubt noted, there is a dearth of suggestions for such practical applications of ACT. My original naive expectations about ACT have been considerably disappointed in this regard. I had thought practical suggestions would naturally flow from the theory as it evolved. That clearly is not the case. Applying ACT to practical problems will be no different than attempting to apply ACT to a new experimental paradigm. That is, practical applications from a theory like ACT will be forthcoming only by dint of much effort [p. 535].

Our view is that this and similar process models, notably that of Norman *et al.* (1975), offer representational and procedural machinery for constructing detailed, functional models of how cognitive performances *might* be executed. Such models could be extended to deal with specific learning processes, such as the means by which orienting tasks enlist processing resources for processing particular kinds of subject matter to facilitate acquisition, improve retention, or increase recall. Munro and Rigney (1977) present an initial approach to this type of explanation within the format of the Norman *et al.* (1975) model. An important aspect of modeling the cognitive effects of learning strategies is to account for depth-of-processing effects. Craik and Lockhart (1972) used the term *levels of processing* to discriminate between semantic and nonsemantic processing. Klein and Saltz (1976) extended the term to apply to different levels of semantic processing as well. Both types of distinction have important consequences for learning theory and practice. Anderson (1976) attempts to treat depth-of-processing effects within the context of his theory:

5. Learning Strategies

> Unlike encoding, the effects associated with depth of processing do not seem confined to the laboratory situation. Much of our real-life success or failure at memory can be related to the depth at which material is processed. In fact, there seems to be some modest potential for the practical application of the ideas associated with depth of processing. Unfortunately, ACT's elaborative encoding of material comes from the formation of production through tedious experience. Thus, one cannot simply "turn on" his deep processing and establish a rich code for some to-be-remembered material. However, what one can do is attempt to transform material from a form for which there is a paucity of elaborative productions into a form for which there is a rich set of elaborations [p. 406].

An unfortunate consequence of this very reasonable approach to depth-of-processing phenomena is that a model of the process must have access to a knowledge base of a size characteristic of human adult long-term memory. The construction of such a data base is, of course, beyond the reach of any present computer simulation project.

Hybrid semantic memory–production system models have the potential for forming an important part of the theoretical base of new theories of instruction and learning. Scholars in this field must be aware, however, that there are no established results from such models that can be simply "applied" to problems in the domain of learning strategies. Rather, new subtheories must be developed within the constraints of this type of model to deal with learning strategy issues.

Information Processing Models of Mental Abilities. Two currently prominent examples of this type of model are Sternberg's (1977) "Componential Analyses of Analogical Reasoning," and Fredericksen's (1978) "Chronometric Analyses of Components of Basic Reading Skills." These models take an atomistic view of informational processing operations, seeking to isolate elementary operations and then to combine them into larger units, finally relating the various levels of conventional mental ability tests via maximum likelihood factor analysis. This research was reviewed capably in Lesgold *et al.* (1978). It is methodologically brilliant work, and represents another, very different, approach to modeling cognitive processes, having the virtue that the models can be tested by parameter estimation techniques.

What role these models will play in research on cognitive learning strategies is unclear at present. It is possible that the methodologies being developed in this area could be used to isolate the processing operations essential to particular intellectual tasks. These isolated operations could then be the focus of instructional efforts. The extent to which the models can be applied in this way is uncertain. For example, it is not clear how the strategy transformations of Neches and Hayes (1978), discussed previously, could be formulated in these models.

Ad Hoc Computer-Simulation Models. There is a long history of ad hoc computer-simulation models of cognitive processes, which probably has its origins in mathematical models of human behavior. The process of constructing such models consists of first, analyzing the specific task of interest, then representing the component subtasks in the form of a flowchart and, finally, writing a computer program to represent this analysis. The computer simulation model described by Jeffries, Polson, Razran, and Atwood (1977) is a recent example. The process of solving problems of the "missionaries and cannibals" type was the focus of the study. The processing operations required to solve the problem were identified through a (largely intuitive) task analysis. A computer model of these tasks was constructed and a statistical model was derived with parameters. The simulation was validated by running the program to estimate parameters for comparison with results from a sample of subjects.

In many earlier computer simulation models, the processing operations that were simulated were embedded in the computer program, and the program was their only description. This made it almost impossible to evaluate the validity of the cognitive processing model, or for anyone else besides the author of the program to deal with it. In the example cited previously, this is not the case. The results of the task analysis are listed as human information-processing operations.

This type of process model, like the others just described, provides mechanisms for trying out plausible descriptions of detailed information-processing operations. These mechanisms might be considered for describing how particular kinds of learning strategies operate, as, indeed, Anderson used the mechanisms of his ACT system for explaining how deep, or elaborative processing might influence storage and retrieval in long-term memory. It could be useful to attempt to explain Neches and Hayes (1978) strategy transformations by means of these or similar mechanisms. Thus, process models could lead to a better understanding of how human information-processing operations *might* function. From this, it might be possible to derive different processing operations in terms of effectiveness for learning; but, teaching students to *use* these processing operations is a different problem, whose solution would depend on Glaser's "Cognitive Engineering," derived from a theory of instruction, instead of a theory of cognition.

With respect to the goal of modeling cognitive learning strategies, the choice between ad hoc computer simulation and the semantic memory–production system models depends upon the investigator's objectives. If a quick and inexpensive model of cognitive performance in a small domain is sought, the ad hoc simulation is an appropriate choice. If, however, the investigator hopes to relate his or her findings to a general model of cognition or to extend the findings to applications outside the domain, a semantic memory–production system model should be chosen.

Conscious and Unconscious Processing. The process models briefly reviewed will have to come to terms, in one way or another, with several dualities in the architecture of the human information-processing system (Rigney, 1978b). Two dualities—the duality of the self and the duality of conscious and unconscious processing—may be thought of as different manifestations of self-direction by metaprocessing control processes that accept outputs from process-

5. Learning Strategies

ing operations that function at preconscious or unconscious levels. Mandler (1975) described some of the functions of consciousness:

1. To serve as a scratch pad for the choice and selection of action systems.
2. To modify and interrogate long range plans; to organize disparate action systems to serve as a higher plan.
3. Participate in retrieval programs from Long Term Memory.
4. Monitor the organism's available activities and initiate new codings and representations.
5. Troubleshoot cognitive processes that normally cannot be brought into consciousness.

In Table 5.1, metaprocessing includes both selectional and self-directional processes. In this taxonomy, these processes include interactions between the two selves—the "doer" and the "watcher of the door." Richardson (1978) has described approaches to dealing with test anxiety, as a probable suppressor or disrupter of learning strategies. These approaches were derived, in part, from clinical behavioral modification techniques; in part, from clinical knowledge of mentally unhealthy relationships between the watcher and the doer; and from other clinical techniques for coping with these relationships.

Spielberger et al. (1979) described an impressive series of studies of test-anxiety reduction, learning strategies, and academic performance. They found that clinical techniques did reduce test anxiety, but did not actually result in improved grade-point average (GPA) in college courses. When these procedures were combined with study counseling, the GPA's of students with previously high test-anxiety and relatively good prior study habits were improved significantly. It could be assumed that test anxiety is a product of unconscious automatic processes aroused by conscious, unhealthy self-evaluation, by the watcher's rumination's over real or imagined deficiencies of the doer. It might be supposed that these ruminations could preempt attentional processes at times when they are needed for performance. In addition, these evaluations could influence intentional processes negatively, so that the student might avoid altogether attempting to learn challenging subject matter.

Conscious and unconscious processing have been intensively investigated by Shiffrin and Schneider (1977). Rigney (1978b) proposed that the conscious-unconscious processing duality is an adaptive mechanism in a processor that has evolved to deal with two kinds of events; those that it has encountered before in some recognizable form and for which it already possesses coping mechanisms; and those events that differ substantially from prior events that require reorganization of existing coping mechanisms at some level (i.e., that require learning). As an adaptive process, learning eventually will result in the automatization of the reorganized conceptual structures. Automatization can be thought of as shifting the ratio of conscious versus unconscious processing toward less use of conscious processing resources, freeing these for coping with unanticipated events and for planning future courses of action. According to this view, conscious processing is dependent on the outputs of unconscious processes, and has relatively limited processing capacity. Where learning strategies fit in this duality is problematic. Some may entail conscious processes; others may function at unconscious levels. Experimenter- or instructional-system-imposed learning strategies could constitute, for those students who do not already use them, an additional burden on limited conscious processing resources, so might tend to interfere with accustomed ways of processing, until the strategies were themselves well learned. Studies of differences between novices and experts should be instructive in this regard. Rigney (1978b) reviewed two such studies. Of these, Hatano, Yoshio, and Brinks (1977) study of abacus operators in Japan suggested strongly that not only had many of the novice's conscious processing operations become automatized in the expert, but also that the expert had learned transformations of many of these operations, possibly along the lines suggested by Neches and Hayes (discussed in a previous section of this chapter). In particular, Hatano et al. found that interfering with the finger movements required to operate an abacus disrupted the performances of (a) novice operators, who had to perform these movements on the abacus; and of (b) advanced intermediates, who did not need the abacus but still had to perform the movements with their fingers; but it did not disrupt the performance of experts. Perhaps, the execution of these "finger computations" had been transformed into some kind of table lookup, or the peripheral motor activity had been inhibited, as in silent reading.

Some learning strategies obviously are consciously controlled; mnemonic systems are an example. But, even here, these seem to be dependent on other well-learned, automatized, or unconscious processes. The keyword method will not work if the set of one hundred keywords is not already well learned. The method-of-loci requires that there be easily recalled loci (e.g., the rooms in one's own house, in which to "store" pieces of the new material to be recalled). Asking students to form mental images of technical concepts will not work unless the students already have some understanding of the concepts.

In summary, there are paradigms for studying conscious and unconscious processing, notably those of Shiffrin and Schneider (1977), but there are no process models that deal with the issues raised by this duality in a way that leads to a better understanding of the nature of learning strategies.

Studies of Cognitive Processes as Learning Strategies

Although, as discussed previously, Anderson proposed an ACT mechanism for explaining depth-of-processing, most process models have not been directly concerned with cognitive processes as learning strategies. Nevertheless, two of these, depth-of-processing and mental imagery, have been investigated intensively by cognitive psychologists, using other methods than process modeling. Of course, attention is recognized as fundamental precondition to all conscious processing, acting both as a kind of interrupt mechanism to switch this processing to higher priority events, and as a kind of amplifying mechanism while this processing is going on. In view of this, it is curious that there are not more studies of the management of attention in learning.

Bower (1972) and Paivio (1971) demonstrated the effectiveness of mental imagery for simple verbal learning, and Paivio advanced the idea of a dual-processing system, in which CVC's, nouns, and the like had two representations: one verbal and one imaginal. Wittrock (1977) reviewed the lateralization evidence for this. Although the positive effects of mental imagery on acquisition and recall of these simple verbal stimuli can be dramatic, these effects have not been found to extend to the more complex subject matter typical of the organized bodies of knowledge taught in training and education (Lutz & Rigney, 1977).

A basic difference in the use of imagery for simple and complex learning seems to be in the fact that students cannot generate mental imagery about concepts they have not already learned. They cannot visualize processes in science if they do not know what these processes are. On the other hand, paired CVC's or paired nouns are composed of well-learned symbols and are easily held in short-term memory while an embedding context of mental imagery is generated.

The studies of Shepard and his associates (Cooper & Shephard, 1973; Shepard, 1975) of mental rotation of mental images also have used familiar stimulus material. For more complex subject matter, mental imagery may have more use as a learning strategy for rehearsing material that is at least partly learned already. For this type of material, imagery could facilitate memory by establishing an integrating context or allowing vicarious practice procedures. Some aviators report using mental imagery to create imaginary scenarios in which they visualize themselves performing critical flight procedures. This use of mental imagery as a "workspace" for cognitive processing represents a different kind of cognitive learning strategy that may be the kind described in accounts of how great men solved problems. Kosslyn and his associates (Pinker & Kosslyn, 1978) have been concerned with exploring the characteristics of this mental workspace; for example, mental images seem to occur in a three-dimensional workspace. This conception of a mental workspace may identify a fundamental cognitive processing capacity. The ability to manipulate processes within this workspace seems to be an important individual difference and suggests the possibility that it could be improved through training.

Contributions from Educational Psychology: A Research Strategy for Relating Cognitive Processes and Aptitudes

Cronbach and Snow (Cronback & Snow, 1977; Snow, 1977) may finally succeed in forcing the methodology for studying cognitive processes to take into account the obvious fact that people differ.

Snow's (1977) reclassification of mental tests in terms of higher level constructs, G, G_f, G_c, and G_v, provides a less cumbersome way of organizing tests of individual differences than the earlier factorial structures (Guilford, 1967). Snow's (1977) compilation of definitions of major human mental abilities in these four categories is instructive.

Snow recommends a strategy for research on aptitude processes, that is, for research relating cognitive processes to individual differences in major human mental abilities. His goal is to find a strategy that will not only guide new research but will also show how prior studies are related to the framework. He recommends that the work be carried out on two fronts: in real instructional settings and in laboratory settings. Experiments done in the latter context are likely to permit the testing of models of the psychological processes responsible for aptitude–treatment interaction (ATI) effects.

Snow identifies four sources of individual differences in processing. People can differ in (*a*) the efficiency or capacity of particular processing components; (*b*) the organization of a sequence of processing components; (*c*) the processing components or sequences they possess; and (*d*) the adaptation of processing to particular tasks. An objective of the course of research he proposes is that aptitude factors (such as his crystallized fluid–visualization ability distinction) be analyzed in terms of such processes. Some empirical studies have already been conducted that show correlations between particular processes and certain aptitudes. Future research will have to combine multivariate experimental and correlational methods.

Snow and his associates have set out to apply these recommendations in a series of studies of ability–process parameter relations in a continuing program of research. In one of the first of these, Snow, Marshalek, and Lohman (1976) investigated some relationships between tested ability variables and processing parameters obtained from memory search and visual search tasks. They used multiple regression methods to regress ability variables on parameters and parameters on ability variables. The correlations between parameters and ability variables were low. They interpreted the overall pattern of correlation in terms of an information processing model in which general ability is the executive function that selects, creates, and implements programs that process and store information.

Contributions from Learning-to-Learn Centers

Many universitites and colleges maintain centers for teaching students who are having trouble attaining minimum standards of scholarly performance. These centers typically perform a number of services related to this problem. Students may be given tests of basic skills, particularly of reading skills; counselors at the centers attempt to diagnose the student's problems, and remedial reading and study skills courses may be available. The more elaborate centers may have libraries of tape cassettes for self-help courses, and may assign tutors to help students whose academic problems are confined to specific courses. These academic service centers have grown up quite outside the research domain surveyed in this report, and may be staffed by personnel who are not aware of what is going on in these research domains.

Because these learning-to-learn centers seldom have the resources, and certainly do not have the mission, to do research aimed at finding the best ways to aid students, their contributions are difficult to assess. A built-in selection process ensures that students who do use these centers are students who need help. Informal discussions with the managers of three of these centers suggest that the ability to locate quickly the information needed and the subsequent comprehension of the material are general problems. Centers are not necessarily restricted to marginal students. In some cases, any student or faculty member may use the center.

The significance of these learning-to-learn centers is that they are the principal institutional mechanisms for bringing students into contact with learning strategies. If these centers achieve a permanent place in educational institutions, they might be aligned with research on the problems they were established to alleviate, and researchers might be brought into contact with the centers. It will be interesting to see if this rapprochement does occur, or if these service centers and the research on learning strategies go their separate ways.

Methodological Issues

Campbell and Stanley (1963) reviewed methodological issues in educational research and described experimental and pseudoexperimental methods they considered to be useful. That such recommendations are not always heeded is easy to verify in any issue of *Educational Psychology*. Research on learning strategies, by and large, has not been distinguished by notably more rigorous methodology (although, as in the rest of educational research, studies vary from bad to good). The most pervasive problem is a simple one: it is not possible for researchers to gain control over enough subjects for a long enough time. They have to piggyback their data collection in training and educational institutions or depend on paid volunteers or students who are fulfilling a requirement to serve as experimental subjects for course credit. This situation drives research in education and training toward the kind of small-sample, short-term studies that Snow (1977) called learning sample tests. But, there are other problems. Not enough is known about the functional architecture of the human processor. Cognitive scientists are just beginning to grapple with this problem. As illustrated in the preceding section, the current models tend to be very limited in scope. Duality of processing in terms of conscious and unconscious levels is a particularly important issue for research on cognitive learning strategies. This duality has been discussed in similar terms by many theorists, but is has not been represented successfully in a general model.

The implications of this duality for research on cognitive learning strategies were discussed by Rigney (1978b). The principal implication is that cognitive learning strategies may operate at two levels. At the conscious level, the student may be given instructions or may use self-instructions to apply some strategy, say mental imagery, to facilitate acquisition and retention. This conscious level is the entrée to the human processor. These instructions can act as a temporary orienting task for the student to follow, requiring the performance of mental operations (which the student understands to be mental imagery) on the subject matter to be learned. These operations use up a certain amount of limited conscious-processing capacity, which is not a problem if the subject matter is very simple, as is the case with paired associates; or if it is already learned well enough to be easily recalled, as is the case with the aviator mentally rehearsing emergency procedures by imagining himself or herself in the aircraft and operating the controls. Otherwise, mental imagining operations may interfere with learning subject matter by already well-learned strategies that function at the lower, unconscious level, and do not use up limited conscious processing resources. Learning strategies operating at the conscious level can be repeated by repeating the instructions again in the new learning situation. But, it is unlikely that they will be evoked automatically by the new learning situation. This view accords with Snow's suggestion that general mental ability, G, may be represented in the conscious level of processing. If this is the case, it should not be expected that the results of "learning sample tests" predict only temporary outcomes, and that extrapolations of learning strategies previously successful on simple subject matter to applications on complex subject matter will not always succeed.

Learning strategies may operate at the unconscious level only after long practice in using them has resulted in automatization. At this level, they would be used automatically by variables in the learning situation, and would operate without a heavy drain on conscious processing resources, so that more of these resources would be available to conscious processing for coping with the new, unfamiliar subject matter. At this stage in our knowledge of the human processor architecture, these views are highly speculative. If they turn out to be substantially correct, then research on learning-to-learn must be prepared to develop suitable paradigms for investigating the effects of strategies of each level. Another problem, which has been a major theme in Glaser's discussions, is how to make theory derived from the traditional experimental methods serve the requirements for a theory of instruction. The road from experiments to prescriptions is not yet heavily traveled. A recent expression of these views was included in Lesgold et al. (1978). The four general requirements they describe for building a theory of instruction highlight the pressing need for more knowledge about

5. Learning Strategies

human-learning processes and *how they can be controlled by instructional variables*. As important mechanisms for facilitating acquisition, retention, and retrieval, in an instructional system, cognitive learning strategies will have to be transportable along Glaser's road, too.

PROSPECTS FOR THE IMMEDIATE FUTURE

Research depends on priorities in society that impact federal funding of research programs. Functional illiteracy and decreasing mental ability scores have been topics for a good bit of hand-writing in the press, as noted earlier. The executive branch has expressed intentions to increase funding of basic research, and to move the Department of Education out of HEW. These good intentions may be negated by congressional perceptions of *their* priorities. The best prediction of support for research on cognitive learning strategies in this climate is no prediction at all. It is clear, however, that massive federal programs in education are often motivated by a desire to quell the demands of minority special-interest groups, and are not grounded in analyses of the real problem in learning and instruction.

Cognitive Process Analyses

The approaches to analysis of cognitive processes, reviewed above, undoubtedly will be continued in some form in the near future. John Anderson's development of his ACT program is a process of successive revisions, with each new model incorporating improvements suggested by limitations in the earlier version. So long as the basic premises of this model and their implementation in code are viable, this computer simulation should continue to demonstrate interesting programmed mechanisms that simulate underlying processes for well-established phenomena in learning: stimulus discrimination, stimulus generalization, and depth-of-processing. One criterion of viability is the ability of the programmed mechanisms to account for more and more detailed experimental data.

Cognitive-process analyses and relating cognitive processes to tested aptitudes—as exemplified by the research of Fredericksen (1978), Hitch (1978), Hunt (1978), Hunt and Lansman (1978), Snow *et al*. (1976), and R. J. Sternberg (1978)—also is likely to continue in the near future. Both sides of the fence will require a long period of sorting out. Snow's (1976) hierarchical organization of tests of mental aptitude may be compelling enough to be adopted by others, and thus may serve as the basis for a restructuring of models of the intellect. On the other side of the fence, studies of cognitive processes seem to fall into two categories: general processes such as attention or rehearsal, and specific task or skill, problem-related processes; as exemplified by reading, analogical reasoning, the river-crossing problem, and mental arithmetic. Because the same human processor is the subject of these studies, it will be important to find some kind of integrating or unifying frame of reference. Perhaps this can be derived from some overall conception of the architecture of the human processor that will eventually emerge from the data of these seemingly disparate approaches.

The great hope of cognitive-process analysis for learning strategies is that it will succeed in describing processes involved in acquisition and retrieval that could be taught as learning strategies, or that it will elucidate enough about the architecture of the human processor to suggest better paradigms for investigating learning strategies and better methods for teaching them. The same thing can be said for computer simulation using some form of semantic network or schema theory, on the assumption that at this point, all these different approaches to studying the same processor are different ways of viewing the *same* elephant.

Processing Resources and Individual Differences

The term *processing resources* is used in different ways. It is used in Table 5.1 to denote a top-level classification of cognitive processes that are presumed to be enlisted by orienting tasks for the processing of different kinds of subject matter. Lansman (1978) described the use of processing resources in one of two theories of attention—the limited-resources model. According to Lansman, in this model, all mental processes draw from the same sources of processing capacity, which she also called processing resources, following Kahneman (1973). Norman and Bobrow (1975) also viewed processing resources as general and limited. They introduced the ideas of (*a*) performance–operating characteristic (POC) to describe the trade-off between two tasks making simultaneous demands on processing resources; and (*b*) a performance-resources function that describes how performance on a task is a function of the amount of resources devoted to it. Thus, a processing task may be either *data-limited,* if an increase in resources will have no effect on performance; or *resource-limited* if allocation of more resources will increase performance. On the other hand, the limited-capacity processor model of attention holds that a bottleneck exists somewhere in the human processor between input and output. This bottleneck is the limited-capacity processor. Some cognitive processes do not use this limited processor (e.g., long-term memory access). These can occur automatically and in parallel, presumably in front of and behind the limited processor. Other processes, notably conscious operations, do require this limited-capacity processor and must be carried out serially. The research of Schneider and Shiffrin (Schneider & Shiffrin, 1977; Shiffrin & Schneider, 1977) supports this model.

It seems best for the purposes of this chapter to distinguish between processing capacity and processing resources. The limited-capacity processor model of attention, with its distinction between controlled and automatic processes accords

5. Learning Strategies

with our views elaborated elsewhere (Munro & Rigney, 1977; Rigney, 1978b). The top-level classification of processing resources outlined in Table 5.1 also seems to fit a broad spectrum of evidence, and it allows for the acquisition of processing resources through learning. In this respect, prior knowledge could be considered synonymous with processing resources. However, a further distinction is required. There must be a general capability for acquiring processing resources. There must be significant individual differences in this capability, because there are ranges of individual differences in processing resources among individuals with substantially similar environmental histories. This could be called processing capacity, but it is a capability that cannot be accounted for simply by theories of attention. The limited-capacity processor model of attention assumes there are automatic parallel processes, but has nothing to say about processing capacity *at this level,* which surely must be where most human information-processing occurs. This is, in fact, the level of processing that is most often the subject of psychological experimentation. It is necessary to distinguish between controlled or conscious, processing capacity, which is very limited; and automatic or unconscious processing capacity, which is much less limited. According to this view, processing resources are to be distinguished from processing capacity. Processing resources are crudely analogous to computer programs, whereas processing capacity is crudely analogous to central-processing unit (CPU) architecture and machine-language instruction set. This is the view taken by Rigney (1978b), where processing capacity was called cognitive capacity.

The top-level classification of processing resources, illustrated in Table 5.1, encompasses cognitive processes that are the topics of research by cognitive scientists, some of which was illustrated in the preceding section. Most of this research is concerned with representational and procedural processes; some is concerned with selectional metaprocessing—primarily attention. As yet, very little deals with self-directional metaprocessing, although self-monitoring is a topic for research outside of cognitive science, in clinical psychology. The categories listed in Table 5.1 might serve, as intended, as a sort of road map for exploring cognitive processes. We expect that research on cognitive processes in the near future will reveal more detailed processing operations that can be fitted into this classification. The cognitive operations required for mental arithmetic (Brown & Burton, 1977; Hitch, 1978) are examples. However, since no one has adopted completion of this classification as a primary mission, progress in doing so is apt to be slow.

Ideally, a taxonomy of processing resources and a taxonomy of orienting tasks should be developed for constructing learning strategies for different kinds of subject matter. Something like this seems to have been the objective of the Training Analysis and Evaluation Group (TAEG) report on techniques for learning (Aagard & Braby, 1976).

Of course, the whole field of mental tests has been concerned with measures of processing resources in terms of individual differences; but, as Snow *et al.* (1976), Sternberg (1977), Hunt (1978), Carroll (1976) and others have argued, mental tests contain very little direct information about cognitive processes. The Snow, Sternberg, and Fredericksen strategies for research, discussed previously, are concerned with process descriptions of aptitude. It will be interesting to see if this line of research flourishes in the near future. Carroll's (1976) analysis of tests as cognitive tasks contains a list of twenty "operations and strategies" that would, according to the view adopted here, be classifiable as processing resources (see Table 5.3).

Trainability of Basic Skills

The impact of functional illiteracy on the military services, is, perhaps, more visible than its impact on society at large. Still, the welfare and unemployment figures cited earlier are not comforting, if, as is reasonable to assume, the majority of these persons lack salable skills. The question of interest is whether any more will be done about this problem in the immediate future than has been done in the immediate past. The courses of action open to the military are remedial reading, higher selection standards, or massive recruitment of women. Of these alternatives, remedial reading scarcely seems to be the responsibility of

TABLE 5.3
Operations and Strategies[a]

1. Identify, recognize, interpret stimulus
2. Educe identities or similarities between two or more stimuli
3. Retrieve name, description, or instance from memory
4. Store item in memory
5. Retrieve associations, or general information, from memory
6. Retrieve or construct hypotheses
7. Examine different portions of memory
8. Perform serial operations with data from memory
9. Record intermediate result
10. Visual inspection strategy (examine different parts of visual stimulus)
11. Reinterpretation of possibly ambiguous item
12. Imaging, imagining, or other way of forming abstract representation of a stimulus
13. Mentally rotate spatial configuration
14. Comprehend and analyze language stimulus
15. Judge stimulus with respect to a specified characteristic
16. Ignore irrelevant stimuli
17. Use a special mnemonic aid (specify)
18. Rehearse associations
19. Develop a special search (visual)
20. Chunk or group stimuli or data from memory

[a] From Carroll, 1976, p. 39 with permission.

the Services, unless it is agreed that this should be a peacetime mission and funding is provided for its accomplishment. But the short remedial reading courses cannot adequately address the problem of deficiencies in prior world knowledge, which accumulates over long periods of frequent use of reading skills. Stitch's ideas about long-term, job-oriented reading training are certainly more appealing than short, one-shot remedial reading courses. It would be of great interest to observe the outcome of such a program.

Research on Learning Strategies

The near-term prospects for research on learning strategies will be determined primarily by the availability of funding and the interest that the various research communities have in doing this research. One reasonable prediction would be that the scope of this research will be narrower and that there will be fewer people doing it. Frontal assaults may, indeed should be replaced by more circumspect approaches that include concern for known and probable human processor achitecture and by more attention to solving or avoiding the methodological problems discussed previously. The outlook is for slow progress, primarily because the rate of generating new information depends on the data rate, which is extremely slow.

PROSPECTS FOR THE LATE 1980s

Priorities in Society

Although it is relatively easy to extrapolate current trends a few years ahead, only a bona fide prophet could predict 10 years in advance, and one of these has not been around for quite some time. Today's societies are in economic, political, and philosophical turmoil. Brushfire military actions flare up almost daily, each with the potential to escalate. This turmoil is bound to influence, if not determine, social priorities. The critical question is whether our society will have sufficient resources and will be willing to allocate them for any quantum increases or grand-scale improvements in the educational system. This seems unlikely, unless some crisis drives priorities in that direction.

Pressures on Military Training

Will the conditions today that are exerting pressures on military training change for better or worse in 10 years? It does appear to be highly likely that the admission of women to military service will increase in the next decade, possibly relieving the shortage of high-quality personnel. But will the basic sources of pressure—short enlistments, increasing complexity of military systems, and inherently slow learning of the human species—change? From here, the prospects are that a relatively large proportion of the military budget will have to be allocated to training.

Resources for Research on Learning Strategies

The safest long-term prediction is that the electronics industry will continue to invent miracles. It has revolutionized the computer CPU, and it will very shortly revolutionize computer storage media. There is very little doubt that, in 10 years, everyone's automatic portable tutor can be a reality, with some forms of speech recognition and voice synthesis, and that the software arts will be vastly more efficient and less expensive. One hopes that a revolution comparable to the CPU and the memory revolution also will have occurred in computer programming and other instructional software production. It is tempting to predict that these three miracles, (the first already here, the second just now occurring, and the third not yet in sight but anxiously awaited), will radically alter structure and practices in training and educational institutions. We expect more effective distribution of training and education and more effective training and education. Everyone's portable automatic tutor will, it is to be hoped, include memory courses in how to learn in its multi-mega-byte.

Will the research communities produce Glaser's instructional theory for realizing instructional technologist's dreams? Certainly the research in cognitive process modeling and simulation, sampled in a preceding section, seems at this time to be robust enough to persist and grow into the late 1980s. We hope, however, that it will not grow in all directions at once. Perhaps work on general processes, such as attention and long-term memory, will have delineated a more detailed and more complete model of the human processor, whereas studies of subject-matter-related processes will have described a rich library of these processing resources. Snow's research strategy for capitalizing on the fact that people differ may lead to ATI-sensitive research paradigms for studying learnings strategies, on the hand, and ATI-sensitive instructional systems, on the other. Perhaps, 10 years is too soon to expect learning about learning strategies to have a place in the curricula coordinate with learning about subject matter.

SUMMARY AND CONCLUSIONS

Learning strategies are cognitive processing operations used by the learner to improve acquisition, retention, and retrieval of representational and procedural knowledge. These processing operations are initiated by orienting tasks that may be self-assigned by the learner or imposed by an instructor or an instructional system. Social and military pressures to improve the effectiveness of education and training; the shift in interest in cognitive psychology to analyzing, modeling, and controlling cognitive processes; and the emergence of new tools in psycholinguistics, computer science, and artificial intelligence have created a favorable zeitgeist for studying learning strategies.

A state-of-the-art assessment of where we are now, and where the field is likely to go in the future, has been attempted in this chapter. Archtypical examples of recent research on learning strategies are described. The possible contributions from cognitive science, educational psychology, and study skills centers are discussed. Methodological issues to consider for research on learning strategies are described. Finally, some comments on the future prospects for research on and application of learning strategies are offered.

Several conclusions are warranted. Attempts to teach students to use more effective learning strategies have been, for the most part, only modestly successful. The short-term nature of these attempts, in which subjects received only a few minutes or a few hours of practice in using the new strategies, is one reason for this.

There probably are two categories of learning strategies, determined by the level at which the human processor uses them—conscious or unconscious. At the conscious level, there are mnemonic devices that can be taught relatively quickly and can be used consciously to good effect. At the unconscious level, the student already uses overlearned or automatized, learning strategies, good or bad, that are difficult to replace with others. This category of learning strategies is likely to require long periods of guided practice as a part of the training procedure.

Although the research on cognitive-process analysis, modeling, and sysnthesis is exciting and has many positive implications for a better understanding of learning strategies and for better methods for investigating them, it is not concerned directly with learning strategies and the special consideration for research that they pose. Because of the great social urgency for reducing functional illiteracy in the population and for teaching citizens marketable skills, research with the objectives of understanding these cognitive processes and how to teach them to those who need them most should be actively pursued.

REFERENCES

Aagard, J. A., & Braby, R. *Learning guidelines and algorithms for types of learning objectives.* TAEG Report No. 23, Orlando, Fla.: Training Analysis and Evaluation Group, March, 1976.

Aiken, E., Duffy, T., & Nugent, W. *Reading skill and performance in a sample of Navy class A schools.* NPRDC Technical Report 77-28, San Diego, Calif.: Navy Personnel Research and Development Center, April, 1976.

Anderson, J. R. *Language, memory and thought.* Hillsdale, N.J.: Erlbaum, 1976.

Anderson, J. R. *Complex learning processes.* Paper presented at the Conference on Aptitude, Learning, and Instruction: Cognitive Process Analyses, San Diego, Calif., March, 1978.(a)

Anderson, J. R., & Bower, G. H. *Human associative memory.* Washington, D.C.: Winston, 1973.

Anderson, R. C. Schema-directed processes in language comprehension. In A. M. Lesgold, J. W. Pellegrino, S. D. Fokkema, & R. Glaser (Eds.), *Cognitive psychology and instruction.* New York: Plenum, 1978.(b)

Anderson, R. C., Spiro R. J., & Anderson, M. C. *Schemata as scaffolding for the representation of information in connected discourse.* Technical Report No. 24, Urbana: University of Illinois, Center for the Study of Reading, March, 1977.

Anderson, T. Study skills and learning strategies. In H. F. O'Neil, Jr. & C. D. Spielberger (Eds.), *Cognitive and affective learning strategies.* New York: Academic Press, 1979.

Atkinson, R. C. Mnemotechnics in second-language learning. *American Psychologist,* 1975, *30,* 821-828.

Atkinson, R. C., & Raugh, M. R. *Application of the mnemonic keyword method to the acquisition of a Russian vocabulary.* Technical Report No. 237, Stanford University, Calif.: Institute for Mathematical Studies in the Social Sciences, 1974.

Atwood, M. E., & Polson, P. G. A process model for water jug problems. *Cognitive Psychology,* 1976, *8,* 191-216.

The beneficent monster. *Time,* June 12, 1978, 24-32.

Bond, N. A., McGregor, D., Schmidt, K., Lattimore, M., & Rigney, J. W. *Studies of verbal problem-solving: II. Prediction of performance from sentence-processing scores.* Technical Report No. 87, Los Angeles, Calif.: University of Southern California, Behavioral Technology Laboratories, June, 1978.

Bower, G. H. Mental imagery and associative learning. In L. Gregg (Ed.), *Cognition of learning and memory.* New York: Wiley, 1972.

Brown, J. S., & Burton, R. R. *Diagnostic models for procedural bugs in basic mathematical skills.* Technical Report No. 3669, Cambridge, Mass.: Bolt, Beranek and Newman, December, 1977.

Brown, J. S., Collins, A., & Harris, G. Artificial intelligence and learning strategies. In H. F. O'Neil, Jr. (Ed.), *Learning strategies.* New York: Academic Press, 1978, 107-139.

Campbell, D. T., & Stanley, J. C. Experimental and quasi-experimental designs for research on teaching. In N. L. Gage (Ed.), *Handbook of Research on teaching.* Chicago, Ill.: Rand-McNally, 1963.

Carpenter, P. A., & Just, M. A. Sentence comprehension: A psycholinguistic processing model of verification. *Psychological Review,* 1975, *82,* 45-73.

Carroll, J. B. Psychometric tests as cognitive tasks: A new "structure of intellect." In L. B. Resnick (Ed.), *The nature of intelligence.* Hillsdale, N.J.: Erlbaum, 1976.

Case, R. Implications of developmental psychology for the design of effective instruction. In A. M. Lesgold, J. W. Pellegrino, S. D. Fokkema, & R. Glaser (Eds.), *Cognitive psychology and instruction.* New York: Plenum, 1978.

Coleman, J. S. *Equality of educational opportunity.* Summary Report, U.S. Department of Health, Education and Welfare, Office of Education. Washington, D.C.: U.S. Government Printing Office, 1966.

Conant, J. B. Slums and suburbs. New York: McGraw-Hill, 1961.

Cooper, L. A. *Spatial information processing: Strategies for research.* Paper presented at the Conference on Aptitude, Learning, and Instruction: Cognitive Process Analyses, San Diego, Calif., March, 1978.

Cooper, L. A., & Shepard, R. N. The time required to prepare for a rotated stimulus. *Memory and Cognition,* 1973, *1,* 246-250.

Craik, F. I. M., & Lockhart, R. S. Levels of processing: A framework for memory research. *Journal of Verbal Learning and Verbal Behavior,* 1972, *11,* 671-684.

5. Learning Strategies

Cronbach, L. J., & Snow, R. E. *Aptitudes and instructional methods: A handbook for research on interactions.* New York: Irvington, 1977.

Dansereau, D. The development of a learning strategies curriculum. In H. F. O'Neil, Jr. (Ed.), *Learning strategies.* New York: Academic Press, 1978.

deGroot, A. D. Perception and memory versus thinking. In B. Kleinmuntz (Ed.), *Problem solving.* New York: Wiley, 1966.

Duffy, T. M. *Literacy research in the Navy.* Paper presented at the Conference on Reading and Readability Research in the Armed Services, Monterey, Calif., October, 1975.

Feigenbaum, E. A. The simulation of verbal behavior. In E. A. Feigenbaum, & J. Feldman (Eds.), *Computers and thought.* New York: McGraw-Hill, 1963.

Fredericksen, J. R. *Component skills in reading: Measurement of individual differences through chronometric analysis.* Paper presented at the Conference on Aptitude, Learning, and Instruction: Cognitive Process Analyses, San Diego, Calif., March, 1978.

Glaser, R., Pellegrino, J. W., & Lesgold, A. M. Some directions for a cognitive psychology of instruction. In A. M. Lesgold, J. W. Pellegrino, S. D. Fokkema, & R. Glaser (Eds.), *Cognitive psychology and instruction.* New York: Plenum, 1978.

Gordon, L., Munro, A., Rigney, J. W., & Lutz, K. A. *Summaries and recalls for the three types of texts.* Technical Report No. 85, Los Angeles, Calif.: University of Southern California, Behavioral Technology Laboratories, May, 1978.

Guilford, J. P. *The nature of human intelligence.* New York: McGraw-Hill, 1967.

Hatano, G., Yoshio, M., & Binks, M. G. Performance of expert abacus operators. *Cognition,* 1977, 5, 47-55.

Hitch, G. J. Mental arithmetic: Short-term storage and information processing in a cognitive skill. In A. M. Lesgold, J. W. Pellegrino, S. D. Fokkema, & R. Glaser (Eds.), *Cognitive psychology and instruction.* New York: Plenum, 1978.

Hunt, E. Mechanics of verbal ability. *Psychological Review,* 1978, 85, 109-130.

Hunt, E., & Lansman, M. Cognitive theory applied to individual differences. In W. K. Estes (Ed.), *Handbook of learning and cognitive processes.* Hillsdale, N.J.: Erlbaum, 1975.

Jefferies, R., Polson, P. G., Razran, L., & Atwood, M. E. A process model for missionaries-cannibals and other river-crossing problems. *Cognitive Psychology,* 1977, 9 412-440.

Judd, W. A., McCombs, B. L., & Dobrovolny, J. L. Time management as a learning strategy for individualized instruction. In H. F. O'Neil, Jr. & C. D. Spielberger (Eds.), *Cognitive and affective learning strategies.* New York: Academic Press, 1979.

Kahneman, D. *Attention and effort.* Englewood Cliffs, N.J.: Prentice-Hall, 1973.

Kendler, H. H. A seductive paradigm. In J. W. Cotton & R. L. Klatzky (Eds.), *Semantic factors in cognition.* Hillsdale, N.J.: Erlbaum, 1978.

Klein, K., & Saltz, E. Specifying the mechanisms in a levels-of-processing approach to memory. *Journal of Experimental Psychology: Human Learning and Memory,* 1976, 2, 671-679.

Kosslyn, S. M. *Imagery and cognitive development: A teleological approach.* Paper presented at the Conference on Aptitude, Learning, and Instruction: Cognitive Process Analyses, San Diego, Calif., March, 1978.

Lansman, M. *An attentional approach to individual differences in immediate memory.* Final Technical Report, Seattle, Wash.,: University of Washington, June, 1978.

Larkin, J. H., & Reif, F. Analysis and teaching of a general skill for studying scientific text. *Journal of Educational Psychology,* 1976, 68, 431-440.

Lesgold, A. M., Pellegrino, J. W., Fokkema, S. D., & Glaser, R. (Eds.), *Cognitive psychology and instruction.* New York: Plenum, 1978.

Logan, R. S. An instructional systems development approach for learning strategies. In H. F. O'Neil, Jr. (Ed.), *Learning strategies.* New York: Academic Press, 1978.

Lutz, K. A., & Rigney, J. W. *The effects of student-generated elaboration during acquisition of concepts in science*. Technical Report No. 82, Los Angeles, Calif.,: University of Southern California, Behavioral Technology Laboratories, September, 1977.

Mandler, G. Consciousness: Respectable, useful and probably necessary. In R. L. Solso (Ed.), *Information processing and cognition: The Loyola symposium*. Hillsdale, N.J.: Erlbaum, 1975.

Miller, G. A., & Johnson-Laird, P. N. *Language and perception*. Cambridge, Mass.: Belknap, 1976.

Minsky, M. A framework for representing knowledge. In P. Winston (Ed.), *The psychology of computer vision*. New York: McGraw-Hill, 1975.

Munro, A., & Rigney, J. W. *A schema theory account of some cognitive processes in complex human learning*. Technical Report No. 81, Los Angeles, Calif.: University of Southern California, Behavioral Technology Laboratories, July, 1977.

Neches, R., & Hayes, J. R. Progress towards taxonomy of strategy transformations. In A. M. Lesgold, J. W. Pellegrino, S. D. Fokkema, & R. Glaser (Eds.), *Cognitive psychology and instruction*. New York: Plenum, 1978.

Newel, A., & Simon, H. A. *Human problem solving*. Englewood Cliffs, N.J.: Prentice-Hall, 1972.

Norman, D. A., & Bobrow, D. G. On data-limited and resource-limited processes. *Cognitive Psychology*, 1975, 7, 44-64.

Norman, D. A., Rumelhart, D. E., & the LNR Group. *Explorations in cognition*. San Francisco, Calif.: Freeman, 1975.

O'Neil, H. F., Jr. (Ed.). *Learning strategies*. New York: Academic Press, 1978.

O'Neil, H.F., Jr., & Spielberger, C. D. (Eds.). *Cognitive and affective learning strategies*. New York: Academic Press, 1979.

Paivio, A. *Imagery and verbal processes*. New York: Holt, 1971.

Pinker, S., & Kosslyn, S. M. The representation and manipulation of three-dimensional space in mental images. *Journal of Mental imagery*, 1978, 2, 69-84.

Richardson, F. Behavior modification and learning strategies. In H. F. O'Neil, Jr. (Ed.), *Learning strategies*. New York: Academic Press, 1978.

Rigney, J. W. Learning strategies: A theoretical perspective. In H. F. O'Neil (Ed.), *Learning strategies*. New York: Academic Press, 1978.(a)

Rigney, J. W. *Cognitive learning strategies and dualities in the human information processing system*. Paper presented at the Conference on Aptitude, Learning, and Instruction: Cognitive Process Analysis, San Diego, Calif., March, 1978.(b)

Rigney, J. W., & Lutz, K. A. Effect of graphic analogies of concepts in chemistry on learning and attitude. *Journal of Educational Psychology*, 1976, 68, 305-311.

Rigney, J. W., Munro, A., & Crook, D. E. Teaching task-oriented selective reading: a learning strategy. In H. F. O'Neil, Jr., and C. D. Spielberger, *Cognitive and affective learning strategies*. New York: Academic Press, 1979.

Rothkopf, E. Z. On the reciprocal relationship between previous experience and processing in determining learning outcomes. In A. M. Lesgold, J. W. Pellegrino, S. D. Fokkema, & R. Glaser (Eds.), *Cognitive psychology and instruction*. New York: Plenum, 1978.

Rumelhart, D. E., Lindsay, P. H., & Norman, D. A. A process model of long-term memory. In E. Tulving, & W. Donaldson (Eds), *Organization of memory*. New York: Academic Press, 1972.

Schank, R. C., & Abelson, R. P. *Scripts, plans, goals and understanding*. Hillsdale, N.J.: Erlbaum, 1977.

Schneider, W., & Shiffrin, R. M. Controlled and automatic human information processing: I. Detection, search, and attention. *Psychological Review*, 1977, 84, 127-190.

Shepard, R. N. Form, formation, and transformation of internal representations. In R. L. Solso (Ed.) *Information processing and cognition: The Loyola Symposium*. Hillsdale, N.J.: Erlbaum, 1975.

5. Learning Strategies

Shiffrin, R. M., & Scheider, W. Controlled and automatic human information processing: II. Perceptual learning, automatic attending, and a general theory. *Psychological Review*, 1977, *84*, 127-190.

Singer, R., & Gerson, R. F. In H. F. O'Neil, Jr. (Ed), *Learning strategies*. New York: Academic Press, 1978.

Snow, R. E. Research on aptitudes: A progress report. In L. S. Schulman (Ed.), *Review of research in education* (Vol. 4). 1977.

Snow, R. E., Marshalek, B., & Lohman, D. F. *Correlation of selected cognitive abilities and cognitive processing parameters: An exploratory study*. Technical Report No. 3, Stanford University, Calif.: Aptitude Research Project, School of Education, 1976.

Spielberger, C. D., Gonzalez, H. P. & Fletcher, T. Test anxiety reduction, learning strategies, and academic performance. In H. F. O'Neil, Jr., *Cognitive and affective learning strategies*. New York: Academic Press, 1979.

Sternberg, R. J. *Intelligence, information processing, and analogical reasoning: The componential analysis of human abilities*. Hillsdale, N.J.: Erlbaum, 1977.

Sternberg, R. J. Componential investigations of human intelligence. In A. M. Lesgold, J. W. Pellegrino, S. D. Fokkema, & R. Glaser (Eds.), *Cognitive psychology and instruction*. New York: Plenum, 1978.

Sternberg, S. Memory-scanning: Mental processes revealed by reaction-time experiments. *American Scientist*, 1969, *57*, 421-457.

Sticht, T. G. Cognitive research applied to literacy training. In A. M. Lesgold, J. W. Pellegrino, S. D. Fokkema, & R. Glaser (Eds), *Cognitive psychology and instruction*. New York: Plenum, 1978.

Sticht, T. G. Developing literacy and learning strategies in organizational settings. In H. F. O'Neil, Jr., & C. D. Spielberger (Eds.), *Cognitive and affective learning strategies*. New York: Academic Press, 1979.

Wagner, H., & Seidel, R. J. Program evaluation. In H. F. O'Neil, Jr. (Ed.), *Learning strategies*. New York: Academic Press, 1978.

Weinstein, C. Elaboration skills as a learning strategy. In H. F. O'Neil, Jr. (Ed.), *Learning strategies*. New York: Academic Press, 1978.

Weinstein, C. E., Underwood, V. L., Wicker, F. W., & Cubbverly, W. E. Cognitive learning strategies: Verbal and imaginal elaboration. In H. F. O'Neil, Jr., & C. D. Spielberger (Eds.), *Cognitive and affective learning strategies*. New York: Academic Press, 1979.

Wittrock, M. C. *Discussant's view of alternative approaches to learning strategies*. Paper presented at the Seminar on Learning Strategies: Measures, and Modules, Carmel, Calif., December, 1977.

6

Evaluation[1]

GARY D. BORICH
RON P. JEMELKA

OVERVIEW OF EVALUATION

One purpose of educational evaluation is to provide decision makers with information about the effectiveness of an educational program, product, or procedure. Within this perspective, evaluation is viewed as a process in which data are obtained, analyzed, and synthesized into relevant information for decision making.

Although most evaluation activities fit comfortably within the bounds of this definition, the specific approach used and procedures employed vary from one evaluation study to another as a function of who is doing the evaluation, the context in which the evaluation is to occur, and the desires and needs of the individual or agency contracting the evaluation. There is basic agreement about the fundamental role of evaluation in education; however, beyond this there is considerable variance in the conceptual frameworks used by practitioners. Indeed, even the ways in which evaluation has been defined in the literature has produced considerable debate.

Bloom, Hastings, and Madaus (1971) point to five different facets of evaluation, not all of which are included in other definitions. These authors pose a broad view of evaluation consisting of the following activities:

---

[1]The work reported in this chapter was supported in part by the Army Research Institute for the Behavioral and Social Sciences, contract number MDA 903-79-C-0558. Views and conclusions contained in this document are those of the authors and should not be interpreted as necessarily representing the official policies, either expressed or implied, of the Army Research Institute for the Behavioral and Social Sciences, or the United States Government.

1. Acquiring and processing the evidence needed to improve the students learning and the teaching.
2. Employing a great variety of evidence beyond the final paper and pencil examination.
3. Clarifying the significant goals and objectives of education and determining the extent to which the students are developing in these desired ways.
4. Instituting a system of quality control in which it may be determined at each step in the teaching-learning process whether the process is effective or not and if not, what changes must be made to insure effectiveness.
5. And, ascertaining whether alternative procedures are equally effective or not in achieving a set of educational ends [pp. 7-8].

As general as these activities may appear, they are not the only purposes for which evaluations can be conducted. Stufflebeam *et al.* (1971), for example, divide evaluation into a four-part process consisting of context, input, process, and product evaluations, each with its own objectives and methods; whereas Hammond (1969), Metfessel and Michael (1967), Provus (1971), Stake (1967), and others conceptualize and partition the process, if not the domain, of evaluation in still other ways.

With evaluators differing on such basic issues, it is not surprising that numerous evaluation paradigms or models can be found in the literature to help shape and guide evaluation activities. The problem for the evaluator becomes one of choosing the conceptualization or model most appropriate to the evaluation problem. Because the evaluation models appearing in the literature are purposely general (so as to be applicable to a wide variety of educational problems), the task of choosing that conceptualization of evaluation most appropriate to a specific purpose becomes even more arduous. One purpose of this chapter is to trace the origins of the problem of choosing the correct conceptualization or model for an evaluation and to identify some of the underlying factors that have contributed to the heterogeneity of opinion concerning the definition, nature, and scope of educational evaluation. To this end we will present an overview of some historical developments that have influenced the growth of educational evaluation. This chronology will provide the foundation for an interpretation of contemporary movements in the field and the extrapolation of these movements to the not too distant future.

Before proceeding, a personal note is in order. We have struggled in this writing to keep separate the idea of where the field of evaluation is going from the idea of where we believe it should be going. As most authors will attest any writing is inextricably tied to their background, training, and philosophy and this chapter is no exception. As Kuhn (1970) has made us painfully aware "an apparently arbitrary element, compounded of personal and historical accident, is always a formative ingredient of the beliefs espoused by a given scientific community (and scientist) at a given time . . . among those legitimate possibilities, the particular conclusions he does arrive at are probably determined by his prior experience in other fields, by accidents of his investigation, and by his own individual makeup [p. 4]." Kuhn's observation leads us to ask who might be the wiser: the scientist who writes about his or her field influenced by his or her own implicit biases and the philosophy of the scientific community, or the objective scholar who chronicles the accomplishments of a discipline with which he or she has only fundamental knowledge? When the Carnegie corporation chose the Swedish sociologist Gunnar Myrdal to write an objective report on the status of the American black, it clearly valued the view of an outsider. Although it is difficult to measure the consequences of either approach, history has shown the value of each. If the reader feels that our interpretation is only one interpretation that may be made from these historical trends, he or she will no doubt be correct.

WHERE WE ARE NOW: HISTORY AND CURRENT STATUS OF EVALUATION

This section briefly reviews the history of educational evaluation, presents the roles evaluation has traditionally played in education, and summarizes the current status of the field.

Educational Developments and Societal Trends Influencing the Growth and Development of Evaluation

In the first three decades of this century the measurement of human abilities grew out of early work by Binet, Thorndike, and Thurstone. This newly developed measurement technology had much appeal to educators and was assimilated into educational practice, giving rise to the development of standardized achievement tests that made possible large-scale testing programs. The accreditation movement also flourished during this early period and with the development of formal accrediting policies for colleges and schools, program evaluation gained a foothold in education. In 1947 the Educational Testing Service (ETS) was established. A national system of research and development centers and laboratories was created in 1966 that provided additional momentum to the field of evaluation through evaluation projects and contributions to evaluation methodology (see Borich, 1974, and Poyner, 1974, for a selection of evaluation contributions from these centers and laboratories).

Impact of Operationalism and the Behavioral Objectives Movement[2]

The concept of behavioral objectives has held a position of importance in the field of evaluation for almost half a century. One origin of the concept of

---

[2]We are indebted to Bloom, Hastings, and Madaus (1971) for the early origins of this movement.

behavioral objectives can be traced to a book by Bridgman (1927) titled *The Logic of Modern Physics*.

In his book, Bridgman pointed to the need to define new constructs by describing the operations used to measure them. Bridgman's concept offered an alternative to the practice of defining constructs by their apparent commonality or lack of commonality with other constructs that had been defined in the same manner. Through the efforts of Bridgman and the parallel efforts of others, the idea of operationally defining constructs became incorporated into the behavioral sciences, where constructs such as "motivation," "anxiety," and "learning" were redefined in terms of the measurement operations used to observe them. The process of tying construct definition to construct measurement became an integral part of the school known as behaviorism to which the behavioral objectives movement owes its beginning.

The application of operationalism to education resulted in the outgrowth of two distinct but related movements. The first is typified by Tyler's "Eight-Year Study of Secondary Education for the Progressive Education Association" (Smith & Tyler, 1942), in which behavioral objectives were used extensively to evaluate "progressive" attempts to apply new curricula and approaches to instruction. Tyler's contribution is significant not only because it offered the first example of how behavioral objectives could be used to construct evaluation instruments and to appraise the effectiveness of curricula, but also because it provided the impetus for many developments that were to follow in the field. Some of the more noteworthy of these were the *Taxonomy of Educational Objectives: The Classification of Educational Goals. Handbook 1. Cognitive Domain* (Bloom, 1956), the *Taxonomy of Educational Objectives: The Classification of Educational Goals. Handbook 2. Affective Domain* (Krathwohl, Bloom, & Masia, 1964), and a popular book entitled *Preparing Objectives for Programmed Instruction* (Mager, 1962) on how to write educational objectives. These volumes, in turn, stimulated an extensive literature on behavioral objectives, both in support of and critical of their application in the schools (Eisner, 1969; Popham, 1969).

A second movement rooted in a behaviorist philosophy was the programmed instruction and related computer-assisted instruction (CAI) movement of the late 1950s and 1960s. Behaviorally stated objectives were central to both these forms of instruction. The development of programmed and CAI depended heavily on the specification and breaking down of content into discrete learnable units having measurable outcomes, for which the concept of behavioral objectives was ideally suited. In this behavioralist setting, several large development and evaluation projects were begun. Of particular note were evaluations of the PLATO and TICCIT CAI projects designed to study the cost and effectiveness of computer-based instruction (CBI) for teaching large numbers of geographically dispersed students (see Alderman, 1978; Murphy & Appel, 1977; and Orlansky & String, 1978, for evaluations of these and other CBI projects).

The Impact of the Curriculum Reform Movement

A major impetus to the development of evaluation was the curriculum reform movement. Spanning roughly the decades of the 1950s and 1960s, the curriculum reform movement was characterized by widespread change in the philosophy, techniques, and materials used in teaching elementary and secondary school children. Most notable were the changes that occurred in the sciences shortly after the 1957 launching of the Soviet satellite, Sputnik. Prior to this unsettling event, curricula for the public schools were written primarily by individuals authoring textbooks that changed only slightly the style and content of earlier versions. Partly because of the inability of any single author to undertake major curriculum reform and partly because of the liability to the author and publisher such reform might present if it was not salable, curriculum changes were slow and for the most part conservative. With Soviet competition in the sciences, however, came the impetus for the federal government to play an increasing role in the field of education, at first through the vehicle of the National Science Foundation (NSF) and later through the efforts of the U.S. Office of Education and the National Institute of Education (NIE). The post-Sputnik era provided the context for new initiatives in the design and development of curricular materials, particularly in the fields of science and mathematics. These initiatives represented not only an effort to reform certain segments of the school curriculum but also to try new approaches to curriculum development that placed decreasing emphasis on the individual author and increasing emphasis on teams of specialists brought together by public monies specifically for the purpose of infusing the school curriculum with the latest scientific advances. New content and innovative ways of presenting it became more palatable, with the burden of risk for a development project shared by teams of specialists sponsored by government monies. Even more appealing was the fact that often extensive discussions, symposia, and workshops accompanied these development projects for the purpose of giving teachers and scientists a significant role in the design and selection of content. This unique integration of theory and practice became a key element in a process that was to become characteristic of the curriculum reform movement.

Also of significance was the fact that with the systematic approach to curriculum development the previously isolated concepts of development and evaluation became parts of a unitary process. Because of the experimental nature of much of the content and approaches used, pilot and field testing of instructional components became logical extensions of the curriculum development effort. It was in this context that projects such as the Biological Sciences Curriculum Study (BSCS), the Chemical Education Materials Study (Chem Study), the Physical Science Study Committee (PSSC), and the School Mathematics Study Group (SMSG) were born. These projects contributed significantly to the field of evaluation by employing development strategies that required the repeated testing and revision of component parts of the curriculum. This process of testing well-defined units of a curriculum during development for purposes of revision and modification was later to be coined "formative evaluation" by Scriven (1967) (see Grobman, 1968, for a review of the curriculum reform movement and a history of the BSCS).

The significant role evaluation played in these projects stimulated efforts at several universities to mount doctoral training programs in the area of evaluation. Training programs were begun at the Ohio State University, influenced principally by Professor Stufflebeam (now at Western Michigan University); the University of Illinois, influenced principally by Professor Stake; and at the University of Virginia, influenced principally by the late Professor Provus. In addition, each of these individuals developed in conjunction with his training curriculum an evaluation model that could be used in evaluating educational programs and curricula. These models would later figure centrally in the development of the field of evaluation.

The Impact of the Elementary and Secondary Education Act (ESEA)

Despite the influence of the behavioral objectives and curriculum reform movements, there was still relatively little emphasis placed on the evaluation of educational programs in the mid-1960s. It was within this context that the U.S. Congress began debate on the Elementary and Secondary Education Act of 1965 (ESEA). This comprehensive and ambitious educational legislation was to make available large sums of money in the form of grants to universities and local education agencies for educational materials, development, and research. As the bill was debated, concern was expressed that there were no assurances that the federal monies made available would actually result in improvements in the quality of education. This concern perhaps was magnified by the general belief that, in the past, educators had done a poor job of accounting for the federal money they spent.

Motivated by this concern, the Congress insisted on a provision to ESEA requiring that grantees submit evaluation reports on the impact of their programs. These guidelines were conveyed to prospective grantees in an ESEA Title III manual published by the U.S. Office of Education (1967), requiring the applicant to:

1. Where applicable, describe the methods, techniques, and objectives which will be used to determine the degree to which the objectives of the proposed program are achieved.
2. Describe the instruments to be used to conduct the evaluation, and
3. Provide a separate estimate of costs for evaluation purposes [p. 48].

6. Evaluation

Although the final version of the bill did not require evaluation of all the programs (titles) under ESEA, there was a clear mandate from those providing federal funds for education that programs using these funds be accountable for the educational programs, products, and procedures they developed and/or implemented. For the first time educators were required to devote time and resources to evaluating their own efforts.

This emphasis on accountability became evident again in 1971, when a rider was placed on routine legislation requiring that *all* ESEA projects be evaluated by the grantee. The current popularity of "sunset" and "sunshine" policies and zero-based budgeting among both state and federal funding agencies reflect this continued emphasis on accountability. These policies require the recipients of funds to justify refunding of their program each year or program cycle, and to make program decisions and expenditures a matter of public record.

Impact of School and Teacher Accountability

The concept of school and teacher accountability emerged as an outgrowth of the ESEA Legislation of 1965 and 1971. Federal agencies and grantees responsible for innovative ESEA programs were only the first to feel the pressure for accountability. Because many of these programs dealt directly with the schools, the accountability demanded of them also raised questions about the school staff who played a prominent role in their implementation. Consequently, teaching effectiveness and the administrative accountability of schools in general often became the focus of attempts to monitor and evaluate federally funded programs. The concepts of "accountability," "cost-benefit," and "quality assurance," filtered down in spirit, if not in substance, to the local school and teacher.

By 1970 community pressures began to bear down on the local school, often demanding accountability in terms of pupil outcome. In some cases school administrators responded to these pressures by concentrating on the more obvious indicators of effectiveness, such as pupil performance on national achievement tests, number of college admissions, and National Merit scholarships. Others began exploring ways to make cost-effective decisions about the operation and management of their school to prove that increased revenues actually produced more effective teaching and learning. School administrators embraced accountability procedures in answer to community pressures for more objectively determined and effective ways to spend school revenue, and to make internal decisions that could be defended to school boards, PTA's, and professional groups.

It was within this context of widespread community concern about higher but apparently unproductive school expenditures that some state governments began discussing legislation requiring the appraisal of school district personnel. A prime example of state-enacted accountability legislation was California's Stull Act passed in 1971, requiring that school boards in that state evaluate their educators yearly and provide recommendations for their professional development. The Stull Act gave local communities a mandate to develop procedures for appraising school district personnel and for periodically reporting appraisal data to the teacher to upgrade his or her performance. One impact of the school and teacher accountability movement on the general field of evaluation has been in the area of process evaluation. To evaluate the performance of teachers, researchers have defined operationally a large number of teacher behaviors or competencies that have been shown to relate to pupil achievement. Many of these teacher behaviors and related instrumentation have been used by evaluators to study the processes with which instructional staff implement educational programs and curricula (see Borich, 1977 and Borich & Madden, 1977, for other contributions of the school and teacher accountability movement).

A summary of the contributions to evaluation associated with operationalism, curriculum reform, ESEA legislation, and school accountability appears in Table 6.1.

Response to the Demand for Effective Evaluation

Although citizens were generally positive about the explicit mandates contained in ESEA legislation and California's Stull Act, it became evident by

TABLE 6.1
Some Contributions Associated with Four Milestones in the Field of Evaluation

Milestones	Contributions
1. Operationalism	Defining constructs by the procedures used to measure them
	Use of behavioral objectives for program design and evaluation
	Programmed instruction
	Computer-assisted instruction
2. Curriculum reform	Increased federal expenditure in education
	New initiatives in instructional techniques and materials
	Cooperation of scientists and teachers on the design of curricula
	Integration of curriculum development and evaluation as a unitary process (formative evaluation)
	Doctoral training programs in evaluation
3. Elementary and Secondary Education Act of 1965	Federal commitment to evaluation
	Federally mandated and funded evaluations
	The principle of refunding contingent on evaluation results
	Project accountability at the local level
4. School accountability	Teacher and administrator accountability
	Pupil behavior as criterion of program (teacher) success
	State-mandated evaluations
	Process evaluation techniques and instruments
	Evaluation as feedback for professional development.

6. Evaluation

mid-1970 that educators were not prepared to implement effectively either of these new mandates. Moreover, the sudden increase in demand for capable evaluators brought about by these mandates exhausted the supply quickly. Few educators had any formal training in evaluation, and often local school personnel were pressed into service as program evaluators.

One obstacle to the implementation of these mandates was the inability of local, state, and federal administrators to apply the mandates. The evaluation concepts created by educators in the preceding decade no longer seemed adequate to answer the questions that now were being asked of these programs. After reviewing the evaluation reports of ESEA programs, Guba (1969) concluded that

> The traditional methods of evaluation have failed educators in their attempts to assess the impact of innovations in operating systems. Indeed, for decades the evidence produced by the application of conventional evaluation procedures has contradicted the experiential evidence of the practitioner. Innovations have persisted in education not because of the supporting evidence of evaluation but despite it [p. 28].

and at another point argued that "when the evidence produced by any scientific concept or technique continually fails to affirm experiential observation and theory arising from that observation, the technique may itself appropriately be called into question [p. 30]."

With the emergence of ESEA came not only a need for new management strategies to monitor these programs but also a need for improved evaluation designs to test their effectiveness.

Reflecting on the current state-of-evaluation practice the report of the Phi Delta Kappa (PDK) national study committee on evaluation (Stufflebeam *et al.*, 1971) concluded that evaluation was "seized with a great illness [p. 4]." The "symptoms" of this illness, as indicated by the PDK committee were

1. *The avoidance symptom:* Evaluation is perceived as a painful process that may expose a school districts' programs or individuals' shortcomings. Evaluation is avoided unless absolutely necessary.
2. *The anxiety symptom:* Evaluation evokes anxiety. The educator as well as the evaluator knows how cursory, inadequate, and subject to error the evaluation process can be. The ambiguity in the evaluation process engenders anxiety in both the educator and evaluator.
3. *The immobilization symptom:* Despite federal requirements to evaluate, evaluative data on educational programs, products, and procedures are still rare. This lethargy and lack of responsiveness is symptomatic of deeper ills.
4. *Lack of theory and guidelines symptom:* There is a lack of unified theory of evaluation. With evaluators differing among themselves about what

evaluation should and should not be, an evaluator in the field is left to his or her own devices for conducting evaluative inquiry; there are few useful guidelines to follow.
5. *The misadvice symptom:* There is ample evidence that evaluation consultants have provided educational practitioners with poor advice. Not only is there a lack of adequate guidelines, but obtaining advice from an evaluation "expert" is no guarantee that a technically sound evaluation report will result.

To the preceding symptoms were added the lack of trained personnel, the lack of knowledge about decision processes; the lack of values and criteria for judging evaluation results; the need to have different evaluation approaches for different types of audiences; and the lack of techniques and mechanisms for organizing, procuring, and reporting evaluative information.

The foregoing suggest that at the beginning of the past decade the relatively new discipline of evaluation was indeed besieged with problems that could be regarded as deficiencies. These deficiencies, though, were themselves symptoms of a more fundamental ill: the lack of an adequate definition of evaluation and the lack of adequate evaluation theory.

Traditional Definitions of Evaluation

The lack of an adequate theoretical base for the discipline of evaluation has often been cited as a factor that has stifled the development of the field and its ability to provide meaningful evaluative data to educational practitioners. Even more problematic, however, is the lack of consensus among evaluators as to how evaluation should be defined.

"Evaluation" has been defined in a number of arbitrary ways. Four definitions that have achieved some popularity during the development of the field are the following.

Evaluation as Measurement

The early definition of evaluation as measurement came to the forefront during the 1920s and 1930s with the rise of the measurement movement in psychology and education. Evaluation received considerable impetus from the emergence of the science of measurement, and it is not surprising that the terms were equated during the 1930s. More current measurement definitions have been expanded to give a broader focus to the term *evaluation* but maintaining the close tie to measurement. Consider the following definition from a measurement text by Thorndike and Hagen (cited in Stuffelbeam *et al.*, 1971): "the term 'evaluation' as we use it is closely related to measurement. It is in some respects more inclusive, including informal and intuitive judgments, . . . [than is] saying what is desirable and good. Good measurement techniques provide the solid foundation of sound evaluation [p. 10]."

Defining evaluation as measurement has the advantage of building directly on the scientific measurement movement with its attendant objectivity and reliability. Furthermore, measurement instruments yield data that are mathematically and statistically manipulable, facilitating the establishment of norms and standards. The disadvantage of this definition of evaluation is that it is totally dependent on the development, administration, scoring, and interpretation of measurement instruments (tests, questionnaires, attitude scales, and so on), which take time to develop and are relatively expensive. This approach also obscures judgments and judgment criteria. Scores become entities unto themselves, whereas concepts behind the scores tend to be obfuscated. A final disadvantage, and perhaps the most important, is that variables that do not lend themselves readily to measurement are often eliminated or ignored (see Ebel, 1965 and Thorndike & Hagen, 1969, for further explication of this approach to evaluation).

Evaluation as Determining Congruence

This widely accepted definition of evaluation is concerned with the congruence between performance and objectives, that is, determining the degree to which the performances of students are congruent with the objectives of instruction. The major proponent of this definition was Tyler who, reporting on his Eight-Year Study of Secondary Education for the Progressive Education Association (Smith & Tyler, 1942), viewed educational objectives as changes in behavior. If a program succeeded in bringing about the desired changes (i.e., if there was a congruence between student performance and the objectives) then the program was judged successful.

A major advantage of this approach is that it forces educators to conceptualize clearly the goals of instruction and requires their full articulation. Further, this emphasis on objectives provides at least implicit criteria for judging the success of a program. Another distinct advantage of this definition is that it allows for the evaluation of educational processes (e.g., teacher behavior) as well as educational products (e.g., student achievement).

One disadvantage of this definition includes the fact that objectives have to be made specific to be measurable, which may obscure important but less specifiable objectives intended by program developers. Another disadvantage is the heavy emphasis placed on *student* behaviors. A new staffing policy or instructional strategy is evaluated in terms of student achievement, and such issues as cost effectiveness, teacher satisfaction, and student discipline may be ignored. A related disadvantage of emphasizing student achievement is that congruence evaluations tend to be ex post facto. Although Tyler's approach allows for evaluation of process, the data emphasized in this approach, that of student performance, are available only at the end of the project when the performance of students is compared to program objectives. Thus, valuable process data often are not collected (or at least not emphasized) and the opportunity for feedback and program modification is often lost (see Furst, 1964, and Tyler, 1950, for a further discussion of this definition of evaluation).

Evaluation as Professional Judgment

The definitions discussed previously place little emphasis on the judgmental process. Attaching value to the data was assumed. In this definition evaluation *is* professional judgment. The most common practice in this approach is site visitation, such as that used in accrediting schools and colleges. A visiting team of experts come to "soak up" the environment, and to use their expertise in rendering a judgment of program effectiveness.

Advantages of this approach include ease of implementation, consideration of a large number of quantitative and qualitative variables (including the context, experience, and expertise of the evaluators), and quick turnaround of results and conclusions. Major disadvantages include the questionable objectivity and reliability of the judgments that are made, the ambiguity of the judgment criteria, and the difficulty in generalizing results of the evaluation to other programs or institutions.

Evaluation as Applied Research

Although evaluation usually has not been defined in terms of research, a sorting through of evaluation studies reveals a strong reliance on the scientific method and an even heavier emphasis on the experimental designs and statistical tools of research. This result is not surprising when considering that the typical evaluator usually is trained extensively in the methodology of research and often only minimally trained in those concepts unique to evaluation.

Despite obvious advantages of classical research methodology, such as experimental control over variables and the statistical power of parametric statistical techniques, there are practical considerations that limit the applicability of these procedures to educational problems. These were presented by Stufflebeam *et al.* (1971) and are updated and summarized in the following list with some extensions and modifications.

1. *Laboratory antisepsis:* Cooley and Lohnes (1976) point out that scientific research attempts to validate the existence of cause-and-effect relationships with the ultimate goal being the development of a consistent and parsimonious theory of natural phenomena. Evaluation research, on the other hand, is concerned with means–end relationships with the ultimate goal being a rational choice between alternatives for action. Because scientific research pursues universal laws, knowledge must be obtained in a context-independent way. Experimental manipulation

6. Evaluation

is used to control all confounding and extraneous variables. The evaluation of an educational program is concerned, however, with all the mitigating variables affecting some educational outcome. "In order to provide useful data, educational evaluation does not need the antiseptic world of the laboratory, but the septic world of the classroom and school [Stufflebeam, *et al.*, 1971, p. 22]." Laboratory research designs require conditions usually not attainable in evaluation contexts.

2. *Effects of intervention:* In scientific research, variables are manipulated by the experimenter to create critical comparisons of the ways variables interact. Thus, the experimenter's intents become part of the data. The evaluator, on the other hand, attempts to assess interactions in a real rather than contrived environment. His or her data collection must be done unobtrusively so as to not confound results.

3. *Terminal availability of data:* Research designs typically attempt to assess the effect of some experimental treatment. The treatment is administered, then data are collected and analyzed. Data for making judgments are available only after the treatment has been administered. This precludes the use of data to refine a treatment, although continuous refinement of an ongoing educational program is a frequent function of evaluation.

4. *Single treatments only:* For purposes of experimental control, scientific research requires that a treatment be evaluated alone. If several treatments are operating simultaneously, their effects will confound each other. Educators, on the other hand, cannot withhold a potentially beneficial educational program because students are concurrently enrolled in other treatments.

5. *Effects of control variables:* Random assignment is generally not possible in educational settings. Thus, to equate treatment groups (to enhance their comparability) evaluators usually match groups on selected control variables such as intelligence levels, ethnic mix, classroom size, socioeconomic status, and the like. The problem with this procedure is that criterion variables (such as measures of cognitive or affective achievement) are often correlated with these control variables causing treatment differences to be obscured.

6. *Inapplicability of assumptions:* Some assumptions underlying the use of parametric statistical procedures may not be met in the usual evaluation setting, for example, when distributions are severely skewed, relationships nonlinear, or group variances unequal.

7. *Restricted decision rules:* Conventional statistical techniques contain decision rules of the simple "go–no-go" variety. A null hypothesis may be rejected or accepted or treatment X may be judged better than treatment Y. Evaluators are often asked to bring their expertise to bear in more complex decision settings.

In a fashion similar to Stufflebeam *et al.* Hemphill (1969) has distinguished research from evaluation along six dimensions: problem selection, replication, determination of data, determination of hypotheses, values, and control. To emphasize the differences between research and evaluation, Hemphill cast these dimensions in parallel form, which are noted in Table 6.2.

Whereas all-exclusive distinctions between research and evaluation are often subjects of controversy, most evaluators and researchers implicitly support a broad separation between these two modes of inquiry. So sharply has the line between research and evaluation been drawn at times that some evaluators contend that the two modes of inquiry are basically incompatible and ultimately must employ different methodology.

Models for Evaluation

Different conceptions of evaluation have spawned numerous paradigms or models for implementing an evaluation study. These paradigms or models, however, represent different conceptions of evaluation more than they do different objectives or contexts for evaluation. Matching a particular type of evaluation problem to a particular model does not seem possible nor does there seem to be an explicit rationale as to why an evaluator might choose one model over another. This has left evaluators without criteria for selecting the most appropriate model for a given evaluation problem.

Some educators and some program developers operate under the assumption

TABLE 6.2
Contrasts between Research and Evaluation[a]

Research	Evaluation
1. Problem selection and definition is the responsibility of the individual doing the study.	Many people may be involved in the definition of the problem and because of its complexity, it is difficult to define.
2. Given the statement of the problem and the hypothesis, the study can be replicated.	The study is unique to a situation and seldom can be replicated, even approximately.
3. The data to be collected are determined largely by the problem and hypothesis.	The data to be collected are influenced heavily if not determined by feasibility.
4. Tentative answers may be derived by deduction from theories or by induction from an organized body of knowledge.	Precise hypotheses usually cannot be generated; rather the task becomes one of testing generalizations, some of which may be basically contradictory.
5. Value judgments are limited to those implicit in the selection of the problem.	Value judgments are made explicit by the selection and definition of the problem as well as by the development and implementation of the study.
6. Relevant variables can be manipulated or controlled by including them in the design.	Only superficial control of potentially confounding variables can be achieved.

[a] Adapted from Hemphill, 1969, pp. 190-191.

6. Evaluation

that a variety of specific evaluation models exist that are readily applicable to their particular educational problem. When the time for evaluation comes, the task is deemed as a simple one of selecting an appropriate model, plugging the program into it, and analyzing the results. Evaluation models generally are not precise or specific and the choice of an evaluation model is itself a value judgment about how an educational program should be evaluated. An alternative to selecting a general model is to adapt a model developed for a specific setting and generalize it to the problem context at hand. Highly specific models are, however, developed within a narrow context and are generalizable to only those settings that have identical or highly similar administrative organizations, funding and political presses, personnel compositions, data-analysis support systems, client populations, educational objectives, and personnel biases about what is and is not important in evaluating a program.

A variety of evaluation models abound in the professional literature. Some are purposively general so as to be applicable to a variety of educational contexts (cf Hammond, 1973; Provus, 1971; Stufflebeam *et al.,* 1971, Metfessel & Michael, 1967; and Stake, 1967), whereas others are developed to meet evaluation needs in a specific setting (cf Belliott, 1969; Dykstra, 1968; Emrick, Sorenson, & Stearns, 1973; and the Interservice Procedures for Instructional Systems Development (IPISD) model, 1975). To underscore their general nature three popular evaluation models are summarized below.

The Discrepancy Evaluation Model

Stage 1

The discrepancy evaluation model developed by Provus (1971) divides evaluation into five stages. Stage 1 documents program description. The evaluator obtains from the program staff a comprehensive description of program inputs, processes, and outputs. These are compared to the staff's definition of the program. Discrepancies are noted and used to modify program definition such that it is congruent with program components.

Stage 2

In Stage 2 field observations are used to determine if the program is being implemented as intended. Discrepancy information is used to modify program implementation.

Stage 3

In Stage 3 it is determined whether program components are engendering the attainment of intermediate or "enabling" educational objectives as intended. It is a check on whether student behavior is changing as expected. Discrepancy information is used to modify either the program components or the objectives. This stage is similar to Scriven's (1967) concept of formative evaluation.

Stage 4

In Stage 4 it is determined whether program components are leading students to terminal program objectives. This stage often uses pre-post behavior change and, sometimes, control versus experimental comparisons. This stage is similar to what is called *summative* evaluation.

Stage 5

In Stage 5 (which is not always applicable) the experimental program is compared to a realistic alternative. An experimental or quasi-experimental design (Campbell & Stanley, 1966) is used to prove that program benefit is commensurate with cost.

The discrepancy evaluation model's components include agreeing on program standards, determining whether a discrepancy exists between aspects of a program and standards governing those aspects, and using discrepancy information to identify program weaknesses. Discrepancy information at each stage leads to a decision whether to proceed to the next stage or to alter either program standards or operations. Advancement to a subsequent stage is contingent on attaining congruence between operations and standards at the previous stage. If congruence is not possible program termination is recommended, although in practice this option is rarely chosen.

Stake's Concept of Evaluation

This concept (Stake, 1967) divides educational programs into three major concepts:

1. *Antecedents:* conditions existing prior to training that may be related to outcomes such as previous experience, interest, and aptitude.
2. *Transactions:* encounters of students with teacher, author with reader, parent with counselor or some educational activity such as the presentation of a film, a class discussion, or working a homework problem.
3. *Outcomes:* measures of the impact of instruction on students, teacher, administrators, parents, or others. These are usually measures of abilities, achievements, attitudes, aspirations, and so on. Outcomes can be immediate or long range, cognitive or affective, personal or communitywide.

To Stake, the descriptive phase of an evaluation involves (*a*) examining the logical contingencies that exist between intended antecedents, transactions, and outcomes; (*b*) determining the congruence between intended and observed antecedents, transactions, and outcomes; and (*c*) determining the empirical contingencies between observed antecedents, transactions, and outcomes. Illogical contingencies, lack of congruence, and, possibly, a failure to establish empirical contingencies aid in identifying program weaknesses (see also Stake, 1975a, b, for extensions and additions to these concepts).

The CIPP Evaluation Model

The CIPP model, developed by the Phi Delta Kappa Commission on Evaluation (Stufflebeam *et al.*, 1971), divides evaluation into four distinct strategies—Context evaluation, Input evaluation, Process evaluation, and Product evaluation, thus the acronym CIPP. The objective of context evaluation is to specify the operational context and to identify problems underlying needs. Input evaluation is concerned with identifying and assessing system capabilities. The objective of process evaluation is to identify defects in procedural design or implementation and to document project activities. The goal of product evaluation is to relate outcome information to objectives, context, and input and process information. If these relations are not specifiable, program weaknesses are suspected.

As can be noted from this overview, evaluation models represent very general aids or heuristics to conceptualizing evaluation designs. Other more technical models embodying more specificity have been developed for highly specialized, idiosyncratic applications, but these have limited capacity for generalization across educational settings (see Borich, 1974, for examples of more specific models).

Models as Heuristics

The desire among evaluators to identify models is understandable because there is the hope that once these models are established they can be used in a large variety of evaluation contexts. However, evaluation does not work that way. The techniques and methods brought to bear in an evaluation are a function of the problem, the clients for whom the evaluation is being conducted, and the amount of time and money that can be devoted to it. Although evaluation is certainly not an art form, evaluation models can communicate only a relatively small set of categories and constructs that might be useful in planning an evaluation. Thus, in part, the problem of choosing the correct evaluation model derives from a somewhat natural tendency to see an evaluation model as more than it is—as a methodology for actually conducting the evaluation—instead of a metamethodology or framework into which more specific constructs and methods must be plugged.

This false expectation for evaluation models has been known to lull educators, with the result that they do not give much thought to the evaluation process.

Further, when it is discovered that there is not a "tight" evaluation model available to provide needed evaluative data, it is often considered a shortcoming of the evaluator. Good evaluation procedures require the input of evaluation specialists early in program planning and development. The frustrations of educators over evaluation often stem from their own failure to consider evaluation issues throughout the educational program development process. Surprising to some is the fact that an evaluator is not an all-knowing guru with a magical bag of tricks (models) that will compensate for the failure to consider properly and plan evaluation activities early in program planning and development. Evaluation models do not provide answers but do provide useful guidelines or heuristics that can help organize thinking about how an evaluation should be conducted. This heuristic role for models, which has not always been appreciated in evaluation theory or practice, has been described by Kac (1969):

> The main role of models is not so much to explain and to predict—though ultimately these are the main functions of science—as to polarize thinking and to pose sharp questions. Above all, they are fun to invent and to play with, and they have a peculiar life of their own. The "survival of the fittest" applies to models even more than it does to living creatures. They should not, however, be allowed to multiply indiscriminately without real necessity or real purpose [p. 699].

Commonalities among Models

Among evaluators a common approach to obtaining useful evaluation data has been to develop their own models that borrow, where appropriate, from existing models in the literature, thus avoiding the model-selection problem. This is

TABLE 6.3
Some Commonalities among Three Evaluation Models

General concept	Provus	Stufflebeam	Stake
Transaction	Transaction		Transaction
Enabling Behavior	Enabling	Instrumental	Immediate
Input Evaluation	Stage 1	Stage 2	Antecedents
Product Evaluation	Stage 4	Stage 4	Outcomes
Process Evaluation	Installation Stage	Process Stage	Congruency
Program Definition	Program Definition Stage	Input Stage	Logical Contingency
Standards	Each Stage		Relative, Absolute
Objectives	Program Definition		Intents
Judgment	Stages 1–5		After Description
Context		Context	
Antecedents			Antecedents

Authors[a]

[a] Wording used by these authors appears in their respective columns.

6. Evaluation

TABLE 6.4
Characteristics of Three Evaluation Models

Characteristic[a]	CIPP	Stake	Provus
1. Purpose of evaluation	To make better, more defensible decisions	To describe and judge the merit of a thing	To uncover discrepancies between standards and performance
2. Implied role of evaluator	Information provider, serves the decision maker	Makes judgments about the effectiveness of a program from descriptions and standards	Compares standards with performance at various stages to revise or terminate program
3. Relationship to objectives	High	High "intents" are objectives	High "standards" are objectives
4. Types of evaluation activities proposed	Context, input Process, product	Description, judgment, logical and empirical contingency, congruency	Program definition, installation, process, product, cost-benefit
5. Unique constructs	Context	Logical contingency	Discrepancy
6. Relationship to decision maker	Integral	Unclear	High
7. Some criteria for judging evaluations	Did the evaluator collect context input, and process and product data?	Did the evaluator look for logical contingencies and collect judgment data?	Did the evaluator collect data and check for discrepancies within each stage?
8. Implications for evaluation designs	Mostly qualitative decisions except for product evaluation, where more quantitative strategies are applicable	Deals mostly with descriptions and judgments. Control group helpful but not necessary, judgments can be absolute	Comparisons between standards and performance at each stage are essential. Control group is needed for cost-benefit stage

[a] Constructs in this column were selected from Worthen and Sanders (1973).

generally the preferred alternative for educators who wish to assure the best match of program purpose and context to an evaluation model. Table 6.3 indicates the fundamental evaluation concepts shared by these three models and where they tie into each model. Table 6.4 provides a specification matrix indicating how each model addresses major considerations in choosing an evaluation design. Taken together these tables provide a means of judging the applicability of the component parts of these models to specific evaluation contexts. Further, they serve to illustrate the commonalities and distinctions encountered in studying established, well-known evaluation models. However, evaluators must be mindful that some models may not apply to the real world. Evaluators must never forsake the complexity of the real world for models that purport to describe it.

PROSPECTS FOR THE IMMEDIATE FUTURE: EMERGING TRENDS IN EDUCATIONAL EVALUATION

Since the initial ESEA legislation of 1965, some evaluators (Apple, 1974; Cooley & Lohnes, 1976; Cronbach & associates, 1980; Guba, 1978; Kaufman, 1972; Patton, 1980; Provus, 1971; Scriven, 1973; Stake, 1967, 1975a,b; and Stufflebeam *et al.*, 1971) have attempted to provide a stronger basis for evaluative theory and in so doing have implicitly or explicitly offered new definitions and theoretical bases for evaluation. These new conceptualizations build on previous ones and can be broken into four types or styles of evaluation: decision-oriented evaluation, value-oriented evaluation; naturalistic evaluation, and systems-oriented evaluation.

Decision-Oriented Evaluation

The PDK National Study Committee on Evaluation (Stufflebeam *et al.*, 1971) defines educational evaluation as "the process of delineating, obtaining, and providing useful information for judging decision alternatives [p. 40]." Provus (1971) similarly defines evaluation as "primarily a comparison of program performance with expected or designed programs, and secondly, among other things, a comparison of client performances with expected client outcomes [p. 12]." It can be seen that these decision-oriented definitions are heavily influenced by Tyler's (1950) congruence definition of evaluation but are of a much broader scope and are oriented toward a decision-tree logic. Inherent in this approach is an emphasis on comparing "what is" with "what should be" and using discrepancy data as a basis for decisions.

The major advantage of this approach is that by following the models associated with these definitions an evaluator is better able to provide the kinds of information desired by decision makers. Acceptance of the decision-oriented stance requires that clearly defined goals and objectives be elucidated prior to the collection of data, thus ensuring the presence of adequate criteria for judging the adequacy or relative merit of a program. The presence of prespecified criteria for judging program effectiveness may, however, be a disadvantage as the following discussion notes.

Value-Oriented Evaluation

Some authors in the field of evaluation have taken exception to the notion of decision-oriented evaluation and its implications for the conduct of evaluative research. The primary criticism of decision-oriented definitions is that evaluation

6. Evaluation

is viewed as a shared function. The role of the evaluator is to provide a decision maker with meaningful information; the decision maker makes the actual judgment of value or merit.

A value-oriented definition of evaluation stresses the value judgments made in evaluating educational programs and describes the act of judging merit or worth as central to the role of the evaluator. Worthen and Sanders (1973) define evaluation as "the determination of the worth of a thing [p. 19]." Scriven (1967) considers the evaluator who does not participate in the decision-making process as having abrogated his or her role. Stufflebeam *et al.* (1971) and Stake (1967) argue that by participating in decision making, the evaluator loses objectivity and hence, usefulness. Differences in these approaches are more than semantic for they imply different evaluation activities.

Within the decision-oriented approach, the evaluator is dependent on the decision maker for the way the decision context is to be defined and for the values and criteria that are to be used to judge program success (these are usually termed program intents, goals, or purposes). Cooley and Lohnes (1976) and Apple (1974) point out that there is no evidence to suggest that the decision maker is any more capable than the evaluator to define decision settings, alternatives, and values. Indeed there may be (and often are) social, institutional, and political pressures on the decision maker that may lead him or her to opt for evaluation procedures that skirt or ignore key evaluation issues. Apple (1974) makes the case that decision-oriented evaluation is a conservative practice not conducive to the acceptance of educational innovation but rather supportive of the status quo. Apple's point is that the limits of the decision-oriented evaluator's work are circumscribed largely by the already developed program, and therefore, the evaluator cannot deal with the issues, concerns, and objectives that predate the program and to which the program is supposed to be responding. Once the program is in place, the evaluator's role is to work with it (i.e., revise or modify it) regardless of whether it is the best means to the desired end.

Scriven (1974) argues that value judgments are a crucial part of all sciences, particularly methodological value judgments, and there is no reason to dismiss them in evaluation. He calls for goal-free evaluation, insisting that all aspects of an educational program should come under the scrutiny of the evaluator and that nothing should be taken as given from the client or agency soliciting evaluation expertise. The following illustrates his point:

> The goal-free evaluator is a hunter out alone and goes over the ground very carefully, looking for signs of any kind of game, setting speculative snares when in doubt. The goal-based evaluator, given a map that, supposedly, shows the main game trails, finds it hard to work quite so hard in the rest of the jungle [Scriven, 1973, p. 327].

Scriven argues that although knowledge of goals is necessary for effective planning and implementation, it is unnecessary in evaluation and may even blind the evaluator to important program effects.

Scriven (1973, 1974) and Apple (1974) also emphasized the social responsibility of the evaluator. Scriven offers the hypothetical example of an educational program aimed at increasing self-sufficiency. After some evaluative activity the evaluator discovers that in addition to fostering self-sufficiency, the program engenders contempt for the weak, sick, old, and congentially deformed. Scriven contends that these findings should count against the program although the program developer might be concerned only with the achievement of the announced and intended goal. The welfare of the consumer is considered a proper concern of the evaluator.

Apple (1974) puts forth a similar argument:

> The tendency in the face of the all-too-usual finding of "no significant difference" is to argue for better teacher training, for better science materials, for more sophisticated administrative systems designs, and the like. However, it may well be that more basic questions must be asked, that even the obligatory nature of the institution of schooling may need questioning, or that educators are asking the wrong kinds of questions.
>
> For example, much low achievement on the part of many students could be attributable to a symbolic dismissal of school itself as a meaningful institution. These students may perceive schools as relatively unresponsive to human sentiments. This is not to argue that schools should be done away with; to take such a position in a knowledge-based economy is somewhat unrealistic. It does signify, however, that educational problems are considerably more fundamental than educators may suppose, and it places responsibility on the individual educator to examine his or her own professional activity in a wider social and political context [pp. 28-29].

The implication of Apple's view for the evaluator has been elucidated by Becker (1974), a sociologist, who foreshadows how the evaluator who fails to give deference to the status quo is likely to be received by the decision maker:

> For a great variety of reasons, well-known to sociologists, institutions are refractory. They do not perform as society would like them to. Hospitals do not cure people; prisons do not rehabilitate prisoners; schools do not educate students. Since they are supposed to, officials develop ways of denying the failure of the institution to perform as it should and explaining those failures which cannot be hidden. An account of an institution's operation from the point of view of subordinates therefore casts doubt on the official line and may possibly expose it as a lie [p. 113].

Becker believes that any approach the sociologist or evaluator might take is inherently value laden and will implicitly support either the subordinate or superordinate point of view. Although this may be true, Becker's comment also raises the possibility that because of the efforts of decision makers to protect the status quo or allow only changes to be made that are congruent with the existing social, political, and organizational structure, evaluators implicitly may be designing evaluations that examine *only* the efficacy of these two points of view, avoiding all other points of view. Such a design is most likely when the goals and objectives for a program must be taken as "givens" and the evaluation designed around them.

Dewey's Conceptualization of Valuation

A cohesive value-oriented theoretical perspective on evaluation has recently been put forth by Cooley and Lohnes (1976). Their stance is based on the early work of John Dewey (Dewey, 1922, 1939) and borrows from Handy's work on the study of values in the behavioral sciences (Handy, 1969, 1970; Handy & Kurtz, 1964). Although the propositions of Cooley and Lohnes's theory of valuation are quite similar to and generally subsume those of Apple, Scriven, Worthen and Sanders, and others, they are put forth in a more direct fashion that has practical implications for some additions to evaluation methodology.

They assert that the value statements inherent in educational programs can themselves "be analyzed into a set of propositions subjectable to empirical investigation and that failure to perform such analyses in evaluation studies is inexcusable [Cooley & Lohnes, 1976, pp. 9-10]." They argue that the values that have guided educational practice have traditionally been determined by politics and custom, and that their validity has not been challenged by educational researchers. They find it curious that value propositions have evaded empirical scrutiny despite educational researchers' heavy emphasis on empiricism. Clear thinking about values in education is considered essential because educational practice is generally influenced by the value attached to desired educational goals. The alternative to rational inquiry into values is the determination of values on the basis of power that places the educational enterprise "at the mercy of special interest groups who commend values favorable to themselves as universals [p. 10]."

A basic premise to Dewey's notions about values and valuations was that values could be mistakenly viewed as absolutes, only if they were considered out of context. When considered *in context,* values lend themselves to elucidation as propositions about real entities (matters of fact), and the error of ascribing to them absolute or universal properties is thus avoided. The task of the evaluator becomes one of ascertaining whether value propositions inherent in an educational setting reflect only convention or tradition or whether they imply empirically testable relationships between educational means and ends.

Consider the hypothetical example in which an evaluator is called in to determine whether an in-service training program for teachers would increase the teachers's appreciation of the difficulties encountered by Spanish-speaking children in a predominantly English-speaking community. The foregoing discussion suggests that the evaluator should consider the context before proceeding. Did school administrators merely assume that a general in-service program would have this effect? Was pressure applied to administrators to improve teacher understanding of cultural differences? Was the program developed just because funds were available? Or because it was politically expedient for an elected school official? Or was it because a survey of teachers, parents, and students indicated that such an in-service program would be beneficial? The latter possibility is desirous but seldom encountered.

The value judgment explicit in the preceding example is that teachers need to have a better appreciation of the educational difficulties encountered by Spanish-speaking children. Also implicit is that the teachers presently are insensitive to these problems, that these students are being shortchanged in their education, and that the administration is quite concerned over this state of affairs. Each of these value propositions may or may not be true and is capable of being determined empirically.

Optimally, the need for such a program would be ascertained before it is developed and implemented. However, this is not always done. Evaluators are usually ignored in program planning, development, and often in implementation. This greatly limits the evaluation expertise that could be brought to bear in the educational setting. Evaluation has much to offer in terms of the "front end" work of educational programming, and significant inroads have been made in the area of needs assessment (see Kaufman, 1972, 1976, 1977). This issue will be discussed subsequently, but it is sufficient to say here that the notions of Dewey (1939), particularly as they are elucidated by Cooley and Lohnes (1976), provide theoretical justification for the involvement of evaluators early in an educational endeavor generally, and for the conduct of needs assessments particularly.

Another significant aspect of Dewey's theory of valuation is that he made no absolute distinction between means and ends. Any educational event or condition (e.g., a particular teaching strategy, student achievement in a particular area, and so on) can be viewed as occupying space on a continuum such that it is simultaneously an end to those events and conditions that preceded it and a means to those that follow. For example, in-service education is a means to improved teacher performance, which in turn is a means to successful educational settings, and so on. Dewey (1922) makes the further assertion that it is only when an end is conceptualized as a means that it is understood fully, appreciated, or even obtainable.

To some extent evaluators have taken means–end relationships into account by dividing outcomes into *enabling* (those that are prerequisite to the attainment of terminal outcomes) and *terminal* (those that are expected at program completion). Provus (1971) carried the means–end continuum one step further by articulating the concept of *ultimate* outcomes, those that are expected sometime after program completion. For the evaluator following Provus' model, terminal outcomes are also enabling in that they, too, become means to still other, ultimate ends. Cooley and Lohnes (1976) have argued that there can be no ultimate outcomes unless one appeals to some higher-order good. Hoban (1977) suggests that these higher-order ends might be chosen from among the values shared by our society such as affection, enlightenment, rectitude, respect, skill, power, wealth, and well-being; concepts with which a philosopher, not an evaluator, would be comfortable. Yet, it would be admirable for the evaluator to make explicit the means–end relationship that is implicit in every evaluation setting,

6. Evaluation

testing its logic and direction against some acknowledged higher-order good at least one step up on the means-end continuum.

The immediate problem for the evaluator is one of determining where to break into the means-end chain for purposes of data collection. Infinite regress is possible in either direction. Cooley and Lohnes suggest that focusing on the present resolves the dilemma. By striving to endow "present educational policies with a more unified meaning [p. 13]," the evaluator establishes a bounded context for evaluative activities. This context cannot, however, be too restrictive. Judging the relative value of several competing ends, for example, is influenced very much by each alternative's role as a means to subsequent ends, and it is through this logic that relative judgments of worth can be made.

> The question is always what kind of world we want. It is never the narrow one of how to maximize some fixed type of gain. . . . The very important principle is that clarification and transformation of aims or goals of education will be a result of, not a prerequisite for, evaluation research [Cooley & Lohnes, 1976, p. 14].

This approach to evaluation also emphasizes that both means and ends are subject to judgments of value. This position is compatible with Scriven's (1967) concepts of formative and summative evaluation. Because the differences between means and ends are seen as superficial, this theory of evaluation poses no restrictions on the evaluation activities that may be pursued in either the formative or summative mode and argues that both modes be used.

Another relevant point made by Cooley and Lohnes is that evaluation should not be conceptualized as a single product (usually a monograph) delivered at the conclusion of an evaluation. Rather, it should be viewed as a process in which the evaluator interacts with all other interested parties for an extended period of time. This allows for resolution of differences in opinion, viewpoint, and interests. Cooley and Lohnes (1976) consider this version of educational evaluation as "a process of conflict resolution through intelligent social deliberation [p. 16]." This approach suggests an interactive mode that allows the emergence of a common conceptualization of the educational program among all involved parties and fosters a consensus of program need, design, implementation, and evaluation.

This version of evaluation also stresses the education of all persons involved in evaluation. Put simply, the evaluation should be a learning experience for all involved. It is not unrealistic to expect that the various parties to an educational endeavor should come to understand more precisely what they are trying to do and why, how their educational programs achieve the results they do, and how each participant may facilitate individually the attainment of successively higher-level educational ends in a meaningful way. Thus, evaluation may be viewed as an educational procedure (or means) itself, which has as its potential ends-in-view a more harmonious, pleasant, and effective educational setting.

A final point about the value-oriented approach to evaluation is that it is inherently humanistic. Educators who consider themselves in the humanistic camp would be attracted to the value-oriented approach because it focuses on the total effects of a program and short- and long-range outcomes as part of a larger means-end continuum. Also, emphasis is placed on the empirical validation of goals and values, thus preventing them from being determined arbitrarily. The conceptualization of a means-ends continuum provides a foresightful vision of ultimate program effects. The goal-free bias inherent in the approach provides a rationale for being sensitive to unknown or unintended program effects. This theoretical view of evaluation has the potential for breaking the traditional mental set of evaluation and provides evaluators with a framework for providing information that can be used to reduce undesirable conditions in society when the amelioration of these conditions is stated as a higher-order end. Cooley and Lohnes (1976) state "what has been missing in controversies over the schools is convincing evidence which relates choices of educational practices to ends which society values, ends which satisfy needs. Generating such evidence is what evaluation is all about [p. 18]."

Cooley and Lohnes's (1976) rediscovery and updating of Dewey's principles of valuation represents a significant addition to evaluation. First, it provides logical and theoretical justification for evaluation concepts, designs, and activities recently called for by other authors in the field (Apple, 1974; Borich, 1979; Kaufman, 1972, 1977; Scriven, 1967, Worthen & Sanders, 1973; Borich & Jemelka, in press). This justification has been sorely lacking. Unguided by a prudential theoretical basis, evaluation has moved in directions not always conducive to the ultimate improvement of educational quality. Second, this theoretical perspective has practical implications for the ways evaluation should be conducted, which are in some ways at variance with traditional approaches. Inherent in this perspective is a call for new methods and new concepts in the field of evaluation, leading to a considerably expanded and more flexible role for the evaluator. Third, this approach is concerned ultimately with the evaluator's responsibility for "doing the right thing" in terms of educational planning and programming and offers a perspective for moving in that direction. This higher-order orientation has not always been present in evaluation theory or practice.

Naturalistic Evaluation[3]

One of the new methods and new concepts implied by Cooley and Lohnes's updating of Dewey's theory of valuation is that of naturalistic evaluation. An outgrowth of ecological psychology (Barker, 1965, 1968), naturalistic inquiry stands in contradistinction to the more formal models of evaluation previously

---

[3]We are indebted to Guba (1978), Willems & Rauch (1969), and Patton (1980) for much of the material on which this section is based. Readers are directed to those works for more on this topic.

6. Evaluation

discussed. Naturalistic evaluation has been referred to as an alternative to conventional evaluation methodology, breaking ties with both traditional forms of instrumentation and traditional methods of data analysis.

Although many definitions of naturalistic inquiry have been offered, Guba (1978) has suggested that naturalistic inquiry differs from other modes of evaluation by its relative position along two dimensions: (a) the degree to which the investigator manipulates conditions antecedent to the inquiry; and (b) the degree of constraint imposed on the behavior of subjects involved in the inquiry. Accordingly, naturalistic inquiry has been defined as "any form of research that aims at discovery and verification through observation [Willems & Rauch, 1969, p. 81]"; as "slice-of-life episodes documented through natural language representing as closely as possible how people feel, what they know, how they know it, and what their concerns, beliefs, perceptions and understandings are [Wolf & Tymitz, 1976-1977, cited in Guba, 1978, p. 3]"; and as "evaluation which attempts to arrive at naturalistic generalizations on the part of the audience; which is aimed at non-technical audiences like teachers or the public at large; which uses ordinary language; which is based on informal everyday reasoning; and which makes extensive use of arguments which attempts to establish the structure of reality [House, 1977, p. 37]." In addition naturalistic studies have been identified by Sechrest (1969) as ones that "(a) do not require the cooperation of the subject; (b) do not permit the subject's awareness that he is being measured or treated in any special way; and (c) do not change the phenomenon being measured [cited in Guba, 1978, p. 5]."

In theory, a naturalistic study consists of a series of observations that are, alternately, directed at discovery and verification. This process supposedly leads to successive reorientations on the part of the investigator toward the phenomena being observed and to further discovery.

Unlike formal evaluation models, the naturalistic evaluator approaches data collection (observation) with a minimum of preconceived categories or notions of what will be seen—as though the behavioral phenomena were being observed for the first time. Any effort to manipulate any part of the program prior to observation or to constrain the behavior of those being observed would reduce the "naturalism" of the method. How data are tabulated and analyzed in a naturalistic study is left up to the investigator and no "best" method is identified, although invariably it includes some form of unstructured observation followed by a piecing together of relationships, patterns, or consistencies in the data, which are used to further channel and focus subsequent observations. Data-recording methods may include impressionistic accounts or ethnographic records[4] of the phenomenon observed. From these accounts more structured

---

[4] A type of observational record associated with the field of anthropology in which behavior is recorded in relation to the context in which it occurs and is ascribed meaning only in relation to that context.

categories of behavior are derived, which then are expanded and verified through still further observation.

Naturalistic inquiry is appropriately considered by its proponents as a tool, technique, or method of viewing behavior and is not viewed exclusively as a mode of evaluation. Thus, as a general methodology—or perhaps metamethodology—its basic tenets would appear compatible with other forms or stages of evaluation that do not classify as experiments (i.e., where conditions are not prearranged and subject responses are not constrained by the activities of the evaluator; e.g., goal-free evaluation). Naturalistic inquiry need not be considered an all-exclusive alternative to conventional models of evaluation when these other forms of inquiry do not constrain unduly the naturalism of the inquiry. Conducive to this line of reasoning is the idea that naturalism is always considered a matter of degree, making trade-offs and multiple approaches to evaluation within this perspective possible.

The extent and manner to which naturalistic inquiry has become inculcated in the present-day thinking of evaluators is of considerable interest. The influence of naturalistic inquiry in this regard has been significant and represents what might be described as the underlying movement away from conventional evaluation models and more formalistic definitions of evaluation—namely, the measurement, congruency, and applied research definitions. Oddly enough, it is a return of sorts to the visitation-type definition of evaluation that was rejected by many evaluators for being too subjective and impressionistic. It represents in spirit, if not method, the value-oriented approach to evaluation. Value-oriented writers such as Dewey, Scriven, and Apple would find solace in the fact that naturalistic inquiry, more than most other methodological perspectives, is likely to yield data unconstrained by preconceived notions about what the program is or is not supposed to do. This perspective seems congenial to the discovery of means-end relationships (Dewey, 1939), side effects and unanticipated program outcomes (Scriven, 1973), and fundamental issues that question the very rationale on which a program is based (Apple, 1974).

Although they did not embrace naturalistic inquiry directly, some evaluators have turned to this approach as a result of what are perceived to be serious limitations to conventional evaluation methods, namely, (*a*) conventional models have been too restrictive in the types of data that can be observed and therefore may be insensitive to unique and unexpected program outcomes; (*b*) conventional evaluation may at times actually contrive data by manipulating dimensions of a program that have no practical value in the real world, and (*c*) conventional modes of evaluation, particularly those ascribed to either the measurement or congruency definitions of evaluation, may actually constrain through formal instrumentation the responses expected of subjects. In response to these limitations several evaluators have developed ''alternative models'' or approaches to evaluation that embody the elements of naturalistic inquiry. These models do not depend on the arrangement of antecedent conditions or constraint

6. Evaluation

of subject response; hence the basic conditions for naturalistic inquiry are met. These models, taken from Guba (1978), are reviewed briefly in the following discussion. (For further explication of naturalistic inquiry see Guba, 1978; Patton, 1980; and Willems & Rauch, 1969.)

The Responsive Model

The first model with some relationship to naturalistic inquiry is the responsive model developed by Stake (1975a,b). The responsive model focuses on important issues and concerns pertaining to a program. According to Stake (1975b), evaluation is responsive if it "orients more directly to program activities than to program intents; responds to audience requirements for information; and if the different value perspectives are referred to in reporting the success and failure of the program [p. 14]." The primary purpose of responsive evaluation is to respond to audience requirements for information and to bring to the foreground different value perspectives that might be held by different audiences. Its methodology, like naturalistic inquiry itself, is nonconstraining. Stake (1975a) describes it in the following terms:

> To do a responsive evaluation, the evaluator conceives of a plan of observations and negotiations. He arranges for various persons to observe the program and with their help prepares brief narratives, portrayals, product displays, graphs, etc. He finds out what is of value to the audiences and gathers expressions of worth from various individuals whose point of view differ. Of course, he checks the quality of his records: he gets program personnel to react to the accuracy of the portrayals; and audience members to react to the relevance of his findings. He does much of this informally—iterating and keeping a record of action and reaction. He chooses media accessible to his audiences to increase the likelihood and fidelity of communication. He might prepare a final written report, he might not—depending on what he and his clients have agreed on [cited in Guba, 1978, pp. 34-35].

These activities are carried out in a series of steps that may be described as (*a*) talking with clients, program staff, and audiences; (*b*) identifying program scope; (*c*) providing an overview of program activities; (*d*) discovering purposes and concerns; (*e*) conceptualizing issues and problems; (*f*) identifying data needs relevant to the issues; (*g*) selecting observers and instruments (if any); (*h*) observing designated antecedents, transactions, and outcomes; (*i*) thematizing or preparing portrayals in case studies; (*j*) winnowing and matching issues to audiences; (*k*) formatting for audience use; and (*l*) assembling formal reports (if any).

The Judicial Model

A second evaluation model with some relationship to naturalistic inquiry is the judicial model. Developed by Wolf (1975), Owens (1973), and Levine (1974), the judicial model is patterned after the administrative hearing in a court of law. The purpose of the judicial model is to illuminate, inform, and adjudicate issues related to the object or activity being evaluated. Advocates or counsels take opposite views with respect to an issue and argue as convincingly as possible their side of the issue. Jury and judge hear testimony from "witnesses" and the presentation of facts regarding the issue, then offer their opinion as to the merit or worth of the program and their recommendations for improvement. Like the judicial process itself, this approach to evaluation assumes that "truth" is more likely to emerge in an adversary setting with two evaluators "pitted" against one another than in the case of a single evaluator using conventional evaluation models and data-collection methods.

Generally, the following steps are employed in the judicial model:

>   1. *Issue generation:* The issues are identified through "fact-finding interviews" with samples of the audiences involved, as in the case of the Stake responsive model.
>   2. *Issue selection:* The purpose of this stage is to delimit the number of issues and to prioritize them, so that they may be manageable in a hearing format.
>   3. *Preparation of formal arguments:* Each counsel or advocate team prepares formal arguments related to the selected issues. Available evaluation or other data may be used (to be introduced as "exhibits" in the hearing stage), and additional evidence may be collected, particularly evidence in the form of depositions from witnesses. Additionally, selected witnesses may be asked to give testimony at the hearing itself.
>   4. *Pre-hearing discovery sessions:* Each advocate team reviews the major argument it intends to make and discloses the main features of its "evidence" for the other. Since the hearing is not a "trial" in the conventional sense, but an effort to determine "truth" as precisely as possible, each side shares its findings with the other so that the hearing may be as comprehensive as possible. In addition, the advocate teams decide on ground rules, e.g., number of witnesses to be called and criteria for determining admissability of evidence.
>   5. *The hearing:* Modeled on an actual courtroom process, the hearing involves an administrative officer and a "jury" or hearing panel. After hearing the evidence, the jury carries out whatever tasks the advocate teams previously agreed to assign to it, which usually involves at least the determination of findings (which may include judgments of worth) and the making of selected recommendations [Guba, 1978, p. 36–37].

The Transactional Model

A third evaluation model with some relationship to naturalistic inquiry is the transactional model described by Rippey (1973). This model supposedly differs from conventional models in that it deals directly with management conflicts and institutional change brought about by the implementation of a program, using what its authors call "open systems theory." Transactional evaluation is a method that studies institutional disruptions brought about by the program and works to ameliorate these disruptions through strategies for conflict management.

Transactional evaluation has five phases (Talmadge, 1975):

>   1. *The initial phase:* Pre-existing unrest or some other troublesome situation exists. A meeting is set up of interested parties under the direction of a "neutral" evaluator working in a nonjudgmental atmosphere.

2. *Instrumentation phase:* During this phase, a "Transactional Evaluation Instrument" (TEI) is developed whose purpose is to provide the evaluator with insight into the perceptions and expectations of various interest groups. The instrument also provides a forum for the sharing of opinions among the groups. The TEI is developed and administered in group sessions, during which (*a*) the evaluator initially formulates issues on the basis of general expressions from the group; (*b*) participants are asked to re-express opinions about them; (*c*) the most representative and divergent of the written responses are carefully worded into items that can be rated on a scale from "strongly agree' to "strongly disagree;" (*d*) the instrument is administered to the group; and (*e*) responses are examined.

3. *Program development:* The program is redefined to reflect those goals and values on which the group can achieve some consensus.

4. *Program monitoring:* Various groups agree to assume responsibility for implementing and monitoring the developed program.

5. *Recycling:* As new conflicts emerge, the entire process is recycled to whatever phase is appropriate [cited in Guba, 1978, p. 38].

The Connoisseurship Model

A fourth model with some relationship to naturalistic inquiry is the connoisseurship model developed by Eisner (1975). This approach views educational evaluation as a form of criticism. In Eisner's view, criticism depends upon connoisseurship—or the private act of appreciating and sensing the subtle qualities of an object or activity. "Critical guideposts" used to conduct the evaluation are essential elements of the connoisseurship approach. These guideposts represent the personal values and concepts formed from tradition, experience, and theories about the standards for judging the object or activity. Guba (1978) characterizes connoisseurs as:

> persons with refined perceptual apparatus, knowledge of what to look for, and a backlog of previous relevant experience. They have the ability to recognize skills, form, and imagination and to perceive the intentions and leading conceptions underlying the entity being evaluated. In effect, because of these characteristics, the connoisseur is himself the evaluation instrument. Having made his judgment, he communicates the qualities that constitute the entity being evaluated, its significance, and the quality of experience engendered by interaction with it, often through the use of rich metaphors [p. 39].

The Illumination Model

Perhaps most similar to naturalistic inquiry is the illumination model developed by Parlett and Hamilton (1977). This approach to evaluation relies heavily on open-ended observations (but also questionnaires, interviews, and tests) to continuously record ongoing events to identify (*a*) critical and nonobvious characteristics of a program; (*b*) the tacit assumptions underlying it; (*c*) interpersonal relationships affecting it; and (*d*) complex realities surrounding the program. In the authors' words:

> Illuminative evaluation takes account of the wider contexts in which education programs function. Its primary concern is with description and interpretation rather than measurement

and prediction. It stands unambiguously within the alternative methodological paradigm. The aims of illuminative evaluation are to study the innovatory program: how it operates; how it is influenced by the various school situations in which it is applied; what those directly concerned regard as its advantages and disadvantages; and how students' intellectual tasks and academic experiences are most affected. It aims to discover and document what it is like to be participating in the scheme, whether as teacher or pupil, and, in addition, to discern and discuss the innovation's most significant features, recurrent concomitants, and critical processes. In short, it seeks to address and to illuminate a complex array of questions [cited in Guba, 1978, p. 40].

Illuminative evaluation is carried out in three stages:

1. Initial observations for the purpose of familiarization with day-to-day reality of the setting(s), largely in the manner of social anthropologists or natural historians
2. More sustained and intensive inquiry into a number of common incidents, recurring trends, and issues frequently raised in discussion
3. Efforts to seek general principles underlying the organization of the program, determine patterns of cause and effect within its operation, and place individual findings within a broader explanatory context [Guba, 1978, p. 40].

Summary of Naturalistic Models

All five of the models presented qualify as naturalistic insofar as they adhere to the two primary conditions set forth by proponents of the naturalistic method: (*a*) they do not manipulate conditions antecedent to the inquiry; and (*b*) they pose minimal constraints on the behavior of participants involved in the inquiry. Although it is always a matter of degree, these five models meet these conditions to a greater extent than do most conventional approaches to evaluation.

However, it can also be noted that the five models are somewhat vague about the precise manner in which observations are to be conducted and the way in which data resulting from them are to be converted into meaningful statements that serve some client group. Conspicuously lacking both in summary and in original documents describing these models are descriptions of the processes by which responsive, judicial, transactional, connoisseurship, and illuminatory accounts of behavioral phenomena are gleaned of their most significant content and communicated to audiences who desire answers to specific questions, some of which may have been fashioned prior to program observation. If naturalistic methods are to enjoy widespread use, the criteria by which value and importance are bestowed on the data may need further delineation within the context of each model. The absence of this delineation may result in what Kaplan (1964) has called "the dogma of immaculate perception [p. 385]." In explaining the importance of values in directing what the inquirer is looking for, Kaplan compares a value-free inquiry (or one that limits itself just to describing what objectively happens) to the position of the esthetes at the turn of the century, who viewed art as a matter of pure form or decoration, "at the cost of making of it an idle song for an idle hour [p. 385]," with no significance for anyone but themselves.

We may also note that the concept of naturalistic inquiry was first introduced as an alternative methodology to present-day conceptions of experimental design and not as an approach to serve the ends of evaluation. Although the authors of naturalistic models have done an exemplary job of making this relationship appealing, the match between naturalistic inquiry and evaluation may not be as great as it might seem at first. The decision-oriented context in which most evaluations occur is not always conducive to the hypothesis-generating and theory-building purposes for which naturalistic inquiry is best suited. Some audiences for evaluation studies may appreciate being confronted with "issues" and "concerns." But other audiences may not be so appreciative if specific questions requiring formal measurement and analysis are left unanswered simply because they require altering antecedent conditions or constraining subject responses. It is because of the diversity of what clients desire and expect of an evaluation that the word "supplementary" rather than "alternative" might be used to place naturalistic methods in their most appropriate framework.

Finally, it is important to note the perspective or mind-set the naturalistic inquirer adopts when studying behavior. This perspective, or *weltanschauung*, (world-view) has been captured aptly by Louch (1966), who, in the context of describing the role of explanation in the study of human action, provides a good portrayal of the naturalistic inquirer and the commonality between the naturalistic and value-oriented approaches to evaluation. In the words of Louch the world of the naturalistic inquirer is one in which:

> Behavior cannot be explained by a methodology borrowed from the physical science. For him, [the naturalistic inquirer] what is needed . . . is not measurement, experiment, prediction, formal argument but appraisal, detailed description, reflection and rhetoric. . . . Human action is a matter of appraising the rightness or appropriateness of what is attempted or achieved by men in each set of circumstances. Its affinities are with morality rather than with the causal or statistical accounts appropriate to the space–time framework of the physical sciences. Its methods are akin to the deliberations and judgments in the law rather than the hypotheses and experiments of physics [cited in van Gigch, 1978, p. 220].

Systems-Oriented Evaluation

While much of the evaluation literature of the past focused on distinctions between evaluation and research and the insensitivity of the latter to detecting the effects of innovative programs, conceptual models were being developed interconnecting the planning, development, and evaluation process. These models, although not distinct from other approaches in their call to infuse the discipline of evaluation with a broader methodology than research, were distinct in their efforts to include within the domain of evaluation, methodologies to improve the process by which programs were being planned and developed. To accomplish this purpose various systematic approaches to instructional development were introduced posing "front-end" or predevelopment tasks for the evaluator, unifying and integrating the previously separate processes of program planning, development, and evaluation.

Kaufman (1972), in the first modern text dealing with educational planning from a systems perspective, defined *system* as "the sum total of parts working independently and working together to achieve required results or outcomes, based on needs [p. 1]"; and the *systems approach* as "a process by which needs are identified, problems selected, requirements for problem solution are identified, solutions are chosen from alternatives, methods and means are obtained and implemented, results are evaluated, and required revisions to all or part of the system are made so that the needs are eliminated [p. 2]."

The particular systems approach articulated by Kaufman represents a type of logical problem solving for identifying and resolving educational problems. Central to this approach is the process of educational planning.

One example of the systems approach applied to planning and evaluation is the *Interservice Procedures for Instructional Systems Development*[5] (U.S. Army Training and Doctrine Command, 1975), a five-volume compendium on the "what-to-do" aspects of instructional systems development. Although it was developed for the military, this work represents a broad application of the systems approach to training that is useful in virtually any type of setting. The Interservice Procedures are divided into five separate and distinct phases to be carried out successively. These phases, as described in the executive summary of the project, are

> *Phase I, ANALYZE.* This phase deals with procedures for defining what jobs are, breaking these into statements of tasks, and using numerical techniques to combine the best judgment of experienced professionals to select tasks for training. Phase I also presents processes for construction of job performance measures and the sharing of occupational and training information within and among client groups. It provides a rationale for deciding whether tasks should be trained in schools, on the job, or elsewhere, and also requires consideration of the interaction between training and job performance.
>
> *Phase II, DESIGN.* This phase deals with the design aspects of the training program within selected settings. Design is considered in the architectural sense in which the form and specifications for training are laid down in careful detail. Phase II reviews the considerations relating to entry behavior of two separate kinds: general ability and prior experience. A rationale is presented for establishing requirements based on the realistic evaluation of both of these factors.
>
> *Phase III, DEVELOPMENT.* This phase refers to the actual preparation of instruction. Determinations are made about how the students will be managed, the kinds of learning experiences they will have, the activities in which they will engage, and the form and

---

[5]Developed at the Center for Educational Technology, Florida State University, under the directorship of R. K. Branson (see also Branson, 1978, for a review of this approach).

6. Evaluation

content of the instructional delivery system. Techniques are presented for the careful review and adaptation of existing materials. Procedures for the systematic design of instruction which can be delivered in a variety of media are also included. Phase III concludes with a procedure for testing and evaluating the instruction to insure that its performance meets expectations.

Phase IV, IMPLEMENTATION. This phase treats the necessary steps to implement the instruction according to the plan developed in Phase III. Two steps highlight Phase IV, that of training the staff in the procedures and problems unique to the specific instruction and actually bringing the instruction on-line and presenting it. The Phase IV effort continues as long as there is a need for the instruction.

Phase V, CONTROL. This phase deals with procedures and techniques for maintaining instructional quality control standards and for providing data from internal and external sources upon which revision decisions can be based. Data collection, evaluation of the data, and decision making about the implications of the data represent the three principal functions described in Phase V. Emphasis is placed on the importance of determining whether the trainees are learning what was intended, and upon determining whether what they have learned is of benefit in carrying out post-training responsibilities [p. 4-6].

These phases describe the functions necessary to analyze instructional needs; design, develop, and implement instruction; and maintain quality control of instruction. Of primary importance is the sequential relationship of functions within and between phases, giving this model its systems perspective.

In a similar manner, Dick and Carey (1978) integrate the processes of planning, development, and evaluation into a ten-step approach. These steps are: identifying instructional goals, conducting an instructional analysis, identifying entry behaviors and characteristics, writing performance objectives, developing criterion referenced tests, developing an instructional strategy, developing and selecting instruction, designing and conducting formative evaluation, revising instruction, and conducting summative evaluation. Their procedure is described in some 200 pages and 10 chapters, which explicate each of these processes and integrate them into a single model. Other approaches have added still further to the language and conceptual repertoire of the systems approach, requiring the evaluator to conduct needs assessments, prepare program specifications, perform task and learner analyses, and define human and material resources. These activities are more than simply terms and concepts, they represent responsibilities that the systems-oriented evaluator is expected to perform.

Central to the systems approach is the blending of the humanistic and behavioristic principles of psychology. The systems approach is considered humanistic insofar that it requires measurement of the needs of those the program is to serve. Through the conduct of needs assessments, the systems approach identifies discrepancies between "what is desired" and "what exists" and uses these discrepancies to provide direction for program development. Later, through program evaluation, the systems approach determines whether the desired state actually has been achieved. Needs assessments play a particularly central role in the systems approach by linking program design to extant needs for the purpose of improving program performance.

The systems approach derives its concepts and tools from a wide variety of disciplines including computer science, engineering, management science, and economics. These tools are employed in the systems approach with the primary purpose of assuring that the program does what it is supposed to do. Accordingly, a systems approach to program development may specify somewhat elaborate procedures for assuring the accuracy and representativeness of the objectives on which a program is to be based; for analyzing the characteristics of learners and the learning task; and for monitoring the development process itself. These responsibilities have resulted in the blending into a single approach of concepts previously limited to either the field of instructional development or to evaluation. This representation in a single approach of what were two previously distinct specialties has not been without its problems.

A question of some importance is whether the evaluator, especially formative evaluator, should be distinct from the developer; or whether these roles represent responsibilities that can be fulfilled by the same individual working within the context of a systems approach. Some evaluators and developers warn that when role distinctions become unclear, as when an evaluator defines program requirements, conducts needs-assessments, and performs learner and task analyses, the program may suffer from *co-option*. Co-option refers to the situation in which the evaluator is so immersed in the values, feelings, and intents of the developer that evaluations are no longer an objective guide to program effectiveness. On the other hand, some evaluators and developers (Butman & Fletcher, 1974; Grobman, 1968) contend that development is tied so closely to evaluation that any separation of roles or functions is at best an artificial distinction that may detract from, rather than add to, the development process. The popularity of "third party" or independent summative evaluations has dissipated to some extent the differences between these perspectives, especially when they are conducted in addition to formative assessments of program effectiveness and when the third-party evaluator has *not* been provided knowledge of the outcome of the previous formative evaluation.

Although little has been written about the role and function of the evaluator within the context of program planning, development, and evaluation, it is not uncommon for a program to be planned and developed in such a way as to either encourage or preclude a certain kind of evaluation; or that once the program has been developed the evaluator is forced to take a certain approach to evaluation, regardless of its responsiveness to clients' needs. The systems approach argues, however, that the evaluator must serve critical functions early in the development process to prevent just such an eventuality. Some of these early evaluation activities are addressed in Part IV. For the systems approach see also Banathy, 1968; Briggs, 1977; Davis, Alexander, & Yelon, 1975; and Interservice Procedures for Instructional Systems Development, 1975.

6. Evaluation

PROSPECTS FOR THE 1980s AND 1990s: IMPLICATIONS OF THE EMERGING TRENDS

The foregoing review of emerging trends has attempted to touch on current evaluation theory and practice. This review has many implications for developers and evaluators of educational programs. These implications can be generalized to a variety of educational contexts whether they are elementary and secondary schools, colleges, graduate schools, inservice education, or military training.

The purpose of this concluding section is to present several major implications of the emerging trends. These implications will be discussed generally and then illustrated with a specific advancement or change in evaluation practice, which (in our opinion) is likely to occur in the not-too-distant future. Whereas the trends discussed previously represent an analysis of where evaluation is heading, the following implications represent signs or examples of the type of changes or advances that might be expected to result from these trends. These implications fall into the areas of systems approaches, naturalistic observation, needs assessment, policy assessment, and the role of the evaluator.

Implications for a Systems Approach

One implication of the emerging trends is that there is a need for a coherent, integrated approach to program planning, development, and evaluation. Arguments have been presented that these activities can be seen as component parts of a unitary process, rather than conceptualized as separate and distinct activities. Program planning, especially, can be conducted with an eye toward program development (which it usually is) and program evaluation (which it usually is not). This implication can be reduced to a call for the application of a systems approach to instructional planning, development, and evaluation.

Kaufman (1972) proposes that a systems approach to evaluation requires the application of a variety of tools and techniques borrowed from the fields of computer science, cybernetics, engineering, management, and operations research. These include simulations, operational gaming, the Program Evaluation and Review Technique (PERT), the Critical Path Method (CPM), the Delphi technique, and other systems analysis techniques. These tools are essentially modeling approaches to problem solving that fall under the rubric of systems analysis. Although some of these modeling approaches have a distinct format and purpose, Kaufman (1972) advocates the use of graphic models for the general purpose of "displaying (or describing) a system and its components and subsystem relationships in a simple, 'at-a-glance' format [p. 16]."

Some recent developments in the field of general systems theory (Churchman, 1968) have suggested that modeling as a means of studying a system may be useful for planning, developing, and evaluating an educational program. Without guidelines on how systems modeling can be used to study educational programs, however, it is unlikely that the resulting models will be either communicative or generalizable across settings or applications. One implication for the not-too-distant future is the emergence of specific systems-modeling techniques for decomposing or breaking down an instructional program (system) into its component parts prior to evaluation. Bloom *et al.* (1971) have already called for the use of such a technique, called a *behavior-by-content* matrix (or table of specifications), for understanding the nature of a developing program and guiding its evaluation. These authors suggest that a breakdown of the learning task "provides the specifications for formative evaluation and other procedures [p. 17]."

Ross, Brackett, and Schoman (Ross, 1977; Ross & Brackett, 1976; Ross & Schoman, 1977) have suggested that a good system-modeling technique should have certain specifiable properties. Although the properties posited by these authors refer to the development and portrayal of very complex systems, they are also applicable to the development and evaluation of educational programs. Their recommendations, with some extensions and modifications to program evaluation, are as follows:

1. Programs are best studied by building a model that expresses an in-depth understanding of the program, sufficiently precise to serve as the basis for program development and evaluation.
2. Analysis of any program should be topdown (moving from general to specific outcomes), modular (take into consideration all component parts), and hierarchic (determine how the parts are tied together, i.e., structured).
3. Program activities should be represented by a model that shows program components, their interfaces, and their place in the hierarchic structure.
4. The model-building technique must represent behaviors the program is to produce, activities the program is to provide, and relationships among behaviors and activities.
5. All planning, design, development, and evaluation decisions should be shown on the program model, which is open to all interested parties for review.

These authors have developed a specific technique, the Structured Analysis and Design Technique (SADT), which meets these requirements and is applicable to the planning and evaluation of instructional programs (see also Borich, 1979, and Borich & Brackett, 1978, for a review of this technique).

Another implication of general systems theory for program evaluation is that a program cannot be understood fully unless its relationship to the system in which it operates is known. Systems theory suggests that the behavioral changes often attributed to an instructional program are not caused by the program alone but the interaction of the program with a milieu of variables comprising the environment of which it is a part. Simply put, systems theory suggests that more forces are at

6. Evaluation

work than the program in effecting program outcomes and the more these other forces can be revealed through specific tools, such as program modeling, the greater the possibility of understanding and evaluating the program. Although sometimes vague and illusive, instructional programs can be described in such a way (i.e., more precisely) that acknowledges the complex schema of person-to-person, person-to-environment, and environment-to-environment relationships in which they operate. To this end, system analytic tools generally and system-modeling techniques specifically can be useful in assisting evaluators in identifying the contextual variables that moderate the effectiveness of instructional programs.

Implications for Naturalistic Inquiry

It is at this juncture that naturalistic inquiry and systems theory became reciprocally supporting concepts. Naturalistic inquiry, primarily procedures for observing behavior in naturally occurring settings, can provide a general tool with which the evaluator can identify and ultimately record the contextual factors that moderate a program's effectiveness. Our increasing awareness of the multidimensionality of the environment in which programs operate has led to the development of general methods by which this environment can be better understood. Naturalistic inquiry provides one such method for accomplishing this.

Recent advances in the behavioral and social sciences have made it increasingly difficult to understand important concepts or principles without viewing the complex whole of which they are a part. The social and behavioral sciences have, in manner of speaking, run out of simple solutions. Or, more correctly, they have found that simple solutions to old problems are inadequate in light of recent discoveries and advancements, which have all but nullified many "simple" views of instruction and behavior. Complexity is a fact of life and problem-solving techniques that recognize this multidimensional environment seem particularly timely. This is why simplistic views of educational programs may no longer be credible and why naturalistic inquiry coupled with systems theory can be a useful tool for describing a program in terms of the larger system, program, or organizational unit of which it is a component part. It is this exteroceptive—as opposed to interoceptive—view that brings systems theory and the aims of naturalistic inquiry together. Programs should not only be designed but also evaluated from a viewpoint that considers the effects larger systems (programs) have on smaller systems (programs). In the language of the systems approach, exteroceptive analyses trace program effects to contexts not included in formal models of evaluation. These models commonly provide only for interoceptive analyses that trace program effects within the bounded context of the program under consideration.

Finally, it is important, but unfortunate, to note that many programs are designed, operated, and evaluated as though they were ends in themselves without considering that all programs are intended to satisfy the requirements of some larger system or program of which they are a part—just as the objectives of a child's homework assignment are determined by the objectives of the unit of which it is a part; and the unit objectives determined by the subject matter of which it is a part; and the subject matter determined by the objectives of the community who determine what is "best" for their children. Here is where the means-end relationship, which often goes unnoticed with conventional evaluation models, could be uncovered and evaluated with the systems approach. Systems theory and naturalistic inquiry provide a basis for identifying the means-end continuum, determining what program goals (ends) are not ends-in-themselves but means to still other ends, and whether the means actually justify the ends.

Consistent with the above notions are the following claims commonly ascribed to the systems approach (adapted from van Gigch, 1978):

1. The systems approach is indispensible in considering the relationships of a particular problem to its environmental conditions and in identifying the factors and variables that affect the program.
2. The systems approach brings out in the open inconsistencies of objectives when treating the various agents that play a part in programs of the same system.
3. The systems approach provides a useful framework in which the performance of the various systems, subsystems, and the whole system can be tied together.
4. The systems approach and its attendant methodology can be used to redesign the existing system and to compare and test the relative worth of alternative programs within the system [p. 30].

Implications for Needs Assessment

A third implication of the emerging trends derives from both the value-oriented and systems-oriented approaches to evaluation. This implication is that needs assessment is an evaluation activity that should be conducted at all stages of program development. Kaufman (1972, 1977) gives top priority to the needs assessment approach to evaluation. Indeed, in Kaufman's recent writing on systems (Kaufman, 1977), six types of needs studies were posited. The functions of these studies are to: identify programs based upon needs (Alpha-type), determine solution requirements and identify solution alternatives (Beta-type), select solution strategies from among alternatives (Gamma-type), implement program (Delta-type), determine performance effectiveness (Epsilon-type), and revise as required (Zeta-type).

To Kaufman, a systems approach is a sequential series (Alpha-Zeta) of needs assessments—a view that is consistent with a systems orientation. This series is presented in Table 6.5 along with some planning and evaluation tools (Kaufman, 1977) that are associated with each type.

Another noteworthy aspect of Kaufman's (1977) approach is that it is hierar-

6. Evaluation

TABLE 6.5
Planning and Evaluation Tools Available for Performing Each of the Functions of a System Approach[a]

Type of needs assessment	System approach function	Possible planning tools associated with each function
1. Alpha-type	Identify problem based upon needs.	Needs assessment (Alpha-type)
2. Beta-type	Determine solution requirements and identify solution alternatives.	Systems analysis, needs analysis, behavioral objectives, front-end analysis, performance analysis.
3. Gamma-type	Select solution strategies from among alternatives.	Systems analysis, cost-effectiveness analysis, PPB(E)S, simulation, operations research–analysis, methods–means selection techniques, gaming.
4. Delta-type	Implement	PERT, CPM, management by objectives management by exception
5. Epsilon-type	Determine performance effectiveness	Testing, assessment, auditing
6. Zeta-type	Revise as required	Discrepancy analysis

[a] After Kaufman (1977).

chical with respect to making faulty assumptions and achieving significant educational change. Kaufman states that the evaluator may start at any level of needs assessment but the further from the top (Alpha-type) the level of entry, the lower the probability of actually achieving a meaningful change in educational practice and the greater the probability of making errors caused by faulty assumptions. Value-oriented definitions of evaluation would require entry at the Alpha-level (to identify needs and design the program). Decision-oriented definitions generally assume a lower entry level, sometimes as low as Zeta-type needs assessment (to revise the program).

Needs assessment usually is conceptualized within a much narrower context than is reflected by Kaufman's taxonomy. However, a wide variety of needs assessment techniques and procedures are reported in the literature. These techniques include goal-setting and goal-rating procedures, strategies for assessing the current status of a program, discrepancy analysis, priority-setting methods, and various specialized techniques (see a review by Witkin, 1977, describing these techniques and their advantages and disadvantages).

Policy Assessment

A fourth implication of the emerging trends is that policy assessments should be conducted early in the planning process. Policies (often confused with the concept of needs) represent a distinct area of inquiry that provides the data on which needs studies are based. Policy studies come before needs studies and are used in deciding the type of needs study that should be conducted.

In a most general sense, policy assessment is the process by which one understands and anticipates the kinds of issues that are expected to result from alternative courses of action. These studies examine systematically the effects on society or any client group that may occur when an educational technology, program, or product is introduced, extended, or modified. Environmental impact statements now mandated of chemical processors, automobile producers, steel manufacturers, and airlines are examples of policy assessments. These assessments may be distinguished from needs studies by their attempt to: (a) clarify goals; (b) identify assumptions behind goals; (c) define the consequences of goals; and (d) portray alternative courses of action (goals). These objectives entail the corollary tasks of identifying the parties who will be affected both directly and indirectly by the technology, program, or product and describing the social, institutional, technological, and economic factors that can change or be changed by the newly developed technology, program, or product.

Contrary to the quantitative data that often earmark needs assessment, policy assessment often results in a mix of hard and soft data. Kaufman's (1977) Alpha-type needs assessment is, in part, a policy assessment when the inquiry is focused on desired goals. However, as Kaufman's taxonomy of needs assessments moves from a Beta- to a Zeta-type, the emphasis shifts from goals to means. As one moves down the list of Kaufman's five remaining types, the focus of the needs study changes to increasingly reflect means (Beta- and Gamma-types) or take means as givens (Delta-, Epsilon-, and Zeta-types). The fundamental difference between policy assessment and needs assessment is that the former focuses on the legitimacy of goals whereas the latter focuses on the legitimacy of means as illustrated in Table 6.6.

In each of the topics in Table 6.6, policy assessment focuses attention on the

TABLE 6.6
Contrasts between Policy and Needs Assessments

Topic of policy assessment	Topic of needs assessment
Should we contain the Soviets in East Africa?	How do we contain the Soviets in East Africa?
What alternatives are available to our energy crisis?	How do we move oil from Alaska's North slope?
Should we teach vocational education subjects to college-bound students?	In what form should we teach vocational education to college-bound students?
Should technological advancements, such as computer-assisted instruction, be used in schools to perform direct instructional functions.	What technological advancements with direct instruction capability are suitable for the schools?

6. Evaluation

goal itself, the assumptions and consequences underlying it, and/or alternative courses of action. Thus, policy assessment is more fundamental than needs assessment, determining the area of inquiry for a needs assessment and the type of needs study most appropriate for a particular course of action. A needs assessment works most effectively in conjunction with a policy assessment that first must determine the appropriateness of a particular course of action.

The methodology of policy assessment is perhaps one of the fastest developing areas in the general field of evaluation. Methodological advancements in this area have spanned a broad array of qualitative and quantitative techniques often combining the two in unique ways. Coates (1976) has identified a large list of these and has provided some documentation as to their use. The following identifies some of the policy assessment techniques that can be used by the evaluator (see also Borich & Jemelka, in press, for an expanded discussion of these).

1. Trends extrapolation and futures-related techniques
   Forecasting of the time of occurence of an event related to a particular goal (Hencley & Yates, 1974)
2. Risk-benefit and fault-tree analyses
   The codification of risks and assorted options under varying conditions of uncertainty (National Academy of Engineering, 1971)
3. Delphi technique
   Consensus forecasting among a panel of experts using cycles of information and feedback without face-to-face confrontation (Linstone & Turoff, 1975)
4. Scenario, gaming, and simulation
   Mathematical and nonmathematical techniques for developing complex statements of future conditions including psychodramatizations of current and existing states and simulations of future states (Abt, 1970)
5. Cross impact analysis
   A process whereby each individual prediction in a forecast is evaluated in relation to the probable truth or falsity of other predictions (Hudspeth, 1973)
6. Morphological analysis
   A process by which all possible questions and answers pertaining to a certain problem are exhausted in a large question by answer matrix (Zwicky, 1957)
7. Decision/relevance tree
   A method for exhausting all possible options and alternatives with regard to a particular problem (Gulick, 1979)
8. Judgment theory
   A procedure which combines interrogation with statistical regression to assign weights to alternative courses of action (Hammond & Summers, 1972)
9. Cost-benefit (input/output studies)
   A class of econometric models using regression analyses for interrelating cost and productivity variables (Leontief, 1966; see also Orlansky & String, 1978)
10. Structural and system dynamic modeling
    A group activity which applies logical reasoning to complex issues to determine interrelationships and networks among the elements of a system (Meadows, Meadows, Randers, & Behrens, 1972)

Perhaps the single most definable quality linking these techniques is the emphasis and importance they place on the participation of a broad mixture of experts and laypersons who are capable of making judgments about the implications of policy. Most of these techniques represent highly democratic processes in which individual opinion is weighted heavily. In contradistinction to some forms of government where policy alternatives must be weighed against their compatability with an accepted ideology, these policy assessment techniques represent democratically oriented approaches to the generation of alternatives and definitions of consequences regardless of their relevance to the existing state of affairs. Thus, they represent relative approaches to problem solving where the criterion is unaffected by any absolute ideology but instead is defined by the best alternative available. This can be both an advantage and disadvantage in that: (*a*) usually a large number of decision alternatives are generated by these methods (as in brainstorming), often making systematic data-tabulation difficult; (*b*) usually small (but not necessarily insignificant) differences can exist among them, making evaluation of differences between alternatives difficult; and (*c*) no appeal to "higher" authority can be made to simplify the process, at least not initially. Only real-world constraints and implications that can be documented by logic or experience may be entered as acceptable data. On the other hand these policy techniques (*a*) provide for a maximum number of alternative courses of action to be discovered, many of which might not have been considered with less democratic methods; (*b*) represent the best mix of opinions and viewpoints, often representing a consensus opinion reflecting the best features of individual viewpoints; and (*c*) lead to identification of alternatives for which there is high probability that practical strategies, solutions, and methods actually exist.

The importance of the field of policy assessment over the coming decade will be linked directly to the extent to which new technological advancements and program development projects create new knowledge gaps and the extent to which the indirect and unanticipated effects of a program prove to be as or more significant than the immediate or planned consequences of that program. The probable occurrence of both of these outcomes should make policy assessment a major development in the field of evaluation.

Role of the Evaluator

By now the reader is no doubt aware of the close and noncoincidental relationships that bind the concepts of systems modeling, naturalistic inquiry, and policy and needs assessment. The interrelationships among these four concepts are never more obvious than when their effects on the field of evaluation are seen through the role of the evaluator. We now conclude with a unifying theme that underpins these four concepts.

The emerging trends depicted in this paper as well as the implications dis-

6. Evaluation

cussed previously forecast an expanding role for the evaluator. This role will be shaped by an increasing tendency to define evaluation broadly and to include within this definition, evaluation activities that are performed prior to program development. The systems approach to evaluation in general and the concepts of naturalistic observation, needs assessment, and policy assessment in particular point to some of the ways the evaluator's role is expanding to include activities performed early in the planning and development process.

The systems approach to evaluation confers on the evaluator a broad array of responsibilities heretofore divided among other specialists. Although leaving the bulk of the planning and development work to these specialists, the systems approach places responsibility with the evaluator for many quasi-evaluation or concomitant activities that, although they are not a direct part of the planning and development process, hold potential for substantially improving the quality of program planning and development. These activities can so influence the design of a program and its evaluation that their completion by the evaluator early in the planning and development process may soon become a standard for good evaluation. An analysis of the systems approach can foreshadow some of these front-end activities that the evaluator soon may be expected to perform.

The systems approach represents the integration of the planning, development, and evaluation processes into a single coherent approach, thus implying an underlining thread by which these processes are linked. The responsibility for providing this link may fall increasingly on the shoulders of the evaluator. The evaluator may be expected to perform this linking function with quasi-evaluation activities that accompany the process of evaluation but that are not themselves part of the act of determining the merit or worth of a thing. Several such activities already have emerged, such as policy assessments for determining the relative consequences of program objectives; needs assessments for determining the most appropriate methods, solutions, and strategies for meeting program objectives; systems-modeling techniques for clarifying and refining program design; and naturalistic inquiry for better understanding the larger system or program in which the program must operate; hence, means–ends relationships. Although these activities can contribute materially to a unified approach to planning, development, and evaluation they are not the only ones. The evaluator can assume many other front-end functions of a logical nature, which help clarify and focus the work of the planner and developer. Determining the representativeness, accuracy, and appropriateness of program objectives; the logic of intended relationships between program components and expected outcomes; the congruency of objectives with planned development activities; and the modeling of intended instructional activities and outcomes to depict hierarchical and sequential relationships among program objectives are other activities implied by an integrated approach to planning, development, and evaluation. These activities can be described as preformative activities, that is, activities performed by the evaluator prior to formative evaluation and even program development. Because preformative evaluation flows from the policy and needs assessment process, it can be expected to influence all aspects of program planning, development, and evaluation.

Traditionally, program planning, development, and evaluation have been viewed as distinct roles or functions related in sequence but not substance. Formal training in evaluation has not always emphasized concepts of instructional design and development and vice versa. Although the notion of formative evaluation has linked program development to evaluation, it has not related evaluation to program planning. With the concepts of systems theory, naturalistic inquiry, and policy and needs assessment, a coherent, unified approach to planning, development, and evaluation can emerge. The further development of these concepts and the linking of them to the planning, development, and evaluation process is an important outcome for the field of evaluation in the decade ahead.

REFERENCES

Abt, C. *Serious games.* New York: Viking Press, 1970.
Alderman, D. L. *Evaluation of the Ticcit computer-assisted instructional system in the community college.* Princeton, N.J.: Educational Testing Service, 1978.
Apple, M. W. The process and ideology of valuing in educational settings. In M. Apple, M. Subkoviak, & H. Lufler, Jr. (Eds.), *Educational evaluation: Analysis and responsibility.* Berkeley, Calif.: McCutchan, 1974.
Banathy, B. *Instructional systems.* Belmont, Calif.: Fearon Publishers, 1968.
Barker, R. G. *Ecological psychology.* Stanford, Calif.: Stanford University Press, 1968.
Barker, R. G. Explorations in ecological psychology. *American Psychologist,* 1965, *20,* 1-14.
Becker, H. Whose side are we on? In G. Riley (Ed.), *Values, objectivity and the social sciences.* Reading Mass.: Addison-Wesley, 1974, 107-121.
Belliott, F. *Design for the Tennessee assessment and evaluation of Title III, ESEA.* Nashville, Tenn.: State of Tennessee Department of Education, 1969.
Bloom, B. (Ed.). *Taxonomy of educational objectives: The classification of educational goals. Handbook 1. Cognitive domain.* New York: McKay, 1956.
Bloom, B. S., Hastings, J. T., & Madaus, G. F. *Handbook on formative and summative evaluation of student learning.* New York: McGraw-Hill, 1971.
Borich, G. (Ed.). *Evaluating educational programs and products.* Englewood Cliffs, N.J.: Educational Technology Publications, 1974.
Borich, G. D. *The appraisal of teaching: Concepts and process.* Reading, Mass.: Addison-Wesley, 1977.
Borich, G. D. A systems approach to the evaluation of training. In H. F. O'Neil, Jr. (Ed.), *Procedures for instructional systems development.* New York: Academic Press, 1979, 205-231.
Borich, G. D., & Brackett, J. Instructional design and evaluation with a structured analysis and design technique. *Educational Technology,* July, 1978, 18-23.
Borich, G. D., & Jemelka, R. *Programs and systems: An evaluation perspective.* New York: Academic Press, in press.

6. Evaluation

Borich, G. D., & Madden, S. *Evaluating classroom instruction: A sourcebook of instruments.* Reading, Mass.: Addison-Wesley, 1977.
Branson, R. K. The interservice procedure for instructional system development. *Educational Technology,* 1978, *18*, 11-14.
Bridgman, P. *The logic of modern physics.* New York: MacMillan, 1927.
Briggs, L. (Ed.). *Instructional design.* Englewood Cliffs, N.J.: Educational Technology Publications, 1977.
Butman, J. W., & Fletcher, J. L. The role of the evaluator and developer in educational research and development. In G. Borich (Ed.), *Evaluating educational programs and products.* Englewood Cliffs, N.J.: Educational Technology Publications, 1974.
Campbell, D., & Stanley, J. *Experimental and quasi-experimental designs for research.* Chicago: Rand McNally, 1966.
Churchman, C. W. *A challenge to reason.* New York: McGraw-Hill, 1968.
Coates, J. Technology assessment—a tool kit. *Chemtech,* June, 1976, 372-383.
Cooley, W., & Lohnes, P. *Evaluation research in education.* New York: Irvington, 1976.
Cronbach, L. & associates. *Toward reform of program evaluation: Aims, methods, and institutional arrangements.* San Francisco: Jossey-Bass, 1980.
Davis, R., Alexander, L., & Yelon, S. *Learning systems design.* New York: McGraw-Hill, 1975.
Dewey, J. *Human nature and conduct.* New York: Henry Holt, 1922.
Dewey, J. Theory of valuation. *International encyclopedia of unified science,* 1939, *2,* 1-67.
Dick, W., & Carey, L. *The systematic design of instruction.* Glenview, Ill.: Scott, Foresman and Co., 1978.
Dykstra, R. Summary of the second-grade phase of the cooperative research program in primary reading instruction. *Reading Research Quarterly,* 1968, *4,* 49-70.
Ebel, R. L. *Measuring educational achievement.* Englewood Cliffs, N.J.: Prentice-Hall, 1965.
Eisner, E. Instructional and expressive objectives: Their formulation and use in curriculum. In *AERA monograph series on curriculum evaluation, No. 3: Instructional objectives.* Chicago: Rand McNally, 1969, 1-30.
Eisner, E. W. The perceptive eye: Toward the reformation of educational evaluation. *Occasional papers of the Stanford Evaluation Consortium,* Stanford, Calif.: Stanford University, 1975 (mimeo).
Emrick, J., Sorenson, P. H., & Stearns, M. *Interim evaluation of the national follow through program 1969-1971: A technical report.* Menlo Park, Calif.: Stanford Research Institute, 1973.
Furst, E. J. *Constructing evaluation instruments.* New York: David McKay, 1964.
Grobman, H. Evaluation activities of curriculum projects: A starting point. *AERA monograph series on curriculum evaluation, No. 2: Evaluation activities of curriculum projects.* Chicago: Rand McNally, 1968.
Guba, E. The failure of educational evaluation. *Educational Technology,* May, 1969, 29-38.
Guba, E. *Toward a methodology of naturalistic inquiry in educational evaluation.* Los Angeles: Center for the Study of Evaluation, University of California, 1978.
Gulick, R. M. Decision analysis as a learning strategy. In H. F. O'Neil, Jr. & C. D. Spielberger (Eds.), *Cognitive and affective learning strategies.* New York: Academic Press, 1979.
Hammond, K., & Summers, D. Cognitive control. *Psychological Review,* 79, 1972, 58-67.
Hammond, R. Context evaluation of instruction in local school districts. *Educational Technology,* January 1969, 13-18.
Hammond, R. Evaluation at the local level. In B. Worthen & J. Sanders, *Educational evaluation: Theory and Practice.* Worthington, Ohio: Charles A. Jones, 1973.
Handy, R. *Value theory and the behavioral sciences.* Springfield, Ill.: Charles C. Thomas, 1969.
Handy, R. *The measurement of values.* St. Louis, Mo.: Warren H. Green, 1970.

Handy, R., & Kurtz, P. *A current appraisal of the behavioral sciences*. Great Barrington, Mass.: Behavioral Research Council, 1964.
Hemphill, J. The relationships between research and evaluation studies. In R. Tyler (Ed.), *Educational evaluation: New Roles, new means, the sixty-eighth yearbook of the National Society of the Study of Education*. Chicago: University of Chicago Press, 1969, 189-219.
Hencley, S., & Yates, J. *Futurism in education*. Berkeley, Calif.: McCutchan, 1974.
Hoban, C. Educational technology and human values. *Audiovisual Communications Review*, 1977, 25, 221-242.
House, E. R. *The logic of evaluative argument*. CSE Monograph Series in Evaluation, No. 7, Los Angeles: Center for the Study of Evaluation, University of California, 1977.
Hudspeth, D. The Cross Impact Matrix. In P. Hencley & J. Yates (Eds.), *Futurism in education*. Berkeley, Calif.: McCutchan, 1974, 115-126.
Interservice procedures for instructional system development (IPISP). Ft. Monroe, Va.: U.S. Army Training and Doctine Command (TRADOC), Pamphlet 350-30, August, 1975.
Jemelka, R., & Borich, G. Traditional and emerging definitions of educational evaluation. *Evaluation Quarterly*, 1979, *3*, (2) 263-276.
Kac, M. Some mathematical models in science. *Science*, 1969, *166*, 695-699.
Kaplan, A. *The conduct of inquiry*. San Francisco: Chandler, 1964.
Kaufman, R. *Educational system planning*. Englewood Cliffs, N.J.: Prentice-Hall, 1972.
Kaufman, R. *Identifying and solving problems: A systems approach*. LaJolla, Calif. University Associates Publishers, 1976.
Kaufman, R. A possible taxonomy of needs assessments. *Educational Technology*, 1977, *17*, 60-64.
Krathwohl, D., Bloom, B., & Masia, B. *Taxonomy of educational objectives: The classification of educational goals. Handbook 2. Affective domain*. New York: McKay, 1964.
Kuhn, T. S. *The structure of scientific revolutions*. Chicago: University of Chicago Press, 1970.
Leontief, W. *Input-output economics*. New York: Oxford University Press, 1966.
Levine, M. Scientific method and the adversary model. *American Psychologist*, 1974, *29*, 661-667.
Linstone, H., & Turoff, M. (Eds.). *The Delphi method: Techniques and applications*. Reading, Mass.: Addison-Wesley, 1975.
Louch, A. R. *Explanation and human action*. Berkeley and Los Angeles: University of California Press, 1966.
Mager, R. F. *Preparing objectives for programmed instruction*. San Francisco: Fearon, 1962.
Meadows, D. H., Meadows, D. L., Randers, J., & Behrens, W. *The limits to growth*. New York: University Books, 1972.
Metfessel, N.W., & Michael, W. B. A paradigm involving multiple criterion measures for the evaluation of the effectiveness of school programs. *Educational and Psychological Measurement*, 1967, *27*, 931-943.
Murphy, R. T., & Appel, L. R. *Evaluation of the Plato IV computer-based educational system in the community college*. Princeton, N.J.: Educational Testing Service, 1977.
National Academy of Engineering. *Perspectives on benefit-risk decision making*. Washington, D.C.: Colloquium, Committee on Public Engineering Policy, National Academy of Engineering, April 26-27, 1971.
Orlansky, I., & String, J. *Cost effectiveness of computer based instruction in military training*. Arlington Va.: Institute for Defense Analysis, Science and Technology Division, 1978.
Owens, T. R. Educational evaluation by adversary proceedings. In E. R. House (Ed.), *School evaluation: The politics and process*. Berkeley, Calif.: McCutchan, 1973.
Parlett, M., & Hamilton, D. Evaluation as illumination: A new approach to the study of innovatory programs. In G. V. Glass (Ed.), *Evaluation studies review annual*, Vol. 1, Beverly Hills, Calif.: Sage Publications, 1977, 140-157.

6. Evaluation

Patton, Q. *Qualitative evaluation methods*. Beverly Hills, Calif.: Sage, 1980.

Popham, W. Objectives and instruction. In *AERA monograph series on curriculum evaluation, No. 3: Instructional objectives*. Chicago: Rand McNally, 1969, 32-64.

Poynor, H. (Ed.), *Problems and potentials of educational evaluation*. Austin, Texas: Southwest Educational Development Laboratory, 1974.

Provus, M. *Discrepancy evaluation*. Berkeley, Calif.: McCutchan, 1971.

Rippey, R. M. *Studies in transactional evaluation*. Berkeley, Calif.: McCutchan, 1973.

Ross, D. Structured analysis (SA): A language for communicating ideas. *IEEE Transactions on Software Engineering*, 1977, SE-3 (1), 16-34.

Ross, D., & Brackett, J. An Approach to structured analysis. *Computer Decisions*, 1976, September, 40-44.

Ross D., & Schoman, K. Structured analysis for requirements definition. *IEEE transactions on software engineering*, 1977, SE-3 (1), 6-15.

Scriven, M. The methodology of evaluation. In *AERA monograph series on curriculum evaluation, No. 1: Perspective of curriculum evaluation*. Chicago: Rand McNally, 1967, 39-83.

Scriven, M. Goal-free evaluation. In E. House (Ed.), *School evaluation*, Berkeley, Calif.: McCutchan, 1973, 319-328.

Scriven, M. The concept of evaluation. In M. Apple, H. Subkoviak, & H. Lufler, Jr. (Eds), *Educational evaluation: Analysis and responsibility*. Berkeley, Calif.: McCutchan, 1974, 55-66.

Smith, E., & Tyler, R. *Appraising and recording student progress*. Adventure in American Education Series, Vol. 3, New York: Harper, 1942.

Stake, R. E. The countenance of educational evaluation. *Teachers College Record*, 1967, 68, 523-540.

Stake, R. E. *Evaluating the arts in education*. Columbus, Ohio: Charles E. Merrill Publishing Company, 1975.(a)

Stake, R. E. Program evaluation, particularly responsive evaluation. Occasional Paper No. 5, Kalamazoo, Mich.: The Evaluation Center, Western Michigan University, 1975.(b)

Stufflebeam, D. L., Foley, W. J., Gephart, W. J., Guba, E. G., Hammond, R. L., Merriman, H. D., & Provus, M. M. *Educational evaluation and decision making*. Itasca, Ill.: Peacock, 1971.

Talmadge, H. Evaluation of local school community problems: A transactional evaluation approach. *Journal of Research and Development in Education*, 1975, 8, 32-41.

Thorndike, R. L., & Hagen, E. *Measurement and evaluation in psychology and education*, (2nd ed.). New York: Wiley, 1969.

Tyler, R. W. *Basic principles of curriculum and instruction*. Chicago: University of Chicago Press, 1950.

U.S. Office of Education. *A Manual for Applicants and Grantees, Title III, Elementary and Secondary Education Act*. Washington, D.C.: Office of Education, Department of Health, Education and Welfare, May, 1967, 48.

van Gigch, J. P. *Applied general systems theory*. New York: Harper and Row, 1978.

Willems, E. P., & Rauch, H. L. *Naturalistic viewpoints in psychological research*. New York: Holt, Rinehart and Winston, 1969.

Witkin, B. R. Needs assessment kits, models, and tools. *Educational Technology*, November, 1977, 17, 5-18.

Wolf, R. L. Trial by jury: A new evaluation method. *Phi Delta Kappan*, 1975, 57.

Worthen, B., & Sanders, J. *Educational evaluation: Theory and practice*. Worthington, Ohio: Charles A. Jones, 1973.

Zwicky, F. *Morphological astronomy*. New York: Springer-Verlag, 1957.

7

Management[1]

ROBERT J. SEIDEL
HAROLD WAGNER

INTRODUCTION

In this chapter we intend to discuss the primary issues of concern to managers of computer-based instructional (CBI) projects. We will describe the management aspects of a variety of projects that have involved the use of the computer for instructional purposes. These management aspects are frequently overlooked until too late. In recent Congressional hearings it was concluded that "regardless of the cost or quality of the CAI [computer-assisted instruction] technology involved, managerial and organizational concerns are an important, if not primary, factor in determining whether a particular CAI project is successful or not [Committee on Science and Technology, 1978, p. 21]." It is our goal in this chapter to describe some of the lessons that managers of CBI systems have learned, with the hope that the mistakes made in the past will not be repeated. We suspect that we, as experts in CBI project management, were asked to write this chapter because we have made more mistakes from which to learn than has anyone else.

We begin this chapter with a general discussion of management in the context of different organizational structures, and relate these structures to the complexities of projects involving instructional use of the computer. It is important to

---

[1]The work reported in this chapter was supported in part by the Army Research Institute for the Behavioral and Social Sciences, contract number MDA 903-79-C-0558. Views and conclusions contained in this document are those of the authors and should not be interpreted as necessarily representing the official policies, either expressed or implied, of the Army Research Institute for the Behavioral and Social Sciences, or the United States Government.

note that CBI systems vary widely in comprehensiveness, complexity, adaptability, and so on. In this chapter, we will *not* discuss those situations in which a single teacher or professor has obtained access to a computer provided by a school system, university, or research grant and plans to incorporate it in his or her course(s). We *will* discuss more complex systems since our focus is on management issues (e.g., interpersonal factors). Furthermore, we will describe specific management problems and issues arising from the varied purposes of CBI projects. Examples of specific projects that illustrate how project *purposes* dictate staffing requirements and resources, types of management functions and activities, and the appropriate evaluation models to apply to the project will be presented.

Selection of Projects

We selected existing projects that highlight important difficulties in project management and for which data were available. Our discussion focuses on specific management functions relevant to the major difficulties encountered in these projects.

The lessons learned and guidelines presented next are based on our own research projects and our knowledge of other projects. Thus, in the final section of this chapter we suggest ways in which managers of future projects that use the computer for instruction can benefit from these previous experiences.

ORGANIZATIONAL STRUCTURES FOR PROJECT MANAGEMENT

In the management literature, several organizational structures are suggested to facilitate the management of projects (Youker, 1977). The most prevalent organizational structure is probably the "functional" organization. It is a pyramid arrangement with top, middle, and lower management spreading downward through the pyramid. The functional units could include such things as research, engineering, accounting, administration, and so on. Another type of structure is labeled the "project" organization, in which the resources for attaining a specific objective are gathered together within a self-contained unit under the leadership of a Project Manager. The third type is called a "matrix" organization; it is multidimensional and attempts to capitalize on the strengths of both the preceding structures. It attempts to combine both the hierarchical structure of the functional organization with a lateral, or horizontal, structure under the leadership of a Project Coordinator. Presumably, the benefit of a matrix organization comes about if one can successfully balance project objectives and coordination across department lines. But, in the words of one management expert, "There is no one perfect organizational structure for managing projects and

TABLE 7.1
Criteria for Organization Design Decisions[a]

Criteria	Functional	Favors matrix	Project
Uncertainty	Low	High	High
Technology	Standard	Complicated	New
Complexity	Low	Medium	High
Duration	Short	Medium	Long
Size	Small	Medium	Large
Importance	Low	Medium	High
Customer	Diverse	Medium	One
Interdependency (within)	Low	Medium	High
Interdependency (between)	High	Medium	Low
Time criticality	Low	Medium	High
Resource criticality	Depends	Depends	Depends
Differentiation	Low	High	Medium

[a] Reproduced from Youker (1977) with the permission of *Management Review*.

similar temporary organizations [Youker, 1977, p. 50]." One should assess the feasibility and viability of using one of these alternative structures based on the unique characteristics of a given project.

There are a number of dimensions or criteria appropriate for making a management decision concerning the type of organizational structure to implement. These criteria are contained in Table 7.1 and reproduced from Youker (1977). For example, if there is a large, complex, and lengthy project (i.e., extending beyond at least one budget cycle), then a *project* organizational structure seems to be appropriate. If, however, there is a situation in which an existing computer-based system is to be implemented—where there is little uncertainty regarding how the hardware or software of the system should be used and there are small course development projects that do not last for more than 3-6 months—then a simple *functional* (departmental) structure would seem to be appropriate. In general, according to Youker,[2] if the components of work within the project do not depend on one another for their accomplishment (low within-project interdependency) then a functional organization would work well. Also, in a functional structure, between-project interdependency is high since departmental staff are aware of all projects. (Later in our discussion we will provide examples of the more sophisticated, lengthy projects in which entire computer systems are under development, as well as examples of shorter lived projects.)

From our viewpoint regarding most large computer-based instructional system projects, either a *matrix* or *project* type or organization would seem to be most appropriate because of the complexity and nature of the technology. The

[2] Dr. Robert Youker, personal communication, March 28, 1979.

hardware-software technology has not yet been standardized, and small curriculum development projects are not the rule. Nevertheless, examples of differing potential organizational structures are conceivable. If the next project would be to upgrade an existing CBI system (e.g., Time-Shared Interactive Computer-Controlled Information Television, or TICCIT) at another school, then the matrix organization makes most sense. The levels of uncertainty regarding use of the hardware or software of the system, complexity of the technology, and within- and between-project interdependency in installing the system would be average. Similarly, the size of effort and time criticality would be average.

If, on the other hand, the implementation were for a large state-of-the-art project using HumRRO's CHARGE (Color Halftone Area Graphics Environment) system, then a Project organization would be natural. Interdependency of hardware and software efforts to implement edge-technology (Swallow, 1974) would be high, as would complexity of integrating innovative layouts of large-scale integrated (LSI) circuitry and chips, and so on. A caveat with respect to the choice of a matrix organization is that a major effort of project coordination must be put forth in order to make it work. Authority, as well as responsibility, must be given to the project coordinator in a matrix organization to enable him or her to draw upon the skills of functional department personnel commensurate with the priorities for accomplishing the project objectives. One of the major activities of the project coordinator is to acquire the staff, organize it, and provide it with the necessary support to facilitate accomplishing the purposes of the project. The project coordinator must be carefully chosen, with interpersonal skills his or her most important asset—technical knowledge and skill are of secondary significance. One of the most important aspects of any organizational structure, whether it be functional, project, or matrix, is that the personality and skills of the leader will determine to a large degree the nature and quality of the work being performed and the timeliness with which it is accomplished (Ford Foundation, 1972, p. 33).

MANAGEMENT ISSUES

In the previous section we briefly discussed a number of possible organizational structures within which management of computer-based instructional projects could take place. Whereas that discussion represented the concept of management from a structural point of view, this section is concerned with a number of issues that have to be dealt with successfully regardless of the organizational structure. We have gleaned these issues from our personal experience in conducting research and development studies, as well as from our understanding of the literature in the field regarding other projects of a similar nature.

Project Purposes: Management Implications

Expectations Must Agree

Purposes fit hand-in-glove with expectations. *For successful project management, the expectations of the sponsor must coincide with those of the researcher or developer, as well as with the hopes and goals of the user of any computer-based system.* The requirements for managing a research and development project are creativity, a type of staffing commensurate with that creativity, and a viewpoint that is oriented more toward establishing the need for further research and development (R&D) than toward the implementation of completed computer-based software, hardware, or courses of instruction. On the other hand, projects that demand products will be used by an instructional, educational, or training system—in which case there are specifications and constraints that must be followed. Thus, the issue in any project is the relative weight to be given to research, development, implementation, and so on. If the goals are not clearly communicated to all concerned, then research and development rapidly becomes research *versus* development (Pohland & Wood, 1978).

One of the most significant problem areas that can arise is a failure on the part of the participants in a project (sponsor, or research–developer, or user) to understand the nature of the project and its products. Francis (1977) states that the requirements of an R&D study and its environment are antagonistic to those of an operational project and its environment. He indicates that disagreements on the philosophies or orientation toward operational training versus R&D have seriously hampered efforts at several sites. The operational teaching versus research issue is basic and cannot be resolved by simple allocation of staff. In fact, as noted previously (Seidel, 1971), the very nature of R&D requires creating divergent or exploratory conditions, whereas instructional implementation demands a convergent set of conditions in which the goal of the project is to maximize performance of students in an operational environment.

It is almost a universal finding that where the expectations of the user differ from those of the supplier of the innovative system, the implementation of the system will fail, or at least will only be partially successful. If the supplier has in mind a research study with a breadboard system, then this should be clearly communicated to the user who must provide the subjects, the facilities, and the site for testing the research hypotheses.

The implementation of the Army's Computerized Training System (CTS) at Fort Gordon (Seidel, Rosenblatt, Wagner, Schultz, & Hunter, 1978b) illustrates a lack of agreement in expectations between the project staff and the school administration and instructional staff. The staff and user expectations for an R&D project were established in one location (Fort Monmouth, New Jersey) where the system was initially to be used in prototype form. At that site, all of the user and staff participants were acquainted with each other and were knowledgeable about computer-assisted instruction (CAI) as a result of earlier studies conducted at the school. Thus, their expectations concerning potential outcomes of the project were in fair agreement. On the other hand, when the system was moved to Fort Gordon, there was no reestablishment of agreement of purpose, although new administrative and user personnel were involved in the implementation. This lack of communication resulted in discrepant expectations on the part of site personnel, which in turn impeded the success of the CTS implementation.

Another example of this confusion and intermingling of purposes is shown by the PLATO (Program Logic for Automatic Teaching Operations) Project implementation at Chanute Air Force Base (Dallman, DeLeo, Main, & Gillman, 1977). The Air Training Command (ATC) was interested in PLATO as an operational teaching device, whereas DARPA (Defense Advanced Research Projects Agency) viewed the PLATO system as a vehicle for doing research and development on computer-based instruction. This confusion initially resulted in the *lack* of an officially approved implementation plan for the project, and thus made effective administration of the project difficult.

At HumRRO, our own research in instructional decision models evidenced a similar problem. Initially, Project IMPACT was established by the Army Research Office as an R&D study to establish the specifications for future CAI systems in the Army. However, during the course of the project, operational sites misinterpreted the nature of the IMPACT project and its products. In spite of numerous information briefings during the course of the project, these users perceived the project's purpose to be operational rather than research and development. Finally, with a change in sponsorships from the Army Research Office to the Continental Army Command in 1971, the project orientation was changed to specifications for an *operational* prototype.

These conflicting expectations affected not only relations between HumRRO, potential users, and the sponsor, but also the activities and expectations among the project staff, especially its morale regarding accomplishment of project objectives. There were some members of the staff who perceived their work as satisfying the new operational requirement, whereas others persisted in working toward the establishment of adequate research and development ideas. Although many useful products came out of this project, the participants were never fully satisfied with the results of their efforts.

In a recent project for the U.S. Postal Service, HumRRO implemented a prototype computer-based training system at a post office site (Wagner, Trexler, Hillelsohn, & Seidel, 1978). The contractual requirements were for the development and validation of the prototype system. In this project, too, there were conflicts in expectations between the sponsor, developer, and user. All three parties tried to achieve different purposes. The sponsor (the U.S. Postal Service) attempted to make a comparison between two training systems; the developer (HumRRO) attempted to install and debug a prototype training system; and the user (the Syracuse, New York Post Office) attempted to train as many personnel as possible within a given period of time to fulfill an operational need. Due to this divergence in purpose and expectations, it is no surprise that none of the parties fully attained their goals.

It follows from this necessity for agreement on project purpose that the design of the computer-based instructional system should be compatible with the accepted purpose. For example, the hardware–software requirements for a CAI system are different from those for a computer-managed instruction (CMI) system. A CMI terminal may require compatibility with optical scanning equipment. The power and configuration of the CMI computer system will differ from that of a CAI system. An example of incompatibility between system design and purpose was seen in the CTS implementation (Seidel *et al.*, 1978b). The original goal of this project was to be CAI. When this objective was changed to CMI, the specifications for the computer system were not changed to agree with the new objective. As a result, an inefficient CMI system was configured out of the previously designed CAI system.

Many other projects, including those of the recently completed NSF-sponsored TICCIT implementations, have discovered the issue of disparity in expectations between the developer and users of the system. They have had to deal with these differences in expectations and modify the goals of the projects to adhere to the practical constraints of the sites where the systems were implemented (Alderman, Appel, & Murphy, 1978; Dallman *et al.*, 1977).

Using Appropriate Evaluation Models

The evaluation model should be appropriate and consistent with project purpose. The focus here is on management implications relevant to the use of an appropriate evaluation model. In Chapter 6 (this volume), Borich discusses various types of evaluation models and techniques. Our intent is merely to illustrate the difficulties that occur as a result of applying evaluation models discrepant with the purposes of a project.

Formative versus summative evaluation. *Formative evaluation is appropriate for testing and improving a prototype system; summative evaluation is appropriate when alternative systems are being compared following a thorough debugging and shakedown period.* Unfortunately, it sometimes happens that although everyone can agree with this distinction in theory, the pressing needs of a sponsor or user and/or the ambiguities of communication may result in differences of opinion as to which evaluation purpose is to be served.

Occasionally, an agreement in purpose among the parties involved has led to implementations that have been successful. A situation that is conducive to such agreement occurs when the sponsor, the user, and the developer are within the same organization. IBM provides a classic example of this in their Field Engineering Division CMI implementation. In this case, the purpose for implementing CMI within IBM was to reduce the costs of training its field engineers. This was known from the outset and resulted in the reduction of the number of education centers from 17 to 3, and the saving of over $6 million (or 50% of the training budget) per year within IBM Field Engineering.[3] A similar case in the implementation of the Computer Curriculum Corporation's basic skills packages. Here, the explicit, accepted purpose is to provide an augmentation to the teaching of reading and mathematics skills by devoting 10-15 minutes a day to drill-and-practice CAI. Users have been satisfied with this instruction, as is shown by the successful and continued use of this type of CAI (Suppes & Macken, 1978).

In this section, we cite a number of examples where this type of ambiguity and difficulty has arisen. In the case of the Army CTS project, a very comprehensive evaluation plan was prepared that included a summative cost-effectiveness analysis of the proposed CAI system. However, this plan was premature on two counts: (*a*) a formative evaluation was required at the time because of the prototype implementation; and (*b*) when the purpose was changed to CMI, a different evaluation model should have been designed consistent with the CMI purpose. In the CTS implementation, the purposes were not universally agreed on. It was quite clear that different expectations existed, and, as a result, the user expected a summative evaluation yielding cost-effectiveness conclusions. The problem is that cost-effectiveness projections from such a prototype implementation are premature and subject to high error. *In a prototype project, project management has to be aware of, and resist if possible, the pressures by training system sponsors or users who are hungry for evidence upon which to base their decisions.*

A similar situation existed in HumRRO's project to develop and implement an automated training system for the U.S. Postal Service (see previous discussion). The hardware and software were prototypes, as was the instructional material. The evaluation plan included formative evaluation and revision to produce a complete validated training system. However, there was a conflict between the requirements for the formative evaluation of the prototype system and the operational requirements of the U.S. Postal Service, which needed to graduate a sufficient number of qualified operators. This problem was heightened by the sponsor's attempts to make an experimental comparison between the new automated instructional system under development and an on-going training system that had been operating for a number of years. What this example highlights is how the effects of disparate expectations and the use of inappropriate evaluation models were compounded when the three parties involved (the U.S. Postal Ser-

---

[3]T. Harvey Long, personal communication, 1978.

7. Management

vice, HumRRO, and the Syracuse Post Office) attempted to serve different purposes.

Another example of a mismatch between project purpose and evaluation model is the evaluation of the Computer-Assisted Remedial Education (CARE) project by the U.S. Office of Education and by the Pennsylvania State University administration. The original purpose for the establishment of this computerized mobile teacher training facility was to serve the needs of handicapped children to a much greater degree than had been the case prior to the implementation of this particular system. This was accomplished by the CARE personnel. The judgment was made, however, to discontinue this kind of instructional delivery system because it cost more than similar teacher training curricula were projected to cost on campus. Therefore, according to the management of the university and to personnel at the U.S. Office of Education, this project was not cost-effective. What was overlooked by the decision makers is that their judgments were based on an evaluation purpose different from the original purpose in establishing this project (Cartwright, 1976). Thus, we agree with Francis's (1977) guidance for appropriately matching decision-making needs based on project purposes with evaluation models and criteria. In his report, Francis provides a comprehensive list of questions that need to be answered before developing the evaluation plan and determining which data to collect and which criteria to apply. (See also Seidel, 1980, for a discussion of matching purposes to appropriate measures of effectiveness.) In its initial plans, it appeared that the National Science Foundation (NSF) sponsored an evaluation project that employed Educational Testing Service (ETS) as the external, summative evaluator of the PLATO and TICCIT implementations, using an evaluation model appropriately matched to the projects' purposes (Alderman, Appel, & Murphy, 1978; Anastasio, 1972; Murphy & Appel, 1977). In this case, the evaluation of educational impact was accomplished by an independent evaluator and initiated as part of the original plan for the implementation. This evaluation was to be based on already existing stable hardware and software systems. Therefore, a summative evaluation would seem to be appropriate. However, the instructional materials should not have been stabilized at the time of the summative evaluation. This did not appear to be the case.

The difficulties that arose in implementation of this evaluation relate more to the administration of the evaluation contract than to the management of the PLATO, TICCIT, or ETS projects. For example, Anastasio cites in the ETS Annual Report (1973) that there were delays in receiving the information on the content and objectives of the courses to be covered and, therefore, they could not proceed with the development of measuring instruments necessary for the evaluation. On the other hand, the University of Illinois Computer-Based Education Research Laboratory (CERL) viewed the ETS external evaluation as preventing efforts to conduct an internal evaluation, as there would be too much imposition on students and teachers (Propst & Slottow, 1977). There was also a disagreement between the parties regarding the formative or summative purpose of the evaluation. CERL viewed NSF as placing too great a burden on the external evaluator. Because of the developmental nature of the project, according to CERL, data should have been collected internally and thereby used formatively, with an external monitor, if necessary, to insure objectivity.

In this instance, the guiding source for such decisions would be the sponsor, NSF. As the coordination, communication, and control of all the projects rested with NSF, it was their job to insure that there was cooperative and complementary progress toward the overall goal of project implementation and evaluation. It is quite clear in a complex implementation project of this nature that *the roles and needs of the independent evaluator, as well as the roles and needs of the developers, must be continually coordinated and clarified in order to prevent any ambiguities regarding project responsibilities and outcomes.*

Process: Internal Project Management

Whether the project's purpose is research or implementation, it consists of a multidisciplinary staff and a manager whose interpersonal skills are critical for relating to people who may speak different technical languages. The particular mix of personnel, that is, more engineers than instructional developers, and so on, will vary depending on the nature of the project. *Maintaining a careful and appropriate balance of staffing is an extremely important part of the manager's job.*

One major problem relates to the issue of personnel turbulence or, conversely stated, the retention or continuity of personnel throughout the life of the project. This problem is related to the organizational structure of the project. In a functional organization, there is a high probability that personnel turbulence will be low. If, however, there is a project or matrix organizational structure, then personnel may be working for more than one supervisor and the project would be continually in danger of losing its personnel either permanently or temporarily with resulting inefficiencies.

All of the projects that have been discussed above have proceeded cognizant of the need for an interdisciplinary mix of people appropriate to the project purpose (Seidel, Hunter, & Wagner, 1978a; Seidel & the IMPACT Staff, 1969). Francis (1977) gives a description of the essential skills needed by the staff of a computer-based instruction project that is derived from the PLATO experience. These skills are in the following areas: administrative-managerial leadership; curriculum coordination; subject matter expertise; instructor experience; instructional design; evaluation-testing; CBE-language expertise; editorial skills; and general support.

In virtually all military implementations, lack of continuity in personnel is a

7. Management

major problem. The CTS project, for example, cites this as a continuing difficulty throughout the life of the project. CTS had a unique problem when the site location change occurred and they lost key personnel who were familiar with the software and hardware, as well as with the project management. In a similar case, the PLATO implementation at Chanute Air Force Base, problems in course development were due in part to changes in project administration and the resulting confusion as to course goals (Himwich, 1977).

An example of the need for continuing training because of personnel turbulence can be found in HumRRO's Project IMPACT. We had a director of instructional programming who was responsible for the supervision of all aspects of instructional development, including the implementation (on-line) of the course materials. During the course of the four-year project, we had four different directors of instructional programming, each of whom had a slightly different background and orientation when they came to the project. Therefore, all required a certain degree of orientation and training to capitalize on their unique abilities and, at the same time, to insure that their focus matched the purpose of the project.

Working on any of these complex projects is a group of authors, or instructional developers. Personnel turbulence, that is heightened in the military environment, requires that a training program be administered to aid these authors in the performance of their job. This is currently recognized in a series of projects supported by the military as well as in the civilian sector, that are directed toward the development of both on-line and off-line instructional development aids.

In a volatile personnel environment, such as that which exists in the military, it is necessary to provide as many management aids as possible to overcome the turbulence problem. Where possible, an automated system would be of great help for managing the manpower loads and scheduling the various tasks to be carried out in the project. Such an approach is exemplified by the automated management system being developed by Courseware, Incorporated (O'Neal & O'Neal, 1979).

There needs to be *serial development of critical system components.* Once again, we in the field of computer-based instruction seem to relearn *the necessity for establishing a stable hardware and software environment prior to developing course materials on the system.* Unfortunately, most of the time, the systems are developed by contractors who must adhere to conflicting "real-world" requirements of the sponsor or users. In many cases, the contractor is not permitted the ideal sequential development of hardware and software; followed by instructional content development, formative evaluation, and revision; followed by a summative evaluation of the implementation.

HumRRO's development of a prototype training system for letter sorting machine operators illustrates this problem. We had to develop and deliver a total instructional system that was to be evaluated as to the training effectiveness and efficiency of the instructional materials. However, we had to deliver the prototype hardware and software base prior to completion of the debugging process. This resulted in numerous problems caused by temporary breakdowns of the hardware components. This, in turn, prevented the adequate debugging of software so that some of our training data were inaccessible or incorrect. A proper validation of a prototype system requires sufficient time for shakedown or debugging. In fact, the debugging should have been completed prior to the installation of course materials or instructional logic on the system. Unfortunately, none of this happened, as our activities and schedule were driven to a large degree by the operational requirements of the sponsor and user (i.e., the U.S. Postal Service).

Another example of an unfortunate attempt at parallel development of system components was the Army's CTS project. In this instance, attempts at the development of instructional materials and use of the hardware and software components were made prior to completion of the acceptance testing. In attempting to meet the acceptance test requirements, the contractor created a *simulated* load on the system, thereby not providing an appropriate job stream test of the software. The result was that the simulation tested acceptably, but with a full load of students it did not (Hunter, 1976). A delay was encountered as a result of having to make the software adequate for the full instructional load to be tested properly. Another outcome was a negative attitude on the part of the users, both instructors and students, as a result of their experience with this unreliable system. There was a lack of confidence by the instructors in the reports generated by this system, so they depended on their own manual system for information that could have been more efficiently provided.

Implementation of PLATO at Sheppard Air Force Base in Wichita Falls, Texas, was unsuccessful during its first phase (Misselt & Call-Himwich, 1978) because of a number of reasons, not the least of which was the premature implementation of the course. However, in the case of the NSF-sponsored PLATO and TICCIT projects, the hardware–software systems had been established in a relatively stable environment for a number of years prior to implementing course materials in a community college environment. While the TICCIT system was a newer development, during the course of the project, stabilization of the hardware and software components did precede any significant development of instructional materials on the system. Earlier CAI systems, such as the IBM 1500 system, represent another example of prior development of a stable hardware and software base. Today, Control Data Corporation in Minneapolis, Minnesota is attempting to develop and market both instructional development aids and curricular materials on a stable PLATO system.

It should be noted that one of the principal reasons for the existence of the stable PLATO hardware base and the IBM 1500 system was that, prior to the delivery to the general public of these CAI systems, a good deal of research and development took place on the hardware and software alone. The PLATO system was funded with millions of dollars of federal and other support over many years. The atmosphere for support of large scale hardware-software development efforts, such as the technology of PLATO and TICCIT, no longer exists in the federal funding patterns. A recent report by the Committee on Science and Technology (1978) illustrates these decreasing amounts and the very low level of support for computer-based instructional research and redevelopment that exists in the federal government today. As a result, many short-term contracts are left that are operationally oriented—even though some projects should have an R&D focus, permitting a more appropriate, sequential process to be applied.

Product: Management of Technology Transfer

From our experience in both civilian and military educational institutions, one of the most important factors contributing to the resistance toward implementing computer-based instruction is a lack of understanding of its advantages and limitations. This problem occurs at a number of levels, from the highest level of institutional administration down to the instructors and students. And their needs for such understanding are different. *For successful implementation, therefore, it is necessary to provide a multilevel training program covering general awareness of computers, discipline-related knowledges, and programming skills.* In a recent survey performed for the National Science Foundation, we found that the institutions serving as exemplars of successful academic computing had a successful computing literacy program in some form (Hunter, 1978). Many of the problems in the CTS implementation (Seidel *et al.*, 1978b) showed that the need for such a training program of computing literacy and orientation was clearly indicated.

A recent HumRRO project for the National Science Foundation, in which computer-based instruction was introduced into four District of Columbia high schools, illustrates the need for and limitations of such a training program (Hargan, Hibbits, & Seidel, 1978). The program we instituted included an awareness level of training for the school principals, as well as workshops to develop BASIC programming skills by the teachers. Moreover, we had continual and frequent meetings with these personnel during the course of the project. Unfortunately, there was a high degree of personnel turbulence at the top management levels during the course of this project. After 1 year of existence, there was a need for additional training at the top management level within this project. This additional orientation was required in order to maintain a continuing base of commitment and communication among the managers of the implementation. Even though we had continual training for new personnel as they arrived on the scene, it was fast discovered that computing literacy and orientation, although necessary, were not sufficient to obtain the required levels of commitment from the participants to insure successful completion of the project.

Implications from this example show that the orientation training did not seem to be as effective with the new personnel as it had been with the initiators of the project. They did not perceive the project as their own, and thus the "not-invented-here" syndrome predominated. From the reports by Abramson, Weiner, Malkin, & Howell (1970), something similar seems to have happened with an implementation of drill and practice in the New York City school system. In that case, the implementation seemed to be successful in the first year of the study; but in the second year, the materials were not implemented in the way they were intended to be used (e.g., the facilities were not used as regularly as had been prescribed).

A clear line of project control is necessary along with a congruent allocation of authority and responsibility. If a single line of authority in a project is lacking, ambiguity in communication can result, as well as a lack of willingness to accept responsibility. For example, in the Army's CTS project, a dual chain of command existed between the school personnel at the implementation site and the CTS project personnel. This was compounded by the fact that the CTS management office was not located at the user school site. The result of this was that the CTS project was viewed as an imposition upon the school.

In working with the D.C. public school system (Hargan *et al.*, 1978), we attempted unsuccessfully to facilitate the establishment of a single chain of authority. One of the last recommendations we made was for the establishment of a coordinator of instructional computing to be given a level of authority commensurate with the system superintendent's office. This did not occur. We learned subsequently that after HumRRO withdrew from its position of "turnkey" manager, much of the computing facilities languished virtually unused for at least 1 year subsequent to our withdrawal.

Frequent communication is necessary for monitoring expectations and understanding. Where a complex innovation such as computer-based instruction is involved, a number of skills within the developing agency is necessary. The various specialists do not speak the same technical languages and therefore require an interpretation through management of the needs, the issues, the necessity for meeting deadlines, priorities, and so on. *Thus, continuous communication mediated by the project manager must exist.* Problems should also be avoided with regard to ambiguities of communication among the developer, the sponsoring agency, and the user. In a DARPA-sponsored implementation of PLATO IV at Sheppard Air Force Base CERL (Computer-Based Education Research Laboratory) personnel noted a definite cooling of relationships when the CERL role was perceived as changed from that of a helpful partner in implementation to that of a summative evaluator. Apparently, these roles and the need to shift from one to the other were not made clear to those at the user site (Seidel, Wagner, Lumsdaine, & Baker, 1976).

That frequent meetings are necessary but not sufficient conditions for maintaining an agreement on expectations is illustrated in the Army CTS project. In this project, there were frequent meetings between the project staff, the contractor, and the user. However, initial establishment of agreed-upon project goals was not accomplished prior to installation of the system at the user site (Seidel et al., 1978b).

That we were able to make some progress in the NSF-supported D.C. school project (Hargan et al., 1978) was facilitated by frequent meetings with teachers and principals of the school. Obtaining as much participation by the principals as we did have in this project established a degree of openness and acceptance which otherwise would have been impossible. In addition, we had quarterly meetings with a board of directors made up of the participating school principals, invited members of the D.C. City Council, and interested parents. This was extremely important for obtaining cooperation in the scheduling of the computer facilities.

An example of a successful implementation of computer-managed instruction, due in great part to efforts at creating a thoroughly communicative environment among all participants, is the Instructional Support System (ISS) of Community School District Number 18 in Brooklyn, New York. This system used an implementation strategy of building consensus directly into the curriculum design process, which led to its acceptance and incorporation into the educational system (Committee on Science and Technology, 1978).

In summary, the issues and examples described in this section illustrate some of the major areas of concern to managers that can determine the success or failure of a computer-based instructional project. These areas can be summarized in terms of control and communications. Control over the resources and activities of the project must be clearly delineated. The lines of communication must be kept open among all parties through frequent meetings, correspondence, and so on (e.g., sponsor, project staff, and user). This is to insure that a commitment by all participants—user, sponsor, and project staff, is continually in effect so that the innovative system can be appropriately developed, used, and evaluated.

LESSONS LEARNED AND RECOMMENDATIONS

What can be learned from the several issues and illustrations presented in the previous section? The studies that we discussed provide bases for the guidance of managers of future computer-based projects. We consolidated this guidance into several prescriptions that primarily involve the management functions of communication and control. These guidelines will be presented and discussed below.

Purpose: Management Implications

Understanding the Nature of the Project

Understanding starts with the project manager. The manager must know whether the project has a research, development, or implementation focus, and whether it will require development of instruction on an existing hardware-software base or require the development of an entire system. The project manager must also understand whether it is to be a CAI or CMI system. Different types of projects will have different products and deliverables. It is the manager's job to make sure that ambiguities about these are minimal and, where ambiguities arise, to resolve them as early as possible.

Clearly Communicating the Project Purpose

Related to the above, the project manager must make sure that the specific objectives to be accomplished, the nature of the instructional goals, the role of the computer, and so on, are all clearly communicated, not just to the project staff but to the sponsor and user as well. A project with the goals of establishing a new hardware and software system requires different managerial emphases than a curriculum development effort using existing systems. The implementation of a computerized instructional system requires different managerial emphases than a research project on the instructional process or studies examining the underlying laws of human learning.

Establishing, Communicating, and Applying Appropriate Evaluation Models

Make certain that an evaluation model is used that is appropriate to the project's purpose. Communicate this model to the project's sponsors and users, and make certain that all can agree on the nature of this evaluation model. For example, if the project has a research focus, is it clear to the sponsor that cost-effectiveness decisions based upon an operational test do *not* apply? Determining whether the evaluation is formative or summative will highlight the data collection procedures that should be undertaken. In a prototype implementation, a formative process is needed, involving iterative development, debugging, testing, and revision of course materials. Only in an operational mode is a summative evaluation appropriate. One problem to be faced is that the manager must not be pressured by the perceived needs of the sponsor for evaluation data that may be inappropriate or premature. One must not attempt to force the use of formative data for summative evaluation as if the data were obtained from an operational system. Only continuing communications with the sponsor can alleviate differences of opinion regarding evaluation purposes. Also, when performing a formative evaluation, reassure the user that the focus of the evaluation is *not* the quality of the current instructor, administrator, or student. It is necessary to emphasize that the quality of the newly developed course or system of instruction is the focus of the evaluation.

If an outside evaluator is employed by the sponsoring agency to summatively evaluate the project, make certain that all parties agree on the appropriateness of the evaluation model, techniques, and criteria *before* such a project is undertaken. If the project is in a formative stage, we believe it is better if the developer performs the evaluation—as objectivity is of no concern at a time when the improvement of the project is the goal of such an activity. However, information can be collected at the same time that will be of use to an outside summative evaluator. It is important to coordinate these activities so that duplication of effort does not occur, antagonisms are not created, and the user's attitudes are not negatively affected. Although we feel that in most cases this is the responsibility of the sponsoring agency, the project manager should interact with the sponsor, evaluator, and user to attempt to obtain a consensus of purpose and a delineation of the roles to be played by all who are involved with the project.

If the project is to result in significant achievements in the quantity or quality of instruction far beyond previous curricular outcomes, then an estimate of the value attributable to this additional achievement is to be made, rather than that obtained from a cost-effectiveness analysis. If using the computer-based instructional system enables the teaching of concepts not attainable without the system, then the judgment must be made as to what appropriate dimensions are to be incorporated for evaluation and what the criteria should be. Generally speaking, in this kind of situation, one must make a "tolerable" cost or value-added judgment (i.e., Is the amount and type of gain worthy of the increment in cost which must be paid in order to attain this gain?).

Finally, any evaluation model must take into account user acceptance as a criterion. No matter how carefully the project activities are planned and executed, the manager must also be concerned with positively affecting the attitudes of the user.

Process: Internal Project Management

Adequate control must be maintained over the allocation of project staff and resources. It is particularly critical that personnel turbulence be held to a minimum when attempting to implement such a complex innovation as computer-based instruction. The project manager is responsible for keeping the staffing mix appropriate to the project purpose and for insuring that project specialists are on the same path toward producing the required products. This means that the manager must possess a sensitivity to the creative contributions that can be made by the staff members from each of the various disciplines, and at the same time insure that the goals of the project are not sacrificed in order to meet the need for creative expression on the part of the staff. The manager, in addition, must try to insure serial completion of the required system components by avoiding pressures to simultaneously develop hardware, software, and course materials. If this cannot be avoided, make sure that critical path planning reflects the realities of the interdependencies and contingencies of the different components under development.

Adequate coordination must be maintained among project staff, sponsors, and users. Coordinating the team efforts, adhering to priorities, meeting the sequential or parallel deadlines, and so on, all imply the necessity for frequent meetings. There is no validated rule as to the number of meetings required per unit of time. However, enough meetings among the staff must be held to allow for the exchange of information and expression of needs and gripes, as well as for encouragement to be provided for progress made and tasks accomplished. In addition, continuous communication must be established and maintained with the system users, as well as with the sponsoring agencies. Even though initial agreements may be attained by written contracts, personal and written communications are necessary thereafter to maintain these agreements. This is especially important when the new technology may disrupt the traditional procedures for administering instruction.

Product: Management of Technology Transfer

One should understand and communicate with appropriate personnel at the sponsoring and user agencies. Knowing who the project sponsor is and how the sponsor operates will place the project purpose and requirements in the proper context. Although this cannot keep the project out of trouble, it will help minimize its difficulties. In addition, the project manager must work with the user in order to encourage commitment on the part of the user and enable the user to have an adequate understanding of project purposes. This communication permits input from the user so that the project manager can see if the user's perceptions or expectations are at variance with project goals and objectives. These discrepancies must be dealt with efficiently in a way that permits the project to progress.

It would be extremely useful in a future study to perform a complete analysis of the major computer-based instructional systems with regard to purpose, and covering all management functions. The foregoing discussion is not intended to be an exhaustive examination of functions by projects. With the proposed study one would be able to develop a Management Guidance Matrix. This would enable a potential CBI user to determine, for a given type of project, the management activities and processes most likely to facilitate successful project management and technology transfer.

7. Management

There is a need to close the loop between research, development, and implementation. As discussed in this chapter, many of the problems in managing computer-based instruction projects emanate from a confusion of purposes, lack of adequate communications and control, and a resulting lack of commitment from user institutions. These can be overcome through the use of an instructional technology evaluation center—a single site to be used for controlled operational testing and development of new technologies. If this site includes an experimental training or educational institution, then the necessary feedback from the user can be obtained in a timely manner. Clear lines of communication and control can be articulated to enable the collection of data, testing and revision of system components, and diffusion of findings and products. Moreover, the commitment by the participants in such a center (e.g., instructors, administrators, researchers, etc.) will have been dictated by the sponsoring agency in its establishment of the center's missions, functions, and organizations. We believe that this type of center can solve many of the problems discussed in this chapter. It remains to be seen whether or not funding policies will change so that this concept can become a reality.

REFERENCES

Abramson, T., Weiner, M., Malkin, S., & Howell, J. *Evaluation of the New York City computer-assisted instruction project in elementary arithmetic, second year, 1969-70.* Research Report 70-16, New York: Research and Evaluation Unit, Division of Teacher Education, City University of New York, October, 1970.

Alderman, D. L., Appel, L. R., & Murphy, R. T. PLATO and TICCIT: An evaluation of CAI in the community college. *Educational Technology,* 1978, **18**(4), 40–45.

Anastasio, E. J. *Evaluation of the PLATO and TICCIT computer-based instructional systems—A preliminary plan.* Annual Report, PR-72-19, Princeton, N.J.: Educational Testing Service, July 31, 1972.

Cartwright, G. P. *Costs of CAI for special education teacher training: Three perspectives.* Paper presented at Society for Applied Learning Technology (SALT), Washington, D.C., 1976.

Committee on Science and Technology. *Computers and the learning society.* Report prepared by the Subcommittee on Domestic and International Scientific Planning, Analysis and Cooperation, Washington, D.C.: U.S. Government Printing Office, June, 1978.

Dallman, B. E., DeLeo, P. J., Main, & Gillman. *Evaluation of PLATO IV in vehicle maintenance training.* AFHRL-TR-77-59, Lowry Air Force Base, Co.: Air Force Human Resources Laboratory, Technical Training Division, November, 1977.

The Ford Foundation. *A foundation goes to school.* Comprehensive School Improvement Program 1960-1970. New York: Ford Foundation, November, 1972.

Francis, L. *Guidelines for establishing and managing a computer-based education site.* MTC Report No. 17, Urbana-Champaign: University of Illinois, Computer-Based Education Research Laboratory, October, 1977.

Hargan, C., Hibbits, N., & Seidel, R. J. *D.C. secondary schools project for adopting computer-aided education.* HumRRO FR 78-11, Alexandria, Va.: Human Resources Research Organization, August, 1978.

Himwich, H. A. (ed.) *Critique and summary of the Chanute AFB CBE project*. MTC Report No. 14, Urbana: University of Illinois, Computer-Based Education Research Laboratory, September, 1977.

Hunter, B. *Report on final acceptance test of CTS (Computerized Training System)*. HumRRO Final Report, FR-ED-76-28. Prepared for U.S. Army Training Support Activities, Fort Gordon, Ga., 1976.

Hunter, B. What makes a computer-literate college? In *Proceedings of Conference on Computers in Undergraduate Curricula*. Denver, Colo.: University of Denver, Department of Mathematics, June, 1978.

Misselt, A. L., & Call-Himwich, E. *Analysis of Sheppard AFB computer-based education project*. MTC Report No. 21, Urbana: University of Illinois, Computer-Based Education Research Laboratory, January, 1978.

Murphy, R. T., & Appel, L. R. *Evaluation of the PLATO IV computer-based education system in the community college*. PR 77-10, Princeton, N.J.: Educational Testing Service, June, 1977.

O'Neal, A. F., & O'Neal, H. L. Author management systems. In H. F. O'Neil, Jr. (Ed.), *Issues in instructional systems development*. New York: Academic Press, 1979, 69-88.

Pohland, P. A., & Wood, C. J. Teachers versus technocrats: An essay review. Review of *Teachers versus technocrats: An educational innovation in anthropological perspective* by H. F. Wolcott. *Educational Researcher*, 1978, 7(10).

Propst, F., & Slottow, G. Chapter 1 in *Demonstration of the PLATO IV computer-based education system*. Final Report, Urbana: University of Illinois, Computer-Based Education Research Laboratory, March, 1977.

Seidel, R. J. *It is 1980: Do you know where your computer is?* Phi Delta Kappan, March, 1980, 481-485.

Seidel, R. J. *Theories and strategies related to measurement in individualized instruction*. Professional Paper 2-71, Alexandria, Va.: Human Resources Research Organization, March, 1971. (Also published in *Educational Technology*, Englewood Cliffs, N.J.: September, 1971.)

Seidel, R. J., Hunter, B., & Wagner, H. Tips for managing CAI projects. *Educational Technology*, 1978, **18**(4), 33-37.(a)

Seidel, R. J., & the IMPACT Staff. *Project IMPACT: Computer-administered instruction concepts and initial development*. Technical Report 69-3, Alexandria, Va.: Human Resources Research Organization, March, 1969.

Seidel, R. J., Rosenblatt, R., Wagner, H., Schulz, R., & Hunter, B. *Evaluation of a prototype computerized training system (CTS) in support of self-pacing and management of instruction*. Final Report 78-10, Alexandria, Va.: Human Resources Research Organization, August, 1978.(b)

Seidel, R. J., Wagner, H., Lumsdaine, A. A., & Baker, E. L. *PLATO evaluation review report*. SR-ED-76-38, Internal Report, Alexandria, Va.: Human Resources Research Organization, September 30, 1976.

Suppes, P., & Macken, E. The historical path from research and development to operational use of CAI. *Educational Technology*, 1978, **18**(4), 9-12.

Swallow, R. J. *CHARGE interactive graphics system terminal: Theory of operation*. HumRRO Tech. Rep. 74-26, Alexandria, Va.: Human Resources Research Organization, December, 1974.

Wagner, H., Trexler, R. C., Hillelsohn, M. J., & Seidel, R. J. *Automated instructional development system: Validation study*. Research Product ED-78-6, Alexandria, Va.: Human Resources Research Organization, March, 1978.

Youker, R. Organization alternatives for project managers. *Management Review*, November, 1977, 46-53.

8

Computer-Based Instruction in Europe and Japan[1]

KARL L. ZINN

INTRODUCTION

The major purpose of this chapter is to provide insight into developments and planning in the United States through comparisons with programs in other countries, particularly in Europe and Japan. It is not practical to summarize all the work that is being conducted in other countries, nor would it be useful for the purposes of this chapter. Rather, this chapter contrasts developments elsewhere in hardware, software, courseware, learning strategies, evaluation, and management. Attention is given to considerations of technical and technological capabilities, pedagogy, economics, politics, and sociology, especially in areas where lessons might be learned from the differences with U.S. computer-based instruction (CBI) experiences.

The countries reviewed include France, Germany, Japan, Sweden, Switzerland, The Netherlands, and the United Kingdom. Some attention is given to activities of international organizations; for example, the International Federation for Information Processing (IFIP), United Nations Educational, Scientific, and Cultural Organization (UNESCO), the Organization for Economic Cooperation and Development (OECD), and the Intergovernmental Bureau for Informatics (IBI). In addition to publications, information was collected through correspondence and personal conversations.

---

[1]The work reported in this chapter was supported in part by the Army Research Institute for the Behavioral and Social Sciences, contract number MDA 903-79-C-0558. Views and conclusions contained in this document are those of the author and should not be interpreted as necessarily representing the official policies, either expressed or implied, of the Army Research Institute for the Behavioral and Social Sciences, or the United States Government.

A major premise of this chapter is that monitoring CBI developments in other countries, with periodic summary and interpretation, provides additional information helpful to planning within national and regional programs.

For other interpretations of CBI developments outside the United States see Howe and Romiszowski (1977); McDonald, Atkins, Jenkins, and Kemmis (1977); Rushby, James, and Anderson (1978); UCODI (1975); and Zender (1975).

HARDWARE AND SOFTWARE

Other countries are experiencing the same options and tradeoffs in hardware and software development that Fields and Paris summarized in Chapter 2 (this volume). Smaller CBI systems used by one student, or perhaps by groups of two or three students at a time, are gaining favor. Lower prices per user station combined with the elimination of communication costs and the increase in reliability are seen as strong points of the smaller systems used in other countries even more than in the United States (Howe, 1978). Although personal, portable, and controllable systems (such as those of Commodore, Radio Shack, Apple, and Atari) appear to be as desirable to consumers in other countries, they are much less affordable in other economies than in the United States.

The push to put computers into homes for educational purposes and into offices and factories for training purposes may have negative consequences since the technology that provides cheap processing is less capable of providing valid and effective courseware. The marketplace in the United States is likely to drive the introduction of computing machinery for education beyond the understanding of its effective uses. Actions by government agencies and professional associations in the United Kingdom are intended to provide direction, assess progress, and inform buyers. Similar actions in the United States would help balance the pressure of market competition.

Knowledge, Data, and Information in CBI Systems

The distinction between knowledge and data (Chapter 2, this volume) is a useful one that is also recognized elsewhere. For example, work on data representation in the United Kingdom (Howe, 1978; Sleeman, 1977) and in Germany (Brunnstein, 1974) is notable. However, studies elsewhere are no further along than similar work in the United States. Arranging a direct access data base for a naive computer user is a very difficult task. What may be different in Europe is the parsimony, that is, the efficiency of computer effort, for processing data structures and text strings. Where projects in the United States may solve problems with bigger and faster machines, projects in the United Kingdom tend to find more efficient algorithms (Annett, 1976b). Each of the two approaches will benefit from the other in the future. Since machines are increasing in speed and

8. Computer-Based Instruction in Europe and Japan   233

memory without increasing in price, the projects with small equipment budgets can take on larger domains of instruction. Because some problems of language processing still are beyond the capabilities of any conceivable machine, clever algorithms are needed regardless of machine size.

Hardware and Software Technologies

Specific characteristics of new computers and peripherals show some interesting contrasts among countries, particularly between the United States and Japan. Because of the graphics requirements and large character set of Japanese writing, special attention has been given to input and display of characters (Sakamoto, 1971; Tanaka, 1975). Typically, there are 12,000 kinds of letters used in an average general circulation Japanese newspaper. Techniques developed for character entry and display may be applied to special character sets in English and to line drawings. The contribution is primarily one of technology for dealing with selection among elements of a rather large set and for display of complex graphics that follow well-established but complex rules. In the selection mode, the input wheel, drum, or matrix could also arrange types of aircraft, elements of an electronic circuit, or members of a complex taxonomy for easy entry. In the display mode, printed output from a large set of graphics is handled economically.

In Japan, high-resolution television displays are used in CBI applications, and will be used more and more in home sets. Popular consumer interest is encouraging the use of flat panel displays. The economics of large production for the consumer market will carry over to displays in educational systems. The application in portable and personal information systems (word processing, information retrieval, records managements, and education) will be very appropriate to personal CBI applications. It is very likely that similar benefits will be obtained in the United States.

Videodisk technology is being actively developed and marketed in the United States by at least two major companies. The two American firms which have developed two incompatible videodisk systems are DiscoVision Associates, which is a partnership between IBM and MCA/Phillips, and RCA. DiscoVision Associates has an agreement with North American Phillips Corporation's Magnavox Company unit to produce the laser beam videodisk players, which are compatible with DiscoVision optical disks. This system costs under $800. RCA has recently announced it will market its mechanical system nationwide for under $500 in 1981.

In Europe, Siemens, Telefunken-Decca, and Thomson-CSF have been producing and marketing their own incompatible videodisk systems. Telefunken-Decca (originally TelDec, but now TED) was the first to be shown in public demonstration in 1970. The TED system has disks that have a playing time of 10 minutes. The TED playback closely resembles an audio phonograph. The RCA system is similar in design to TED. The Thomson-CSF system, like the MCA system, employs a sophisticated reflected optical design with a laser source. However, these systems are not interchangeable. Thomson-CSF has been focusing its marketing efforts in Europe, but is now beginning to actively market its system in the United States. In the spring of 1980 they signed an agreement with the Xerox Corporation to develop jointly optical-disk technology for data-storage applications.

Very Large Scale Integration (VLSI) will provide greater speed and capacity in personal machines used in education and training. The electronic industries of Japan are cooperating on this next generation of hardware in ways which may advance beyond developments in the United States (Japan Institute, 1974; Mackintosh, 1978). Already Japanese companies have a major role in several U.S. computer products. Except for organized efforts to maintain leadership (e.g., Texas Instruments), some business experts expect Japan to take over computer manufacture just as it has taken over the manufacture of electronic components (*Business Week,* September 18, 1978).

In general, software developments in the United States lead other countries. However, some useful observations may be made about the relation of software decisions to courseware development and applications.

Manufacturers of CBI systems in Europe have not given attention to software or courseware, perhaps because the systems are not viewed as dedicated to instructional use only. General or multipurpose systems have larger markets but require greater expertise to apply. Thus limiting the people willing to do the authoring. Courseware aids and special patterns into which curriculum can be loaded are much needed by many of the projects outside the United States.

In overseas educational settings it is expected that teachers will do the authoring. In France they are given a year off to learn about computer applications in education and programming in their own subjects (Hebenstreit, 1977). Then during the following summers they are expected to produce computer-related units. Much more staff time needs to be committed and more technical assistance provided, to make full use of the power of computer assistance for learning in the French schools.

In France, a new language (LSE: Language Symbolique d'Enseignement) was developed especially to serve as a first language for computer studies as well as for teacher-programmed simulations and learning exercises (McLean, 1977). Productivity of French teachers authoring materials may not have been as great as if prepared by professional staff, but the gains in acceptance of the computer studies program in local schools will more than compensate for not having had professionally prepared materials sooner.

Interactions between People and Machines

The same considerations for comparing hardware and software developments in the United States and abroad are applicable in the study of interactions between people and machines overseas. Research and development (R&D) activities are quite successful in providing more attention to human factors in hardware and software design in some projects (notably, Camstra, 1977; Hartley, Lovell & Sleeman, 1976; Kollerbauer, 1979; and Nievergelt, 1978). The results are not dramatic, and the prescriptions for hardware and software design are not unusual, but that students do report satisfaction with the interactive systems can be attributed to the sound design of the projects.

In summary, R&D dealing with the hardware and software of CBI systems is progressing well in Europe and Japan. Projects in the United States can benefit by following their example, especially in the areas of exploiting consumer products, facilitating input of complex symbol sets, authoring with procedure-oriented languages, and dealing effectively with natural language processing and information structures.

COURSEWARE

The analysis of instructional materials and process provided by Bunderson in Chapter 3 (this volume) establishes a context in which developments in the United States rate highly. Neither the courseware products nor the procedures for developing them are as impressive in Europe and Japan.

Comparison is difficult and generalizations are risky since in any country, and particularly in the United States, one observes great diversity in approach and technique for technology in training and education. Nevertheless, one can draw the conclusion that on the whole, courseware in the United States is more concerned with process than with content. The reverse tends to be true elsewhere, at least in the United Kingdom (Annett, 1976a; Howe & Delamont, 1974), Sweden (Baath & Mansson, 1977), and Germany (Hallworth et al., 1974). This may be especially valid in the United Kingdom in light of their continuing debate over the purpose of the computer in education. There are those in the United Kingdom CBI community who see the computer as a means of implementing existing educational objectives more effectively, and there are those who see the computer as a tool for innovation—something which will change the nature of education.

Overseas, at the college level, in particular, acceptance of technological aids to learning and teaching depends on the excellence of the materials (i.e., courseware) or at least on favorable reviews by persons recognized in the discipline. Attention to process can displace, or appear to displace, work on substance. As a result, some effective, carefully prepared materials are not accepted by many college teachers. On the other hand, in industrial and military training the results usually speak louder than the credentials of those who prepared or reviewed the materials.

Major courseware development efforts in Europe (e.g., the Lufthansa training system, Keuther, 1976) and Japan (e.g., Hosoi, Hikawa, Nojima, 1974; Tanaka, 1974) have followed the empirical approach (in contrast with an artistic and analytic approach, Chapter 3. Some work at the Open University, incorporating computer assistance with other modes of self-instruction, blends artistic and analytic approaches (Open University, 1978).

However, most of the courseware development is done by individuals and small groups, usually without the differentiated roles discussed by Bunderson in Chapter 4 (this volume). The results of such efforts are often creative, but on the average they are less productive than is characteristic of corresponding projects in the United States. Part of the problem may be the need to combine technical skills with subject expertise and some experience with instructional strategy. Interpretations of developments in Europe (Rushby, James, & Anderson, 1978) reflect the same concerns expressed by Bunderson (Chapter 4) that authors may become too distracted with the details of delivery. That is to say, managers of courseware development projects (and some critics) are concerned with the apparently low productivity of authors who attempt to do all the work themselves.

The approach to courseware development influences the choice of authoring (or programming) languages and vice versa. Programming languages used for CBI in Germany, The Netherlands, and the United Kingdom tend to be procedural rather than specific to CBI. ALGOL and APL (a Programming Language), for example, are popular for that purpose. This choice of language somewhat favors individual work by versatile authors rather than team projects; and systematic courseware development projects tend to favor languages dedicated to CBI. Planning for acceptance of new applications plays a role in language determinations as well.

A strategy of learning aided by complex computer programs is demonstrated by programs at Leeds University (Hartley & Sleeman, 1973; Sleeman, 1974; Sleeman, 1977) that have some knowledge of what they teach. In chemistry, psychology, and other subjects, the authors have set out to teach problem-solving skills by including some model of the student's understanding in the programs along with some general teaching strategy. This representation of the student includes procedures that replicate to some extent the problem solving of the student as well as his or her current state of knowledge.

In summary, breakthroughs in authoring will be slow in coming and they are not likely in the present education projects in Europe and Japan. Some innovations in courseware development in the United Kingdom are predicted for CBI in industrial training (Miles, 1977a) and military training (Miles, 1977b), but these innovations do not show in the information presently available from R&D projects.

Although non-U.S.A. R&D has little to offer in the area of courseware processes, "intelligent" CAI projects in France, Germany, and particularly the United Kingdom have much to contribute. Two major research projects at Leeds and Edinburgh are briefly summarized as follows.

Researchers in the United States made the first applications of artificial intelligence and automatic languages processing to computer-based learning (e.g., Carbonell, Uhr, Wexler, Simmons, Papert, Collins, Goldberg, and Koffman; see Chapter 3). Some of the United Kingdom projects are strongly influenced by developments in the United States, but make original contributions as well. Work at Leeds (Hartley, Lovell, and Sleeman, 1976) assumes sufficient knowledge in the machine for teaching materials to be generated as needed, rather than prestored in detail. In training for medical diagnosis, the knowledge base is a probabilistic matrix relating symptoms with diseases. In the analysis of nuclear magnetic resonance spectra, the computer procedures are able to solve the same problems given to the students; indeed, the program can solve problems submitted by the students. In elementary algebra, the basis of knowledge is in the processing of mathematical sentences. All of these programs are able to generate an indefinite number of examples and to match them with a model or profile of the student's performance according to built-in decision rules (Annett, 1976b).

The University of Edinburgh project shares with Leeds the common aim of creating a viable system for research. This project originated in the Department of Machine Intelligence (Howe, 1978), now the University of Edinburgh Department of Artificial Intelligence. The earliest programs were for instruction in languages and mathematics in which a diagnostic error matrix was used to control the degree of difficulty of questions put to the student. The major effort then went into devising programs that allowed for exploration by students in problem solving as well as presentation of information and testing of knowledge. This is an interesting departure on programs in the United States, which initially only gave students the opportunity to ask questions of the data base and not to explore it directly. Representation of the subject matter for this purpose requires new modes of representing structure.

The Edinburgh project also is attempting an intermediate solution to the problem of processing unconstrained ("natural") language input (Howe, 1978). Rather than aspire to "understand" any sentence typed in, in many cases it may be sufficient to judge whether or not the sentence entered by the student is an adequate paraphrase of one of a number of reference sentences stored as part of the knowledge base. The approach has been to construct a semantic representation of the input sentence and each possible target sentence and to determine which pairs can be considered synonymous.

LEARNING STRATEGIES

The information on learning strategies provided by Rigney and Munro in Chapter 5 is exceptional for its organization, conceptual clarity, and completeness. Any project concerning development or research with computers in education and training would do well to relate to the context provided there. Computer-based instruction in Europe and Japan can contribute to this area only in particular instances of strategy and may also offer some supporting theory. No explicit R&D on learning strategies is being reported overseas.

The most notable work outside the United States in the area of strategies for courseware is that of Gordon Pask in the United Kingdom. Because the contributions of Pask and his colleagues are quite unusual, they are described in this section in some detail.

In one series of studies on the organization of material and individual learning styles, Pask (1976b) identified two types of learners using very simple measures. "Serialists" approach a topic as a set of elements to be worked through; in one study, it was probability and statistics. These learners appear to learn and to recall a body of information as a series of items related by simple links. In contrast, "holists" work in quite global terms, getting the bigger picture and then filling in details as necessary. They prefer to begin with a conceptual organization and deal with complex structures. The evidence shows that training is more effective when access to the material accommodates and encourages an individual's preferred style of learning. In Pask's experiments, an individual's "style" is predicted by a separate measure. Training is least effective when a deliberate mismatch is introduced, frustrating the holist or serialist.

The instrumentation of Pask's training environments is very clever. The learner is presented with a representation of the training materials which at the same time conveys the organization and accumulates data on how individuals work through it. Control of sequencing can be determined by the apparatus, decided by the learner, or "negotiated" by some exchanges between the learner and built-in higher-level strategies (Pask, 1976a). These ideas were adapted for "learner-control strategies" in the TICCIT (Time-Shared Interactive Computer-Controlled Information Television) system curriculum in which users are shown where they stand in the "map" of curriculum and can negotiate how to achieve the specified goals.

Drawing upon philosophy, linguistics, and engineering as well as cybernetics, Pask (1975) has conducted analytic studies of conversations related to learning and has proposed methods by which content areas can be analyzed for more effective discourse between student and (automated) teacher. Those who are expert in the subject can construct a map of the content that relates the various elements of content. The teacher–author constructs explanations that show how one topic is derived from another. These explanations can be represented in a network with nodes for the topics, arcs indicating steps in a derivation (or interpretation), and clusters of arcs showing a complete derivation (Pask, 1976a). The designer of computer-based instruction must decide where to begin and how to move through some parts of a map of the domain. However, the learner has his or her own conversation with the domain, exploring nodes, arcs, and arc clusters,

8. Computer-Based Instruction in Europe and Japan

which may go beyond the original tutorial conversation but is still provided for by the overall description of the domain. The computer can assist the student in this exploration, as well as check for understanding and identify ineffective attempts at discovery.

Pask is working on ways of prescribing training materials and procedures that take into account the structure of the subject, the preferences and tendencies of the learner, and the "conversations" that improve the results between learner and automated procedure. A secondary and highly significant result is a "laboratory for learning" in which individuals can explore their own abilities and preferences for learning activities, and perhaps modify them to fit better with the training situations in which they wish to work. This additional contribution of Pask to individual learners (improved skills applied to any materials) may turn out to be more important for education overall than his guidance for teacher-authors (improved training materials developed for specific situations).

EVALUATION

The many dimensions of educational evaluation so well laid out by Borich in Chapter 6 are lost on a typical CBI project in Europe. In most projects (in the United States as well as abroad) data are collected and interpreted for the purpose of establishing benefits associated with the costs or other special considerations of technologically based instruction. Evaluations were required of projects in the UK National Development Programme in Computer-Aided Learning (NDPCAL) as part of an effort to encourage the transfer of educational packages among the sites (Hooper, 1977). Considerable material was required to support the transfer of educational packages from one site to another. Evaluation procedures have been oriented to providing the kind of information that would be helpful in these transfers. Of course, much more than evaluative data is involved in the transfer of curriculum packages.

A practical matter of evaluation was brought up in some conversation and correspondence about planning and evaluation. It was discussed briefly in two of the United Kingdom interpretations (Rushby, 1977; Howe, 1978), but it needs more attention than it generally has received. Of concern is the difficulty of evaluating a rapidly changing technology. Computing in education has been based on expensive equipment of rather limited scope. A careful scientist should not be willing to make simple extrapolations from experiences with equipment and procedures that lead users to consider computer efficiency more important than learner convenience. Most research on CBI has used systems that have been made obsolete by a revolution in microelectronics, and restrictive terminals and slow data rates have provided only a small window on the capabilities of computer-learning aids. New research will be done in the United Kingdom in a context which is quite different in both qualitative and quantitative ways.

According to researchers outside of the United States, computing equipment will be available in much larger numbers. Training and education will enjoy the use of 1000 times more single-user computers than there are now time-sharing terminals. Many of these personal devices will have a communicating option so that they can talk with other personal computers directly and with a central time-sharing system. Moreover, these inexpensive and portable computer devices will be more responsive to individual needs. The design of personal computers makes possible more rapid data rates, thus facilitating graphics, sound, and other modes of communication between the computer program and the user.

Personal control of computing equipment is expected to be an important factor in increased use of that equipment in education and training. Systems will be personalized for convenience, and also will gain certain intangible characteristics associated with being owned and entirely under the trainee's own control.

Computing will be common in everyday life. People will know about computers and their uses, and access to time-sharing systems and single-user machines will be common for personal use. Home entertainment and schedule planning are certain to be among the applications; education and information retrieval applications are also likely if personal computers can be coupled with the large but inexpensive storage capabilities of videodisks or their equivalent (Fields & Paris, Chapter 3; Bunderson, Chapter 4).

Dramatically lower costs require rethinking the evaluations of computer contributions. For example, trainees (or students) could have access to readily used word processing and records handling systems based on microcomputers. Predictions are difficult to make regarding the impact on training assignments, grading, job seeking, and other aspects of student and professional life. Increased student research can be facilitated, and not just in computer studies and engineering. Laboratory instrumentation and complex computation aids have been implemented for nearly all sciences and some social sciences.

The difficult point for evaluation is that many of these applications are self-justifying; managers, professors, and others making decisions about how to use resources look mostly at the positive changes in curriculum brought about through computer assistance. In some disciplines, equipment will be purchased as any other equipment is purchased for laboratories, or recommended for student purchase, as are calculators (previously slide rules) and dictionaries. However, some of the changes will be so dramatic as to require more careful attention, such as deliberation by curriculum panels, reviews by technical experts, and assessment by teams of social scientists.

Educational psychologists and other educational researchers in the United States are leaders in the field of evaluation almost to a fault. In other words, if anything is to be learned from projects in Europe and Japan in the area of educational evaluation, it may be that the United States should more often assume a common sense approach to assessment and the perspective of a decision maker faced with a continually changing technology.

MANAGEMENT

Management in its broadest sense includes considerations of securing adoption in various school and training settings. In France, decisions are derived from research studies and field experience, but political factors are important since the curriculum is implemented nationwide and affects schooling throughout the entire country (McLean, 1977). In Sweden, the education system is highly decentralized, so field studies play an important role in developing acceptance at the local level as well as in determining what materials will be effective in the different settings (Berg & Ostergren, 1977).

Some lessons to be learned from projects in Europe and Japan in the area of management, broadly defined, are described briefly under the headings: technology, pedagogy, economics, and politics.

Technology Considerations

Countries with limited resources for CBI have managed them carefully, sometimes with very positive results. In the United Kingdom National Development Programme in Computer-Aided Learning (NDPCAL), standards for software and communications were established by which the materials produced were more likely to be transportable (Hooper, 1977; Peterson & Sessions, 1978). Guidelines and other provisions for program exchange became conditions for funding, and a clearinghouse and other sources of technical information were maintained (NDPCAL, 1977). A study of possible futures for CBI was conducted to aid in planning (Miles, 1977a,b).

Pedagogical Considerations

The national educational program in France, being part of a centralized educational system, is able to operate a rather tight system of trial and feedback. Additional teachers are trained each year, adding to the base of experience throughout the entire system. Teachers author materials while still working in the classroom, providing closer contacts with the students who are the end users (Hebenstreit, 1977). This approach encourages a double loop feedback process which helps the teacher as well as the student. Trials with the use of microcomputers were so successful that the Charge de Mission a l'Informatique, coordinator of computing in all levels of education, is considering the installation of 10,000 microcomputers in high schools throughout France.

Since the French program brings computer students into the school curriculum, the program is based on the experience of both computer educators and potential employers from industry and government. Authoring materials have been prepared for use in various sciences as well as mathematics and computer studies directly, and always with a foundation in concepts of computer science (procedure, data structure, etc.).

Thus, research plays a significant role in management in France. Design and data collection are shaped by information needs for planning the national program, and decision makers respect the input from pedagogical studies.

Economic Considerations

The computer industry in Japan is creating a new generation of computers through nationwide cooperation and along with it new markets for microelectronic products (Japan Computer Institute). Already Japan dominates consumer electronics, and has a good chance at a major share of computers used in research and training (Bylinsky, 1978). Japan's *Plan for an Information Society: A National Goal toward the Year 2000,* initiated in 1972, reflects their commitment to a broad program involving industry, education, and government in joint projects for the development of advanced communication and computing processes. Funds have been invested by the government and by the industry association, in anticipation of tangible benefits to industry and society.

Political Considerations

Decision making in education in Sweden is quite decentralized. Nevertheless, the national project to put CBI in schools involves key decision makers and educational leadership (Kollerbauer, 1979). In its initial design the project favored local perceptions of needs and resources, as well as national plans. Attitudes toward technology and concerns about privacy were taken into account in the design of hardware and communications for CBI. To the extent this approach to design (involving the participation of all concerned persons) is successful, the national project in Sweden will have a broad base of support.

One management concern that appears too seldom is the factor of individual purchases by students, trainees, and families of electronic aids or computers. In some training situations the personal acquisition of powerful, pocket electronic devices used as crutches may be a detriment; in others it may be a highly recommended performance aid for continuing use. In educational situations private purchases may be the only way much computing is made available in public education in the near future.

NEEDED DEVELOPMENTS

Further development of CBI in the United States will interact with a number of needs and issues related to the technology as well as to educational applications. Three such issues are listed in this section. In addition, this section includes a list of areas for possible action and a set of recommendations for the United States, which are derived from experiences elsewhere.

Microelectronics technology, with rapidly decreasing costs that depend on greatly expanded usage, requires that producers find new markets for computers and related technology in education as well as throughout society. Appropriate uses in education require planning for and managing of the design of the technological aids and their introduction into educational activities and institutions. Personal computing products developed in Japan will be marketed aggressively in the United States and will be taken up in the next few years by many people for entertainment and small business purposes. The equipment in which industry is investing large sums of money for the personal computer market will not serve educational purposes well without attention to considerations of design specifically for educational purposes.

Education throughout the world faces similar problems of financing, access, credibility, and the like. Certain of these difficulties can, in part, be eased by appropriate uses of technology, if resources are available at the right time and place for research, development, evaluation, demonstration, diffusion, and operation. Otherwise, significant opportunities to aid all learners, and in particular the disadvantaged, the handicapped, the gifted, and the isolated learners, will be lost. The national program in France appears to have seized the opportunity in a timely way.

General literacy in computing and information systems will be needed by consumers as well as vendors, employees as well as managers, and learners as well as scholars, if society is not to be disrupted by a revolution encouraged by rapid growth of technology needed to support today's "information society." Computer literacy can begin in elementary school or sooner. However, because of the rapid introduction of the technology in many areas, computer literacy training must be carried on in colleges, professional schools, certification programs, on-the-job training, community education, and public media reaching the homes. The United Kingdom has designed (although not yet funded) a national program that would establish literacy in microcomputers throughout the work force and perhaps for most consumers as well.

Areas for Possible Action

Productive national programs in Sweden and the United Kingdom illustrate the benefits of coordination of planning and funding at the national level. Many important matters, for example, goals, standards, and credibility, can be accomplished only through national discussion and action. The funding necessary to realize the benefits of computing in training and education in the United States can no longer be handled piecemeal through many different agencies. The commitment to excellence in education and to effective use of technology must come from the top. Information systems in education and society cut across many areas of concern and consumer groups: research and development; the handicapped and the gifted; elementary, secondary, and vocational training areas; and a wide variety of professionals. Useful information and good advice on these matters has been accumulating for over 15 years in the form of recommendations of national commissions (Carnegie Commission on Higher Education, 1972; Commission on Instructional Technology, 1970; National Academy of Sciences, 1966; President's Science Advisory Committee, 1967), professional organizations, and review projects.

Designated centers with strong financial support and good visibility could provide sites of excellent training, research, and development in the United States as they have in the United Kingdom. Potential users urgently need the most current information, the best training, and an optimal environment for development activity. Residencies would provide an opportunity for individuals to get away from regular responsibilities to initiate new work. Research opportunities would be increased significantly by bringing together creative individuals with necessary resources and a variety of learning environments. Large-scale exploration of technological opportunities and basic concepts of learning would become practical. Alternative systems and approaches to curriculum could be compared within the same environment. Such a program in the United States could be extremely important to courseware development due to the size and diversity of the various enterprises for education and training.

Immediate action to recognize computing and information processing as a significant part of basic education would set in motion the process of curriculum revision necessary to the information age. In a few years, all students in public schools would become familiar with computers, programming, and applications, by about the eighth year of school. Teachers for these students could then assume student familiarity with computers and the ability to utilize personal equipment in future educational environments. Future employees and trainers will be able to build on basic skills with computers and information processing while including microelectronics products in performance situations.

Courseware development in the United States requires special attention, since computer use in education and training is a new industry, as yet untested and lacking clear incentives for developers and distributors. Commercial publishers cannot be expected to initiate high-risk ventures, and yet they may be left behind if the computer vendors try to provide courseware. Universities and colleges have much to contribute since most textbooks originate there today. Furthermore, individual authors need to see rewards, both academic and economic, for their efforts.

Just as in Japan, a blue ribbon committee in the United States could give careful attention to the social implications of dramatic changes in availability of information and automatic processing. As has been described (Fields & Paris, Chapter 3), every elaborate clipboard or binder will have a small pocket for a specialized calculator. Every reference book or procedures guide will have imbedded within its cover an information processor suited to the subject. Each desk encyclopedia will include sounds and animations and a microprocessor which conducts searches of the entire text as well as selects from the contents, index, and cross references. Planners need to consider the implications of new modes of representation and communication with machines; new skills for learning, problem solving, and creative activities; new roles for teachers and managers; and new situations for learning at home, on the job, and in the community. Administrators need to plan systems so that increased dependency on information machines, for assessment of ideas as well as retrieval of information, will not become an inappropriate crutch.

Communication between machines and people needs careful attention. As long as the students (or other casual users) need to type on a keyboard and watch for text and numbers and simple diagrams to appear on a special screen, these machines will have a rather narrow application in training and education. However, when a user can talk to the machine and get a response in printed text as well as in spoken words and other sounds, and can see the effects of directives in the actions of equipment such as models and tools, then the computer will fit into a much larger world of learning and performance.

Recommendations

The most notable difference between the United States and other countries (on curriculum and management as well as hardware and software) is the management of federal funds and the establishment of national goals, priorities, and projects. Although having a less centralized educational system than those in France and Japan, and with less control over funding than in the United Kingdom and Sweden, the U.S. government can still exercise appropriate and useful control and encourage sound developments.

One kind of U.S. national program would be federal funding for computers in the schools similar to programs which put language labs and other media assistance into public education (DISPAC, 1978). Funding of development centers for computer-related curriculum and other actions providing incentives for authors and publishers to prepare and distribute quality materials would create directions and reward contributions.

Other kinds of activity can encourage computing in education and training without the formality of the national programs in France, Japan, and the United Kingdom (Molnar, 1977). When a large company within the industry establishes a major program for computer use in education and training the successful products will have major impact. For example, Control Data Corporation has put much into development and marketing of the PLATO (Programmed Logic for Automatic Teaching Operations) Computer-Based Education System, and Texas Instruments has developed impressive, hand-held learning aids, which are selling very well in "learning centers" of department stores.

During the last 15 years, many CAI projects have worked on spelling programs, some of them with audio. All of the approaches have been very costly to deliver to students. Use of a tape recorder as the audio delivery medium presents major problems in reliability, and use of audio response units is very expensive. Except for experiments with touch tone telephones (which have not been found to be very convenient for entry of alphabetics), the terminals have always been rather expensive, that is, from $500 to $5000. Then Texas Instruments introduced a spelling aid, "Speak and Spell," complete for $50. Its built-in vocabulary of 250 words can be extended by plug-in modules at $15; the quality of audio exceeds most audio response units; the purchasing decisions are made by parents, kids, and teachers, rather than by educational institutions. Texas Instruments built on its own basic research in speech synthesis, borrowed some technical ideas from other CAI projects, perhaps gained encouragement from some of the more successful ones, and designed attractive materials with the advice of spelling experts. None of the CAI projects could have assembled the resources necessary to do what Texas Instruments did. The instances of PLATO and "Speak and Spell" are small compared with what is probably coming.

If Mattel does more than just put the CTW (Children's Television Workshop) logo on its home education packages, and gets quality learning materials into peoples' homes through its $250 computer, that one action by a toy company will do more to provide motivating exercises for practice in math and language skills than anything a national program would put into schools.

Federal policy should take into account the incentives and resources for development by commercial organizations and at the same time consider the impact of marketing educational materials directly to homes in the context of leisure time and recreational activities.

The United States does not have the only innovative projects working in these areas, as is apparent on reading reports of developments elsewhere in the world. Extending communication, processing knowledge and building personal and interpersonal skills are important areas for future development of computers in training and education.

REFERENCES

Annett, J. *Computer-assisted learning: 1969-1975*. A report prepared for the Social Science Research Council, London, 1976. (a)

Annett, J. *Report on a research seminar on computers in education*. University of Warwick, Department of Psychology, 1976. (b)

8. Computer-Based Instruction in Europe and Japan

Baath, J. A., & Mansson, N.O. *CADE: A system for computer-assisted distance education.* Malmo, Sweden: Hermonds Skola, 1977.

Berg, B., & Ostergren, B. *Innovations and innovation processes in higher education.* Stockholm, Sweden: National Board of Universities and Colleges, 1977.

Brunnstein, K. Structuring and retrieving information in computer-based learning. *International Journal of Computer and Information Sciences,* 1974, **2**(2).

Bylinsky, G. The Japanese spies in Silicon Valley. *Fortune,* February 27, 1978.

Camstra, B. *Make computer-assisted instruction smarter.* Computers and Education, 1977, **1**, 177–183.

Carnegie Commission on Higher Education. *The fourth revolution: Instructional technology in higher education.* New York: McGraw-Hill, 1972.

Commission on Instructional Technology. *To improve learning: An evaluation of instructional technology.* New York: R. R. Bowker, 1970.

Hallworth, H. J., Brahan, J. W., Har, J., Hunka, S., Lee, W., & Oliver, W. P. *Computer-aided learning in the Federal Republic of Germany.* National Research Council of Canada, NRC 14946, 1974.

Hartley, J. R., & Sleeman, D. H. Towards more intelligent teaching systems. *International Journal of Man-Machine Studies,* 1973, **5**, 215–235.

Hartley, J. R., Lovell, K., & Sleeman, D. H. *The use of the computer as an adaptive teaching system.* Final report to SSRC. Computer-Based Learning Project, University of Leeds, 1976.

Hebenstreit, J. New trends and related problems in computer-based education. In B. Gilchrist (ed.), *Information Processing 77,* IFIP, North-Holland, Amsterdam, 1977.

Hooper, R. *National development programme in computer-assisted learning: Final report of the director.* Council for Educational Technology, London, 1977.

Hosoi, M., Hikawa, K., & Nojima, E. *Some aspects toward practical CAI software.* The Soken Kiyo, July, 1974, **4**(2).

Howe, J. A. M. Artificial intelligence and computer-assisted learning: Ten years on. *Programmed Learning and Educational Technology,* 1978, **15**, 114–125.

Howe, J. A. M., & Delamont, S. *Towards an evaluation strategy for CAI projects.* Bionics Research Reports, No. 15. School of Artificial Intelligence, University of Edinburgh, 1974.

Japan Computer Usage Development Institute. *Social and economic effects of information-oriented investment.* Tokyo, Japan, 1974.

Keuther, K. *FRITS: Free reservation, information, and travel services.* West Germany: Lufthansa Training Division, 1976.

Kollerbaur, A. Princess: A project with a user-oriented, interdisciplinary approach to computer-based education. *THE Journal,* February, 1979.

McDonald, B., Atkins, R., Jenkins, D. & Kemmis, S. The educational evaluation of NDPCAL. *British Journal of Educational Technology,* 1977, **8**, 3.

Mackintosh, I. M. Large-scale integration: Intercontinental aspects. *IEEE Spectrum,* 1978, 51–56.

McLean, R. S. Interactive computing in secondary schools in France. *Creative Computing,* 1977 (January–February), 54–56.

Miles, R. *Computers in industrial training and management development in the 1980's: A future study report.* Technical Report No. 19. National Development Programme in Computer-Assisted Learning, Council for Educational Technology, London, 1977. (a)

Miles, R. *Computers in military training in the 1980's: A future study report.* Technical Report No. 18. National Development Programme in Computer-Assisted Learning, Council for Educational Technology, London, 1977. (b)

Molnar, A. R. National policy toward technological innovation and academic computing. *THE Journal,* September–October, 1977, **4**, 39–43.

National Academy of Sciences. *Digital computer needs in universities and colleges.* A report of the Commission on Uses of Computers, National Research Council, Washington, D.C., 1966.

NDPCAL. *Project summaries and program index.* National Development Programme in Computer-Assisted Learning, Council for Educational Technology, London, 1977.

Nievergelt, J. ACSESS: The automated computer science education system (at the U of I). *Creative Computing,* March-April, 1978, 96-99.

Pask, G. Conversational techniques in the study and practice of education. *British Journal of Educational Psychology,* 1976, **46,** 12-25. (a)

Pask, G. *The cybernetics of human learning and performance.* New York: Hutchison, 1975.

Pask, G. Styles and strategies of learning. *British Journal of Educational Psychology,* 1976, **46,** 128-148. (b)

Peterson, J. W. M. & Sessions, A. E. A transportable authoring system. *Computers and Education,* 1978, **2,** 331-334.

President's Science Advisory Committee (PSAC). *Computers in higher education.* Washington, D.C.: U.S. Government Printing Office, 1967.

Rushby, N. J., James, E. B., & Anderson, J. S. A. A three-dimensional view of computer-based learning in continental Europe. *Programmed Learning & Educational Technology,* 1978, **15,** 152-161.

Sakamota, T. *The development of educational technology in Japan.* Bulletin of the Unesco Regional Office for Education in Asia, 1971, **6,** 40-48.

Sleeman, D. H. A problem-solving monitor for a deductive-reasoning task. *International Journal of Man-Machine Studies,* 1974, **7,** 182-211.

Sleeman, D. H. A system which allows students to explore algorithms. In R. Reddy (ed.) *Proceedings of the International Joint Conference on Artificial Intelligence,* 780-786. Cambridge, Mass.: MIT, 1977.

Tanaka, S. On an equation of cost-effectiveness of CAI systems. In O. Lecarme and R. Lewis (eds.) *Computers in education.* Proceedings of the IFIP World Conference, North Holland, Amsterdam, 1975.

UCODI. *Computer-assisted instruction project descriptions (in Europe and Japan).* International Center for Documentation Coordination and Research Incentive (UCODI), Heverle, Belgium, 1975.

Zender, R. F. (ed. and translator) *Computers and education in the Soviet Union.* Englewood Cliffs, New Jersey: Educational Technology Publications, 1975.

SUPPLEMENTARY READING:

Abbatt, F. R., & Hartley, J. R. Teaching planning skills by computer. *International Journal of Mathematical Education in Science and Technology,* 1973, **5,** 665-671.

Daly, D. W., Dunn, W., & Hunter, J. The computer-assisted learning (CAL) project in mathematics at the University of Glasgow. *International Journal of Mathematics Education in Science and Technology,* 1977, **8,** 145-156.

DISPAC (Subcommittee on Domestic and International Scientific Planning, Analysis, and Cooperation of the House Committee on Science and Technology *Hearings on computers and the learning society.* Washington, D.C.: U.S. Government Printing Office, 1978.

Fielden, J. The financial evaluation of NDPCAL. *British Journal of Educational Technology,* 1977, **8,** 190-200.

Gains, B. R. Foundations of fuzzy reasoning. *International Journal of Man-Machine Studies,* 1976, **8,** 623-668.

Hartley, J. R. An appraisal of computer-assisted learning in the United Kingdom. *Programmed Learning and Educational Technology,* 1978, **15,** 136-151.

8. Computer-Based Instruction in Europe and Japan

Hartley, J. R., Sleeman, D. H., & Woods, Pat. Controlling the learning of diagnostic tasks. *International Journal of Man-Machine Studies,* 1972, **4,** 319-340.

Henderson, Diane D. (Report on the) Second World Conference on Computers in Education of the International Federation for Information Processing. Virginia: Mitre Corporation, McLean, 1975.

Hooper, R., & Toye, I. (Eds.) *Computer-assisted learning in the U.K.: Some case studies.* Council for Educational Technology, London, 1975.

Howe, A., & Romiszowski, A. J. *International yearbook of educational and instructional technology.* Association for Applied Learning and Educational Technology, London, 1977.

Japan Computer Usage Development Institute. *The plan for an information society: A national goal toward the year 2000.* Tokyo, Japan, 1972.

Kawasaki, Zenshiro. A New Expression Method for Decision Logic in Learning Diagnosis and Treatment. *Computers and Education,* 1978, **2,** 335-337.

Lee, B. and Burrows, J. CAL in the Open University. *CALNEWS 8,* London: Council for Educational Technology, 1977.

Leiblum, M. A pragmatic approach to initiating a computer-assisted instruction service and some problems involved. *Programmed Learning and Educational Technology,* 1977, **14,** 243-249.

McKenzie, J. Computers in the teaching of undergraduate science. *British Journal of Educational Technology,* 1977, **8,** 214-224.

McMahon, H. F. Progress and prospects in computer-managed learning in the United Kingdom. *Programmed Learning and Educational Technology,* 1978, **15,** 104-113.

McMahon, H. F. and Anderson, J. S. A. Implementing a CML system: The tutors role in course development and teaching. In P. Hills, and J. Gilbert, (eds.) *Aspect of Educational Technology.* London: Kogan Page, 1977, **11,** 150-156.

McMahon, H. F., Anderson, J. S. A., & Barton, J. C. Student response to differentiated learning tasks in CML. *Programmed Learning and Educational Technology,* 1977, **14,** 168-175.

O'Shea, T. and Sleeman, D. H. A design for an adaptive self-improving teaching system. In J. Rose (Ed.) *Advances in Cybernetics and Systems.* London: Gordon and Breach, 1973.

Pask, G. & Scott, B. C. E. CASTE: A system for exhibiting learning strategies and regulating uncertainties. *International Journal of Man-Machine Studies,* 1973, **5,** 17-52.

Rushby, N. J. (ed.) *Computer managed learning in the 1980's: A future study report.* Technical Study Report No. 16, National Development Programme for Computer-Assisted Learning, London, 1977.

Self, John A. Student models in computer-aided instruction. *International Journal of Man-Machine Studies,* 1974, **6,** 261-269.

Smith, P. A U.K. project in computer-assisted learning in engineering science. *Computing and Graphics,* 1977, **2,** 151-154.

Tanaka, S. *Principles of development of software at the learner-centered computer-based learning systems.* Paper presented at the Conference on Computer-Based Learning (RGU), Hamburg, Germany, 1974.

UCODI. *File on the computer in education in Germany, Parts 1 and 2.* UCODI Bulletin, 11 and 12. International Center for Documentation Coordination and Research Incentive (UCODI), Heverle, Belgium, 1976. (a)

UCODI. *File on the computer in education in The Netherlands.* UCODI Bulletin 9. International Center for Documentation Coordination and Research Incentive (UCODI), Heverle, Belgium, 1976. (b)

van Hees, E. J. W. J. Computer-managed learning at the university level in the Netherlands. *Educational Technology,* April, 1976, 28-31.

Watanabe, S. *Computer-assisted instruction: A system and its assessment in Japan.* International Conference on Computers and Communications, 1972, 87-94.

Author Index

Numbers in italics refer to the pages on which the complete references are listed.

A

Aagard, J. A., 151, *155*
Abelson, R. P., 139, *158*
Abramson, T., 224, *229*
Abt, C., 203, *206*
Aiken, E., 131, *155*
Alderman, D. L., 102, 112, *122, 123*, 164, *206*, 217, 219, *229*
Alexander, L., 196, *207*
Anastasio, E. J., 219, *229*
Anderson, J. R., 137, 139, 140, 141, *155, 156*
Anderson, J. S. A., 232, 236, *248*
Anderson, M. C., 137, *156*
Anderson, R. C., 137, *156*
Anderson, R. H., 85, *90*
Anderson, T., 133, *156*
Annett, J., 233, 235, 237, *246*
Appel, L. R., 164, *208*, 217, 219, *229, 230*
Apple, M. W., 180, 181, 182, 186, 188, *206*
Atkins, R., 232, *247*
Atkinson, R. C., 134, *156*
Atwood, M. E., 137, 142, *156, 157*
Avner, A., 114, *123*
Axtell, R. H., 119, *123*

B

Baath, J. A., 235, *247*
Baker, E. L., 225, *230*
Baker, F. B., 24, 26, *64*
Banathy, B., 196, *206*
Barker, R. G., 186, *206*
Bass, R. K., 102, *125*
Becker, H., 182, *206*
Behrens, W., 203, *208*
Bell, A., 119, *123*
Belliott, F., 175, *206*
Bennik, F. D., 106, *123*
Berg, B., 241, *247*
Berkowitz, M., 15, *20*
Binks, M. G., 144, *157*
Bloom, B. S., 161, 163, 164, 198, *206*, 208
Bobrow, D. G., 82, *90*, 150, *158*
Bobrow, R. J., 119, *123*
Bond, N. A., 137, *156*
Borich, G. D., 163, 168, 177, 186, 198, 203, *206*, 208
Boutwell, R. C., 111, *124*
Bower, G. H., 133, 135, 137, 139, 145, *156*
Braby, R., 151, *155*

251

Brackett, J. W., 108, *123*, 198, *206*
Brahan, J. W., 235, *247*
Branson, R. K., 105, *123*, 194, *207*
Braswell, J. S., 102, *123*
Bresee, J., 106, *124*
Bridgman, P., 164, *207*
Briggs, L., 196, *207*
Brooks, F. P., Jr., 116, *123*
Brown, J. S., 118, 119, 120, *123*, 134, 151, *156*
Brunnstein, K., 232, *247*
Bunderson, C. V., 93, 102, 105, 106, 107, 109, 111, 113, *123*, *124*
Burton, R. R., 119, 120, *123*, 151, *156*
Butler, A. K., 106, *123*
Butman, J. W., 196, *207*
Bylinsky, G., 242, *247*

C

Call-Himwich, E., 222, *230*
Campbell, D. T., 147, *156*, 175, *207*
Camstra, B., 235, *247*
Carbonell, J., 119, *123*
Carey, L., 195, *207*
Carpenter, P. A., 137, *156*
Carroll, J. B., 152, *156*
Cartwright, G. P., 219, *229*
Case, R., 138, *156*
Churchman, C. W., 197, *207*
Clinton, J. P. M., 102, *123*
Coates, J., 203, *207*
Coldeway, N. A., 109, *124*
Coleman, J. S., 98, *124*, 129, *156*
Collins, A., 118, 119, *123*, 133, *156*
Conant, J. B., 129, *156*
Cooley, W., 172, 180, 183, 184, 185, 186, *207*
Cooper, L. A., 137, 145, *156*
Craik, F. I. M., 133, 140, *156*
Cronbach, L. J., 145, *156*
Crook, D. E., 133, *158*
Cubbverly, W. E., 133, *159*

D

Dallman, B. E., 216, 217, *229*
Dansereau, D., 9, *21*, 133, *156*
Davis, C., 105, *124*
Davis, R., 196, *207*

deGroot, A. D., 139, *157*
Delamont, S., 235, *247*
DeLeo, P. J., 216, 217, *229*
Dewey, J., 183, 184, 188, *207*
Dick, W., 195, *207*
Dobrovolny, J. L., 133, *157*
Duffy, T. M., 131, *155*, *157*
Dykstra, R., 175, *207*

E

Ebel, R. L., 171, *207*
Eisner, E. W., 164, *207*
Emrick, J., 175, *207*

F

Faust, G. W., 93, 102, 106, 109, 111, *123*, *124*
Feigenbaum, E. A., 132, *157*
Fletcher, J. L., 196, *207*
Fletcher, T., 143, *159*
Fokkema, S. D., 137, 141, 148, *157*
Foley, W. J., 15, *21*, 162, 169, 170, 172, 173, 175, 177, 180, 181, *209*
Francis, L., 215, 219, 220, *229*
Fredericksen, J. R., 137, 141, 149, *157*
Freedman, C. R., 105, 106, *124*
Furst, E. J., 172, *207*

G

Gephart, W. J., 15, *21*, 162, 169, 170, 172, 173, 175, 177, 180, 181, *209*
Gerson, R. F., 133, *159*
Ghesquere, J., 105, *124*
Gillman, 216, 217, *229*
Gillogly, J. J., 85, *90*
Glaser, R., 137, 138, 141, 148, *157*
Goldberg, A., 119, *124*
Goldstein, I., 118, 120, *123*
Gonzalez, H. P., 143, *159*
Gordon, L., 137, *157*
Grignetti, M., 119, *124*
Grobman, H., 166, 196, *207*
Guba, E. G., 15, *21*, 162, 169, 170, 172, 173, 175, 177, 180, 181, 186, 187, 189, 190, 191, 192, *207*, *209*
Guilford, J. P., 146, *157*
Gulick, R. M., 203, *207*

Author Index

H

Hagen, E., 171, *209*
Hallworth, H. J., 235, *247*
Hamilton, D., 191, *208*
Hammond, K., 203, *207*
Hammond, R. L., 15, *21*, 162, 169, 170, 172, 173, 175, 177, 180, 181, *207, 209*
Handy, R., 183, *207*
Hanson, A., 83, *90*
Har, J., 235, *247*
Hargan, C., 223, 224, 225, *229*
Harris, G., 118, 123, 134, *156*
Harris, W. P., 107, *124*
Hartley, J. R., 235, 236, 237, *247*
Hastings, J. T., 161, 163, 198, *206*
Hatano, G., 144, *157*
Hayes, J. R., 138, 141, 142, *158*
Hebenstreit, J., 234, 241, *247*
Hemphill, J., 173, 174, *207*
Hencley, S., 203, *207*
Hermanns, J., 106, *124*
Heuston, D. H., 96, *124*
Hibbits, N., 223, 224, 225, *229*
Hikawa, K., 235, *247*
Hillelsohn, M. J., 216, *230*
Himwich, H. A., 220, *230*
Hitch, G. J., 149, 151, *157*
Hoban, C., 184, *207*
Hooper, R., 239, 241, *247*
Hosoi, M., 235, *247*
House, E. R., 187, *208*
Howe, A., 232, *249*
Howe, J. A. M., 232, 237, 239, *247*
Howell, J., 224, *229*
Hoyt, W. G., 106, *123*
Hudspeth, D., 203, *208*
Hunka, S., 235, *247*
Hunt, E., 149, 152, *157*
Hunter, B., 104, *124*, 215, 217, 220, 222, 223, 225, *230*
Hunter, G., 68, *90*

J

James, E. B., 232, 236, *248*
Jeffries, R., 142, *157*
Jemelka, R., 186, 203, *206, 208*
Jenkins, D., 232, *247*

Johnson-Laird, P. N., 139, *158*
Judd, W. A., 133, *157*
Just, M. A., 137, *156*

K

Kac, M., 178, *208*
Kahn, R. E., 77, *90*
Kahneman, D., 150, *157*
Kaplan, A., 192, *208*
Kastner, C., 104, *124*
Kaufman, R., 180, 184, 186, 194, 197, 200, 201, 202, *208*
Kelley, A. C., 50, *64*
Kemmis, S., 232, *247*
Kendler, H. H., 133, *157*
Keuther, K., 235, *247*
Klein, K., 140, *157*
Kollerbaur, A., 235, 242, *247*
Kosslyn, S. M., 137, 145, *157, 158*
Krathwohl, D., 164, *208*
Kuhn, T. S., 162, *208*
Kurtz, P., 183, *207*

L

Lansman, M., 149, 150, *157*
Larkin, J. H., 135, 136, *157*
Lattimore, M., 137, *156*
Lee, W., 235, *247*
Leontief, W., 203, *208*
Lesgold, A. M., 137, 138, 141, 148, *157*
Levine, M., 189, *208*
Lindsay, P. H., 139, *158*
Linstone, H., 203, *208*
Lockhart, R. S., 133, 140, *156*
Logan, R. S., 104, 105, 108, *124*, 133, *157*
Lohman, D. F., 146, *159*
Lohnes, P., 172, 181, 183, 184, 185, 186, *207*
Louch, A. R., 193, *208*
Lovell, K., 235, 237, *247*
Lumsdaine, A. A., 225, *230*
Lutz, K. A., 137, 145, *157, 158*

M

McCombs, B. L., 133, *157*
McDonald, B., 232, *247*
McGregor, D., 137, *156*

McIsaac, D. N., 26, *64*
Macken, E., 218, *230*
Mackintosh, I. M., 234, *247*
McLean, R. S., 234, 241, *247*
Madaus, G. F., 161, 163, 198, *206*
Madden, S., 168, *206*
Mager, R. F., 164, *208*
Main, 216, 217, 229
Malkin, S., 224, *229*
Mandler, G., 143, *158*
Mansson, N. O., 235, *247*
Markle, D. G., 110, *124*
Markle, S. M., 93, 109, 110, *124*
Marshalek, B., 146, *159*
Masia, B., 164, *208*
Meadows, D. H., 203, *208*
Meadows, D. L., 203, *208*
Merrill, M. D., 109, 111, 113, *124*
Merriman, H. D., 15, *21*, 162, 169, 170, 172, 173, 175, 177, 180, 181, *209*
Metfessel, N. W., 162, 175, *208*
Michael, W. B., 162, 175, *208*
Miles, R., 236, 241, *247*
Miller, G. A., 139, *158*
Minsky, M. A., 139, *158*
Misselt, A. L., 222, *230*
Molnar, A. R., 245, *247*
Morningstar, M., 102, *125*
Munro, A., 133, 137, 140, 151, *157*, *158*
Murphy, R. T., 164, *208*, 217, 219, *229*, *230*

N

Neches, R., 138, 141, 142, *158*
Negroponte, N., 70, 83, *90*
Newel, A., 139, *158*
Nievergelt, J., 235, *248*
Nojima, E., 235, *247*
Norman, D. A., 137, 139, 140, 150, *158*
Nugent, W., 131, *155*

O

Oliver, W. P., 235, *247*
Olsen, J. B., 109, *124*
O'Neal, A. F., 106, 107, 108, *124*, 221, *230*
O'Neal, H. L., 106, 107, 108, *124*, 221, *230*
O'Neil, H. F., Jr., 8, 9, 15, 20, *21*, 107, *124*, 134, *158*
Orlansky, J., 3, 14, *21*, 164, 203, *208*

Ostergren, B., 241, 247
Owens, T. R., 189, *208*

P

Paivio, A., 145, *158*
Parlett, M., 191, *208*
Pask, G., 238, *248*
Patton, Q., 180, 186, 189, *208*
Pellegrino, J. W., 137, 138, 141, 148, *157*
Peterson, J. W. M., 241, *248*
Pinker, S., 145, *158*
Pohland, P. A., 215, *230*
Polson, P. G., 137, 142, *156, 157*
Popham, W., 164, *208*
Poynor, H., 163, *208*
Propst, F., 219, *230*
Provus, M. M., 15, *21*, 162, 169, 170, 172, 173, 175, 177, 180, 181, 184, *208, 209*

R

Randers, J., 203, *208*
Raphael, B., 82, *90*
Rauch, H. L., 15, *21*, 186, 187, 189, *209*
Raugh, M. R., 134, *156*
Razran, L., 142, *157*
Reddy, D. R., 83, *90*
Reif, F., 135, 136, *157*
Reigeluth, C. M., 109, *124*
Richardson, F., 143, *158*
Riesman, E., 83, *90*
Rigney, J. W., 128, 133, 134, 137, 140, 142, 143, 144, 145, 148, 151, *156, 157, 158*
Rippey, R. M., 190, *208*
Romiszowski, A. J., 232, *249*
Rosenblatt, R., 215, 217, 223, 225, *230*
Ross, D., 198, *208, 209*
Rothkopf, E. Z., 138, *158*
Rubin, M., 104, *124*
Rumelhart, D. E., 137, 139, 140, *158*
Rushby, N. J., 232, 236, 239, *248*

S

Sakamota, T., 233, *248*
Saltz, E., 140, *157*
Sanders, J., 179, 181, 186, *209*
Schank, R. C., 139, *158*

Author Index

Schmidt, K., 137, *156*
Schneider, W., 143, 144, 150, *158, 159*
Schoman, K., 198, *209*
Schulz, R. E., 106, *124*, 215, 217, 223, 225, *230*
Scriven, M., 166, 176, 180, 181, 182, 185, 186, 188, *209*
Seidel, R. J., 104, *124*, 133, *159*, 215, 216, 217, 219, 220, 223, 224, 225, *229, 230*
Sessions, A. E., 241, *248*
Shepard, R. N., 145, *156, 158*
Sherwood, B. A., 105, *124*
Shiffrin, R. M., 143, 144, 150, *158, 159*
Simon, H. A., 139, *158*
Singer, R., 133, *159*
Sleeman, D. H., 232, 235, 236, 237, *247, 248*
Slottow, G., 219, *230*
Smith, E., 164, 171, *209*
Snow, R. E., 145, 146, 147, 149, 152, *156, 159*
Sorenson, P. H., 175, *207*
Spielberger, C. D., 9, *21*, 133, 134, 143, *159*
Spiro, R. J., 137, *156*
Stake, R. E., 162, 175, 176, 177, 180, 181, 189, *209*
Stanley, J. C., 147, *156*, 175, *207*
Stearns, M., 175, *207*
Sternberg, R. J., 137, 139, 141, 149, 152, *159*
Sternberg, S., 133, *159*
Sticht, T. G., 133, 138, *159*
String, J., 14, *21*, 164, 203, *208*
Stufflebeam, D. L., 15, *21*, 162, 169, 170, 172, 173, 175, 177, 180, 181, *209*
Summers, D., 203, *207*
Suppes, P., 102, 119, *124, 125*, 218, *230*
Swallow, R. J., 214, *230*
Swinton, S. S., 102, *123*

T

Talmadge, H., 190, *209*
Tanaka, S., 233, 235, *248*
Taylor, S. S., 105, *125*
Theis, D. J., 78, *90*
Thiagarajan, S., 106, *125*
Thompson, C., 105, *124*

Thorndike, R. L., 171, *209*
Trexler, R. C., 216, *230*
Turoff, M., 203, *208*
Tyler, R. W., 164, 171, 172, 180, *209*
Tymitz, B., 15, *21*

U

Underwood, V. L., 133, *159*

V

van Gigch, J. P., 193, 200, *209*
Vinsonhaler, J. F., 102, *125*
Volk, J. W., 102, *125*

W

Wagner, H., 134, *159*, 215, 216, 217, 220, 223, 225, *230*
Weiner, M., 224, *229*
Weinstein, C. E., 133, *159*
Weiss, D. J., 104, *125*
Wicker, F. W., 133, *159*
Willems, E. P., 15, *21*, 186, 187, 189, *209*
Wilson, T., 106, *125*
Winston, P. H., 85, *90*
Withington, F. G., 69, *90*
Witkin, B. R., 201, *209*
Wittrock, M. C., 145, *159*
Wolf, R. L., 15, *21*, 189, *209*
Wood, C. J., 215, *230*
Worthen, B., 179, 181, 186, *209*

Y

Yates, J., 203, *207*
Yelon, S., 196, *207*
Yoshio, M., 144, *157*
Youker, R., 212, 213, *230*

Z

Zelkowitz, M. V., 116, *125*
Zender, R. F., 232, *248*
Zwicky, F., 203, *209*

Subject Index

A

ARPANET, 76–77
Artificial intelligence, 83–87, 88, 237–239
Authoring languages, 92, 103, 108, see also Instructional systems development; specific projects

B

Basic skills, 129–132, 152–153
Behaviorism in educational evaluation, 163–164
Bubble memories, see Electronic storage technology

C

Cable television, 75
CAI, see Computer-assisted instruction
CARE, see Computer-Assisted Remedial Education
CBI, see Computer-based instruction
CHARGE, see Color Halftone Area Graphics Environment
Charge-coupled devices, see also Electronic storage technology
CMI, see Computer-managed instruction
Cognitive process
  analyses, 149–152
  models, 139–145
Cognitive psychology, 132–133
Cognitive science, 128, 133, 137–145
Color Halftone Area Graphics Environment, 214
Communications technologies, 6, 74–77
Computer-assisted instruction, 98, 99, 102–104, 108, 112, 118, 164, see also Authoring languages; Instructional systems development
Computer-Assisted Remedial Education, 219
Computer-based instruction
  advantages of, 3
  courseware, 235–237
  definition, 1
  in Europe and Japan, 18–20
  evaluation of, 14–16, 239–241
  hardware, 232–234
  learning strategies, 237–239
  management of, 212–229, 241–242
  needed developments, 243–246
  software, 234–235
Computer languages, 82, 102–104, 108, see also Authoring languages; Software
Computer-managed instruction, 4–5, see also Training School environment
  administrative, 53–54
  curriculum, 53–54
  diagnosis and prescription, 53
  evaluator capabilities, 61–63
  hardware system, 55–58
  performance profile, 52–53
  reports, 52–55

Computer-managed instruction (cont.)
  scheduling, 54
  software modules, 45–50
    administrative, 46–47
    assessment, 47–48
    file maintenance, 49–50
    major module controller, 45–46
    reporting, 48–49
  software system concept, 38–55
    curricular file contents, 41–42
    data base, 40
    data-base management package, 50–51
    instructional resources file, 44–45
    introduction, 38–39
    student administration file, 44
    student instructional history file, 43–44
    system overview, 27–38
    utility routines, 51
Computer-related functions
  data-base management, 37–38
  man-machine interface, 37
  system generation, 38
Computerized testing systems, 104
Computerized Training System (Army), 215, 216–218, 220–221, 222, 223, 224, 225
Conventional presentational packages, 99–100
Cost effectiveness of CBI systems, 2–3
Courseware
  definitions of, 7, 91–92
  delivery system, 94–99
  future delivery systems, 120–122
  intelligent courseware, 118–120
  process aspects, 104–109
  product aspects, 99–104, 117
CTS, *see* Computerized training system

D

Decision-Oriented Evaluation, 180
Drill-and-practice, 102–103, 119

E

Educational evaluation
  contrasts between policy and needs assessment, 202
  contrasts between research and evaluation, 10, 174
  current trends, 180–196
  definitions, 170–174
  emerging trends, 197–206
  facets, 161–163
  history of, 163–170
  models, 174–180, 226–227
  needs assessment, 200–201
  policy assessment, 201–204
  role of evaluator, 204–206
Educational psychology, 145–149
Education and training systems, 1–3
Electronic displays, 72–73
Electronic storage technology, 77–79
Elementary and Secondary Education Act, 166–170
ESEA, *see* Elementary and Secondary Education Act
Evaluation, 11–13, *see also* Educational evaluation
  in CBI system management, 217–220, 226–227
  in Europe, 239–241
Expert systems, 82–83, 85–86, 89–90

F

Floppy disks, *see* Electronic storage technology

H

Hardware, 55–58, 94, 95
Hardware and software, 5–7, 65–90, 213–214
  in Europe and Japan, 232–235

I

ICAI, *see* Intelligent computer-assisted instruction
Individualization of instruction, 25–27, 67, 92, 96–97
Information processing, 80–85
Inputting and outputting hardware, 69–74
Instructional management functions, 5
  data collection, 32–33
  diagnosis and prescription, 33–34
  performance monitoring, 34–35
  reporting, 36–37
  resource allocation/scheduling, 35–36
Instructional strategies, 65–67
  definition of, 65
Instructional systems development, 91–93, 104–109

Subject Index

Intelligent computer-assisted instruction, 8-9, 80-87, 118-120
Intelligent courseware, *see* Courseware; Intelligent computer-assisted instruction
Interservice procedures for instructional systems development, 105-106, 194-196
IPISD, *see* Interservice procedures for instructional systems development
ISD, *see* Instructional systems development

K

Knowledge representation, 67-69
  in Europe and Japan, 232-234

L

Large magnetic disks and tapes, *see* Electronic storage technology
Large-scale integration, 68, 80-81, 86-87, 88-89
Learning strategies
  basic skills, 129-132, 152-153
  cognitive processes, 144-149
  cognitive psychology, 132-133
  cognitive science, 128, 133, 137-139
  conceptual geography, 128
  definition, 127-129
  educational psychology, 145-149
  in Europe, 237-239
  functional illiteracy, 129-130
  military training, 130-132, 153-154
  overview, 9-11
  processing resources, 150-152
  process models, 139-144
  text, 135-136
  verbal learning, 134-135
LSE, *see* Authoring languages
LSI, *see* Large-scale integration

M

Management, 16-18, 212-229
  issues, 214-223
    evaluation models, 217-220
    internal management, 220-223
    technology transfer, 223-225, 228-229
  organizational structure, 212-214
  recommendations, 225-229
Man-machine, 37, 87-89

Mass memories, *see* Electronic storage technology
Microcomputers, 80-81
  literacy in, 243
Military training, 99, 130-132, 153-154

O

Operating systems, 81-82
Optic fibers, 68-69

P

Packet switching, 76-77
Paper transmission, 2, 20, 71-72
Performance aids, 104
PLANIT, 102
PLATO, *see* Program Logic for Automatic Teaching Operations
Program Logic for Automatic Teaching Operations, 66, 110, 114-115
  evaluation of, 164, 219
  management of, 216, 222-223
Programming languages, 108, 236, *see* Authoring languages
Project Impact, 216, 221
Psycholinguistics, 132

R

Replication of courseware, 97-99, 101-103
Research and evaluations, contrasts between, 10, 174
Rule-example-practice strategy, 102, 105

S

Semiconductor and core memories, *see* Electronic storage technology
Software, 38-55, 85-87, 115-116
Speech, 68, 73-74
Staffing, 220-223, 227-228
System-concept document, 25-27
Systems-oriented evaluation, 193-196, 197-199, 205

T

TAL, *see* Authoring languages; TICCIT
Technology transfer, 223-225, 228-229

Texas Instruments
  Little Professor, 66-67
  Speak and Spell, 246
TICCIT, see Time Shared Interactive Computer-Controlled Information Television
Time Shared Interactive Computer-Controlled Information Television, 95, 102-103, 105, 110-116, 119-120, 238
  contrasts with PLATO, 115
  evaluation of, 164, 219
  management of, 217, 222-223
  TAL, 112
Training School environment, 24-25
  components of, 27-30
    administration, 29
    CMI system, 29
    instructional, 29
    logistical, 30
    marketplace, 28
    personnel, 29
TUTOR, see Authoring languages

V

Value-oriented evaluation, 180-186
Very Large Scale Integration, 234
Videodisks, 79, 100, 106
  as courseware media, 117-118, 121
  in Europe and Japan, 233-234
VSLI, see Very Large Scale Integration